American Freemasons

Three Centuries of Building Communities

Mark A. Tabbert

National Heritage Museum
LEXINGTON, MASSACHUSETTS

New York University Press
NEW YORK AND LONDON

National Heritage Museum, Lexington, Massachusetts
www.monh.org

New York University Press, New York and London
www.nyupress.org

Library of Congress Cataloging-in-Publication Data

Tabbert, Mark A.
    American freemasons: three centuries of building
communities / Mark A. Tabbert.
        p. cm.
    Includes biographical references and index.
    ISBN 0-8147-8292-2 (alk. paper)
    1. Freemasonry—United States—History. 2. Freemasons—
United States—Charities. I. Title

HS515.T32 2005
366'.1'0973-dc22

                                                    2005041540

Designed by Susan Marsh
Typeset in ITC Bodoni by Duke & Company
Technical drawings by Mary Reilly Graphics
Printed and bound by CS Graphics, Singapore

HALF TITLE PAGE: *First row.* Frank S. Land (1891–1959), Henry Price (1697–1780),
Arthur A. Schomberg (1874–1938). *Second row.* Unknown American Freemason,
ca. 1860, Harry S. Truman (1884–1972), Joseph Brandt (Thayendanegea) (1742–1807).
Third row. Albert Pike (1809–1891), James W. Hood (1831–1918),
James J. Davis (1873–1947).

TITLE PAGE: *George Washington Laying the Cornerstone of the National Capitol,
18 September 1793.* Allyn Cox, Alexandria Virginia, 1952.
Copyright George Washington Masonic National Memorial Association.

10 9 8 7 6 5 4 3 2

To Richard Harris Curtis

A good colleague, close friend and Masonic Brother

In Appreciation

AMERICAN FREEMASONS is a joint publication of the National Heritage Museum in Lexington, Massachusetts, and the New York University Press. Individuals and organizations have provided funding for this publication. Without their timely and generous support, this book would not have been possible. At the core of this philanthropic endeavor, the benevolent nature of Freemasonry proved itself a living principle of this project's success.

Special recognition for financial support goes to:

Grand Lodge of Masons in Massachusetts
Supreme Council, 33°, Northern Masonic Jurisdiction, USA

Generous support was also received from:

Harry R. and Doreen T. Brahmstadt; Connecticut Council of Deliberation; Masonic Foundation of Michigan; Maine Consistory; Massachusetts Consistory; Mount Olivet Chapter of Rose Croix, Boston; New Hampshire Consistory; Scottish Rite Valley of Chicago, Illinois; Scottish Rite Valley of Cincinnati, Ohio; Scottish Rite Valley of Columbus, Ohio; Scottish Rite Valley of Dayton, Ohio; Scottish Rite Valley of Detroit, Michigan; Scottish Rite Valley of Portland, Maine; Scottish Rite Valley of Reading, Pennsylvania; Scottish Rite Valley of Southern New Jersey; Scottish Rite Valley of Central Jersey; Verdon D. Skipper; Richard V. Travis; Wisconsin Masonic Foundation.

The Square and Compasses: Emblem of Freemasonry

THE SQUARE AND COMPASSES surrounding the letter "G" form the standard emblem of American Freemasonry. The square teaches Masons to be honest and true in their actions. The compasses teach Masons to circumscribe their desires and act in moderation. The "G" represents geometry and is the initial for the name of Deity. Just as geometry is central to an understanding of the physical world, so is God central to Masons' lives.

Ancient Free and Accepted Masons

THIS TITLE IS COMMONLY USED throughout most of the country, although the first word does not appear in the title of grand lodges in some states. It appears in this book as AF&AM (or F&AM). The words have multiple definitions. The word "Ancient" usually refers to the Ancient Grand Lodge of England founded in 1756, and its use demonstrates the lineage to that grand lodge. The word also refers to being old or originating in remote times, similar to the way the word is used by Boston's Ancient and Honorable Artillery Company. The word "Free" usually indicates a freeborn man or one who is not a serf or in bondage. It also relates to the skill of working in freestone, that is, the art of designing, carving and sculpting stone. The term "Accepted" refers to the gentlemen who were not stonemasons but were "accepted" into stonemasons' lodges. It also denotes the acceptance of the fraternity by the British Crown and the Church of England.

Contents

Foreword

SINCE ITS ESTABLISHMENT in 1975, the Scottish Rite Masonic Museum and Library at Lexington, Massachusetts, has produced hundreds of exhibitions and public programs that celebrate and interpret the history and culture of the American people. The Scottish Rite museum — popularly known as the National Heritage Museum — was founded by the Scottish Rite Freemasons in the Northern Masonic Jurisdiction of the United States and was presented as a gift to the American people at the time of the bicentennial of the Battle of Concord and Lexington. The exhibitions have ranged from studies of the British view of the American Revolution and the life and times of George Washington to the American diner and the banjo, America's first instrument.

Part of its core mission during the past 30 years has been to collect, preserve and interpret the artifacts, publications and documents that represent the history of Freemasonry and other fraternal organizations. As this book points out, members of fraternal associations have played vital roles in building and sustaining this country. The museum's exhibitions on American history are well known and have been viewed by millions of visitors. What may be less well known are the catalogues and books that make up an important part of the intellectual legacy of this institution.

Among the catalogues that have accompanied museum exhibitions on Freemasonry are three that were prepared by curator of collections Barbara Franco: *Masonic Symbols in American Decorative Arts* (1976), *Bespangled, Painted and Embroidered: Decorated Masonic Aprons in America, 1790–1850* (1980), and *Fraternally Yours: A Decade of Collecting* (1986). In 1994, the museum published *Material Culture of the American Freemasons* by John D. Hamilton, curator of collections.

It was not the intent of the museum's founders that all exhibitions would be about Freemasonry, yet all projects undertaken by the National

Heritage Museum are built around the Masonic principles of increasing one's knowledge and providing further enlightenment about the subject being presented. Any attempt to focus on Freemasonry in America through an exhibition has been difficult, because the subject matter is so complex. It was out of this dilemma that Mark A. Tabbert, the museum's curator of Masonic and fraternal collections, was assigned the task of curating his first exhibition on Freemasonry. After the opening of "To Build and Sustain: Freemasons in American Community" in 2002, Mark was encouraged to publish a companion catalogue. As he began to work on the project, he decided that the book would be more than just a catalogue of the artifacts and label copy from the gallery's vignettes. It would expand upon the limited space within a gallery and serve as a lasting repository of documented research that supports the reasons why millions of men have been attracted to the Masonic fraternity for more than three centuries. The wealth of information in our Van Gorden-Williams Library and the ever-expanding items in our fraternal collections have been valuable assets in Mark's research.

American Freemasons has two audiences. Members of the Masonic fraternity will find that this book contributes to a greater understanding of the background of the organization. Hopefully they will gain an even greater appreciation of their fraternity. The book was written, however, with the non-Mason in mind. A single publication cannot possibly cover all aspects of such a complex institution, but this book provides the non-Masonic reader with insight into the basic history and philosophy of a fraternity that has often been looked upon as a "secret society." *American Freemasons* opens the door and allows you to walk in. Perhaps its easy-to-read and visually stimulating format will inspire others to research areas within the wide spectrum of fraternalism in America.

Frequently we hear from relatives of deceased members who discover a Masonic apron, jewel, hat, sword, cipher book or other paraphernalia in a dresser drawer or an attic trunk. Flea markets and Internet sites display fraternal regalia on a regular basis. Yet this material offers little meaning without some knowledge of the principles and symbolism of the organization. *American Freemasons* can serve as an important source in your search for more knowledge.

JOHN H. OTT
Executive Director
National Heritage Museum
July 2004

Preface

I BECAME INTERESTED in Freemasonry while working at the Historical Society of Western Pennsylvania in Pittsburgh in August 1993. Like most young Americans, I had a vague understanding of the fraternity. I certainly remember walking past the Masonic temple in my hometown in Iowa, and I was aware of neighbors who were Freemasons or active in Masonic groups like Eastern Star and Rainbow for Girls. I certainly remember Shriners' parades as a kid. On the other hand, I distinctly remember making jokes about how Freemasonry was an international conspiracy, a weird hybrid of the Jesuits, communists and James Bond's nemesis, "SPECTRE." In fact, I probably had the same opinion that most Americans still have about the Masonic fraternity — that Freemasonry is comprised of good and generous men, while the fraternity itself is a worldwide conspiratorial secret Order. After meeting my first "real" Freemason, Herb Wolstoncroft, who kindly gave me a tour of the Masonic temple in Pittsburgh, I realized that many other men whom I respected were also Masons. Through this process, I came to understand that the men who join Freemasonry are indeed kind and generous. This realization, along with the gentle encouragement of Jim and Eva Ann Elmer, caused me to seek membership in a Masonic lodge in 1998.

When I began my graduate history and museum studies program at Duquesne University in 1993, I decided to concentrate on American Freemasonry and fraternalism. In 1995, I completed an internship at the Scottish Rite Masonic Museum of Our National Heritage. (The name has since been shortened to National Heritage Museum.) Four years later, I became its curator of Masonic and fraternal collections. For the past five years, I have written many articles, curated several exhibitions, read countless books, and met scores of Masons. I was installed Master of my adopted Masonic lodge in Arlington, Massachusetts, in October 2004. Looking back at these landmarks along my journey, I am even more convinced that Masons are truly genuine. More importantly, they are almost completely incapable of entering into a conspiracy (except to do good) or keeping a secret (except in hiding private acts of kindness). Through this book, I hope the reader might receive a similar appreciation.

According to Freemasonry's lectures, "It is necessary there should be wisdom to contrive, strength to support and beauty to adorn all great and important undertakings." Nowhere is this truer than in the progress of this book and the people who made it possible. "The wisdom to contrive" comes from the founders of the National Heritage Museum who determined that its mission would be, first, to tell the story of America and, second, to collect, preserve and interpret American Masonic and fraternal history. These founders were the leaders of the Scottish Rite Freemasons of the Northern Masonic Jurisdiction, Sovereign Grand Commanders George A. Newbury and Stanley F. Maxwell. They created a plan, supervised the construction and developed an endowment through voluntary contributions from Scottish Rite Masons as a gift to the American people in 1975. Their leadership and generosity continued through their successors, Francis G. Paul, Robert O. Ralston and now Walter E. Webber. Supporting and advising these leaders were such good men as Louis L. Williams, John H. Van Gorden, James F. Farr and Sidney R. Baxter along with donations of money, time and artifacts from thousands of individual Masons. The impetus for this book, however, comes from John H. Ott, the museum's executive director, and Richard H. Curtis, editor of *The Northern Light.* It was John who gave me an opportunity in 1999 to curate an exhibition on American Freemasonry. After the opening of the exhibition in 2002, it was the insistence of Dick Curtis that the exhibition's story should become a book. Without John's guidance and Dick's patience and perseverance, the exhibition would never have opened and this book would never have been published.

Supporting the founders' wisdom is the work and legacy of the museum staff. Starting with the first museum directors, Clement M. Silvestro and Thomas J. Leavitt, who were assisted by Raymond Wilkinson and June Cobb, the museum has presented over 200 exhibitions, hundreds of public programs, educational lectures, classes and tours and welcomed more than two million visitors in 30 years. Punctuating the stories of American culture and history were those of American Freemasonry and fraternal orders. They were told through the dedicated efforts of my predecessors, Barbara Franco and John D. Hamilton, and librarians Gloria Jackson and Nancy Wilson. For 30 years, they built and organized the Masonic collections. In this process, they wrote dozens of articles and created files of information. From these sources, they produced numerous exhibitions and wrote seminal books on the material culture of American Freemasonry and fraternalism. Without their "strength to support" the collections, the research for this book could not have been documented so easily.

Some of the museum's tens of thousands of objects, archives and photographs have become the ornaments of this book. As much as this is a written history of American Freemasonry, it is also a display of Freemasons' love of beauty. The diversity of things that carry Masonic symbols is mind-boggling. From dice to dolls, from furniture to photographs, from buttons to buildings and even the street plan of Sandusky, Ohio, Freemasons have, in an almost obsessive manner, proclaimed themselves an integral part of American culture. But this obsession is more than simply pride or promotion. As a museum curator, I believe that all artifacts can teach as much about people from the past as photographic images or even documents. This is especially true with Masonic artifacts, for I view them as physical expressions of the abstract concept of fraternity. Every lapel pin, apron, gavel and piece of regalia contains a spark of the love millions of men have had for each other, their lodges and Freemasonry as a whole.

Using the work of the museum's founders and the builders of the collections, I have endeavored to arrange the material culture and historical record of American Freemasonry into an accessible, educational and enjoyable book. Like Freemasonry itself, this book is a compilation of many elements, yet I hope it remains unique in its presentation.

This book is the by-product of the National Heritage Museum's exhibition, "To Build and Sustain: Freemasons in American Community." Soon after it opened in 2002, there was a realization that a great deal of information had to be cut to meet the confines of the gallery. Although reluctant to begin another long-term project, I was compelled by the enthusiasm of Dick Curtis and Cynthia Purvis to begin writing.

Despite the goal to tell the greater story, this book, like all histories, fell inevitably short. No history is definitive. All barely dig beneath the surface of the complex and bewildering emotions, thoughts and actions of our ancestors. This book contains only bits of relics, writings and images of past Masons who have surfaced through the shifting sands. Still buried across this country are great libraries, museums and lodges filled with the history, love and pride of Freemasonry and many other American fraternal organizations. The narrative, illustrations and citations within the book do not represent the entire history of Freemasonry, nor is it even the "treasure map" to the history. At best, it is "a word or key to a word" to discover more insight.

Freemasonry does not presume to articulate anything new in the world;

on the contrary, it remains determined to preserve what is well known and obviously true. So it is with this book. It is not a new interpretive work, but rather an arrangement of older knowledge synthesized with recent scholarship. Its endnotes and bibliography are to aid the curious toward deeper knowledge.

This book would not have happened without Richard H. Curtis, to whom this book is respectfully dedicated. Besides initiating the project in August 2002, he also sustained it through the many months to its completion. During this long process, he relentlessly edited my spelling and grammar, and patiently listened to my long-winded explanations of convoluted paragraphs and awkwardly written sentences. Compulsive about typos, punctuation and capitalization, he did the best he could with what I gave him to edit. If there remain any factual errors within this book, then I am wholly responsible for them.

In every book, in every undertaking and in every life, there are those to thank and those to remember. First and foremost, I want to thank Robert O. Ralston, who approved and sponsored this project, and Walter E. Webber, who continued the support through its completion. Secondly, I wish to thank all those who read and reviewed a draft of the manuscript: William D. Moore, Kirsten Nord Hammerstrom, Richard E. Fletcher and my father, L. E. Tabbert. I also wish to express my particular gratitude to Basilios E. Tsingos and Kamel Oussayef, friends and brother Masons who volunteered to read the book and whose wise counsel and deep intelligence kept the book on an even path. My sincere thanks go to other readers who read sections or chapters of the book: Robert L. D. Cooper, R. A. Gilbert, Steven C. Bullock, Steven Kantrowitz, Keith L. Yates, Richard B. Burgess, Paul D. Fisher, Chernoh Sesay Jr., Alan E. Foulds, Douglass L. Ziedelis and my sister Merrie Tabbert. I also thank Cynthia M. Purvis, of Museum Publishing Partners, who was the catalyst for this project. She arranged for a co-publisher and printer, secured the wonderful talents of designer Susan Marsh and ultimately had faith in my ability to tell this story.

The support, encouragement and patience I have received from the National Heritage Museum staff are immeasurable. John Ott along with Hilary Anderson, director of exhibitions and collections, oversaw the development of the book and the exhibition from whence it came. While I would like to list the museum's complete staff, I am limited by space to particularly thank Maureen K. Harper, Tom Keaney, Julie Hall Williams, Catherine Swanson, Patricia J. Robin, Julie Triessl, Sue Williams, Jill Aszling, Elysa Engelman, Esther Fenerjian and James P. Malmfeldt. But of all the staff, I am most grateful for Helaine Blonder Davis. Through her help, the bibliography was compiled, quotations checked, citations found, and on many occasions she unknowingly supplied timely kind words of encouragement.

Numerous other historians, researchers and brother Freemasons both in Massachusetts and around the country helped me to appreciate the fraternity and research its history. Among the multitude to thank, I can only recognize Donald G. Hicks Jr., John H. Niebaum, Gregory Klemm, Thomas W. Jackson, George Seghers, S. Brent Morris, Diane Clements, Cynthia Alcorn, Heather Calloway, Larissa Watkins, William Krueger, Ray Coleman, Theda Skocpol, Arturo deHoyos, Matt Bucher, Pamela Lindsten, Rabbi Alvin I. Lieberman, Abby Peck, Glenys Waldman, Gaylord Strand, Jeffrey Charles, Stephen Patrick, Dustin Smith, Dick Browning, Thomas Savini, Napoleon Burton Jr., Leslie A. Lewis, Pierre Mollier, Kelley Connolley, Evert Kwaadgras, Norman L. Christensen and Richard V. Travis. Lastly, I want to thank all the members of the Masonic Library and Museum Association who helped me with my research e-mails.

Since arriving in Massachusetts over five years ago, I have met many new friends, but I particularly want to thank Mark and Betty Kelly, Diane Zipoli, Jennifer Doucette, Alex Bird, Alan Harper Jones, Elisabeth Carr-Jones, Robert E. Palmer Jr., Frank S. Maniscalco, Michael S. Podymaitis and Frank P. Foster Jr. Freemasonry's traditions and the brothers who live them have been my great comfort and guide. I am most grateful to be chosen to speak for those traditions and to be called "brother" by so many wonderful men.

My deepest appreciation goes to those closest to me. To each is owed a unique dept of gratitude which words can never express. To my parents, Le Tabbert and Gloria D. Kemp, my step-father, Laverne J. Kemp, and my brothers and sisters. To the family who "adopted me," Jim and Virginia Garnjobst, and my "brothers" Jordan and Joe Garnjobst. And lastly to my "Masonic parents," Jim and Eva Ann Elmer. Through the years and all the changes in my life, they have remained the fixed points by which I have navigated.

Lastly, to God, from Whom all blessings flow and for Whom I have endeavored to work my appointed craft to the best of the abilities He has given me.

Laborare est Orare.

M.A.T.

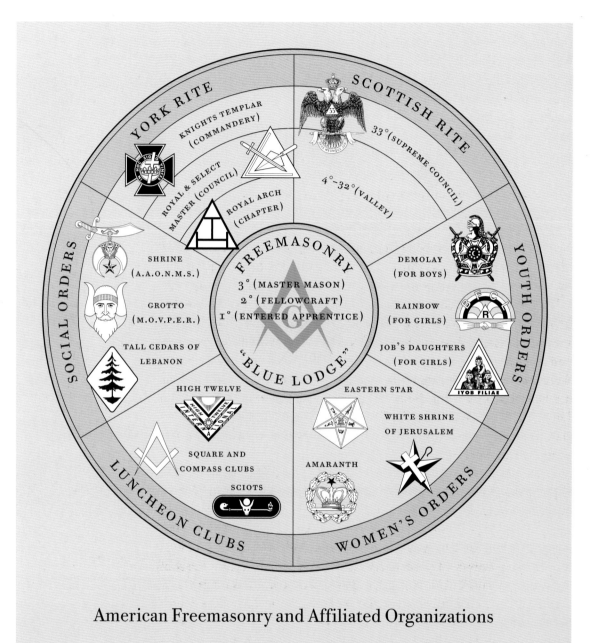

American Freemasonry and Affiliated Organizations

Introduction

"There is nothing new in the world except the history you do not know."

— HARRY S. TRUMAN, 1952 [1]

ON OCTOBER 15, 1948, three weeks before election day and in the midst of the political fight of his life, President Harry S. Truman spent the evening attending a Masonic lodge meeting in Beech Grove, Indiana. Earlier that day, Truman was giving a "whistle-stop" speech in Kokomo when he spotted in the crowd a sailor from his presidential yacht. He invited young Seaman Donald Bauermeister and his father to ride along on the presidential train down to Indianapolis. During the journey, Mr. Bauermeister mentioned to the president that his son Donald was receiving the third degree in Freemasonry at Beech Grove Lodge No. 8 that night. Knowing Truman to be a Mason, the father invited the president to attend. Much to the surprise of the Bauermeisters, Truman accepted the invitation.

Following a major speech at the Indianapolis War Memorial, Truman slipped away from the crowd and was driven to Beech Grove five miles away. Despite attempts by the Secret Service and Masonic leaders to keep the visit a secret, scores of local citizens and many prominent Freemasons awaited the president's arrival in the small town. Truman had been a Mason for nearly 50 years and had served as Grand Master of the Grand Lodge of Missouri, yet the local Masons still followed protocol and examined Truman's Masonic credentials before he could enter the lodge. The Secret Service agents and presidential aides who were not Masons were made to wait outside the lodge door. After the degree ceremony, Brother Truman requested permission of the lodge Master to address the brethren before the close of the meeting, and he asked if he could keep the Masonic apron that he had worn as a token of his visit. [2]

Truman's visit was not an attempt to seek votes. It reflected his genuine interest in the Masonic fraternity and the fraternity's importance in his life. The fact that the President of the United States, with all his major concerns, would interrupt campaigning for the sake of honoring one sailor speaks volumes about the man Harry Truman. But it also reveals an extraordinary loyalty and respect many Freemasons have toward the Masonic fraternity and toward each other as fraternal brothers. Exploring that relationship is at the heart of this book.

Freemasons, like those in Beech Grove, gather in local groups called lodges. These lodges are private clubs that admit only those who meet prescribed requirements. For instance, Harry Truman was admitted, but some of his aides and Secret Service agents were not. Portions of the initiation rituals and certain modes of membership recognition (principally, certain passwords and handshakes) constitute the confidential or "secret" aspects of the lodge. The centuries-old initiation ceremony that Donald Bauermeister received and Harry Truman witnessed is designed "to unite men of every country, sect and opinion and conciliate true friendship" among them.[3]

The private aspect of Masonic membership becomes especially important when it intersects with the American populace. The United States was founded on the proposition that all men are created equal and that they are endowed by their Creator with inalienable rights to life, liberty and the pursuit of happiness. The dynamic relationship and tension between the privacy of restricted Masonic lodges and the openness of America's public communities constitute the principal catalyst of this book. It is the story of men, like Harry Truman, who find refuge from the broader world as "Brother Truman" within a lodge, yet use the principles inculcated and reinforced in the lodge to function more effectively as "Mr. President" in the world. And it is the story of how the private Masonic lodge, like the one in Beech Grove, relates to the American community in which it resides.

Our story begins when disparate men come together and are united through Freemasonry's rituals, symbols and obligations into the community of the lodge. Through a progression of three initiation rituals, a man assumes the identity of a Freemason. He takes upon himself an obligation to obey the rules and regulations of the fraternity and is instructed that Freemasonry never recognizes a man by his wealth or appearance. Regardless of his past achievements or limitations, the fraternity and his lodge recognize him as a brother and equal. He is informed that the three tenets of brotherly love, relief and truth should guide his future conduct.

The privacy of the lodge and Freemasonry's focus on character building does not mean the fraternity is monastic or merely a school for philosophical contemplation. On the contrary, the new Mason is charged to adhere to his Masonic tenets by strengthening his personal relationships and becoming a better father, husband, son and citizen.

Purpose of the Book

"At leisure hours, study the liberal arts and sciences; and improve in Masonic disquisitions, by the conversation of well-informed Brethren, who will be as ready to give, as you can be to receive, instruction."

— WILLIAM PRESTON, 1796[5]

This book seeks to explore and understand how generations of Masons have been exposed to the tenets of Freemasonry and have practiced them in public. To fulfill this purpose is to provide an explanation of what Freemasonry is, why American men have joined it for nearly 300 years, and what Freemasons have done and continue to do. The use of quotations from Masonic initiation ceremonies and the symbols used by Masons to explain their ethical tenets will provide the reader with a deeper insight into Freemasonry's basic philosophy and a member's desire to participate.

Part One begins with a basic explanation of some of the legendary and historical origins of the fraternity. Borrowing heavily from three distinct sources, a group of independent, preexisting Masonic lodges came together in London in 1717 to form a so-called "grand" lodge with certain supervisory

606   SYRIA MOSQUE, PITTSBURGH ATHLETIC ASSOCIATION AND MASONIC TEMPLE,

SCHENLEY DISTRICT, PITTSBURGH, PA.   SA·H231

"The tenets of your profession as a Mason are Brotherly Love, Relief and Truth."

— THOMAS DUNCKERLEY, 1769[4]

SCHENLEY DISTRICT (OAKLAND), PITTSBURGH, PA

This postcard shows the Masonic Shriners' Syria Mosque (left), the Pittsburgh Athletic Association (center) and the Masonic Temple (right). The neighborhood is also the home of the University of Pittsburgh, Carnegie Library and Museum, Soldiers' and Sailors' Memorial and numerous other cultural and civic institutions. The Masonic temple was sold to the university in 1993.

Minsky Bros. & Co., Pittsburgh, PA, ca. 1935. Author's collection.

powers. From this point on, Masons traveled in various directions and adapted the fraternity to fit different locales. In the American colonies, it attracted the social and political elite, entrepreneurs, artisans, farmers and even free African-Americans. Through revolution, war and the establishment of the new republic, Freemasonry was transformed into a forum for equality, liberty, enterprise and civic virtue. By the 1820s, however, its considerable prestige created resentment and fear among some Americans. These attitudes and suspicions about the fraternity helped to fuel the flames of a scandal that caused many political, religious and community leaders to join together to denounce the fraternity, which suffered greatly as a result.

Part Two shows how Freemasonry found new ways to rebuild itself and to grow as the nation expanded in the 1800s. Successive generations of Masons employed the tenets inculcated in thousands of lodges throughout America to build the fraternity and also create new organizations to serve rapidly changing communities. Part Two begins to explore some of the most important reasons for the fraternal involvement of millions of American men, who sought (1) self-improvement, (2) dramatic ritual performance, (3) health and death benefits and (4) social life. Part Three examines life in the 1900s, when they found three more reasons to join: (5) business networks, (6) family participation and (7) community service.

The book does not make predictions for the future of Freemasonry. It simply relates the past to the present and shows how Freemasonry's tenets —first established in the 1700s—continue to adorn both the lodge and America today. Hopefully, the reader will gain a greater understanding of the interaction between the private Masonic lodge and the public environment of American community.

Freemasonry's Symbols and Rituals

"The tools and implements of architecture, symbols the most expressive! Imprint on the memory wise and serious truths, and transmit unimpaired, through a succession of ages, the excellent tenets of this institution."

— WILLIAM PRESTON, 1772 [6]

Freemasonry cannot be understood apart from its rituals and symbols and the way in which its members have interpreted and employed them. The nature of its rituals —their complexity, beauty and symbolism—distinguishes Freemasonry from all other voluntary associations. The initiation rituals attempt to foster brotherly love between the members of the fraternity, impress upon the mind of new Masons the necessity of relief, and encourage the new Mason to be a seeker and lover of truth.

The origin of Freemasonry and its rituals are obscure. While individual lodges are known to have existed in Scotland and England in the 1600s, it was not until 1717 that four London lodges publicly organized a grand lodge to supervise and coordinate the work of individual lodges. The year 1717 is thus referred to as the origin of organized Freemasonry. Yet neither researchers nor speculators have been able to conclusively determine when, where and how Freemasonry was born.[7] Some Masonic writers have been eager to argue that its rituals are divinely inspired and ancient. Many scholars contend that the founders merely wrote rituals laced with architectural and biblical metaphors. Regardless of its obscure origins, Freemasonry now operates throughout the world in tens of thousands of lodges and counts nearly three million men as fraternal brothers.[8]

Freemasonry and other voluntary associations have easily thrived in free and open societies. Unlike many other human institutions, however, the fraternity has persisted through the modern world's cruelest, oppressive and prejudiced communities. In the 20th century, religious fanaticism, communism, fascism, racism, commercialism and hedonism have all sought to dismiss, discredit or destroy it.[9] Nonetheless, Freemasonry still survives. Its rituals are its strength and the keystone that has united its members for four centuries.

The act of instructing and receiving instruction through the initiation rituals constitutes the basic operation of the lodge. Freemasonry is deeply rooted in an oral tradition. In some grand lodges the rituals are never written out, while in others, they are reduced to writings that employ codes. By passing the rituals from mouth to ear and from one generation to the next, Freemasonry has been sustained. The emphasis on preservation and continuation of knowledge reflects the worldly concerns of Freemasonry's founders.

The lessons taught in the rituals are interwoven with ideas central to the European Enlightenment of the 17th and 18th centuries. It is no coincidence that the exponents of the Enlightenment found that Freemasonry resonated with their way of thinking. Enlightenment philosophers, mathematicians, and scientists believed that human beings and their society could be improved by a search for knowledge, rational study and systematic applications.[10]

In the spirit of the Enlightenment, William Preston sought to improve himself in Masonry. More than 50 years after the formation of the first grand lodge in London, Preston, a Scotsman, visited London Masonic lodges to gather their oral rituals and lectures. His 1772 book, *Freemasonry*

Entered according to Act of Congress, in the year 1866 by James T. Hill, in the Clerks Office of the District Court of the District of Massachusetts.

Illustrated, contains the fraternity's first organized, rational and literary published lectures. Preston's work went through nine editions in his lifetime, and much of it today still constitutes Masonic ceremonies throughout America. Preston was, in part, motivated to codify the rituals and teachings so that the fraternity's message could be preserved against "the lapse of time, the ruthless hand of ignorance and the devastation of war." [11]

Freemasonry, as understood and portrayed by Preston, professes to be a universal charitable institution that teaches a system of morality to all men of good will who believe in God, referred to as the Grand Architect of the Universe. Freemasonry maintains its universality, because its tenets transcend time and culture. The fraternity thus uses tools and implements of architecture as the basis for its universal language. Like all languages, Masonic symbolism is taught incrementally to make complex lessons of life easier to understand and master. The stages of initiation and knowledge in Freemasonry are called "degrees." Rather than the titles of academic degrees (bachelor, master or doctor), Freemasonry uses the terms Entered Apprentice (first degree), Fellowcraft (second degree) and Master Mason (third degree) to describe a progression from the "darkness" of ignorance of Masonic principles to the "light" of their knowledge.

Freemasonry's symbolic language and its instructional system are derived mostly from medieval stonemason guilds. To differentiate themselves from stonemasons, Freemasons employ the terms "operative Masonry" and "speculative Masonry." While stonemasonry is the craft of building edifices, Freemasonry professes to be a "craft" devoted to building better men. Operative masons were organized in lodges or guilds and were taught ways to use tools to improve stone for construction. Speculative Masons call their organizations "symbolic" lodges and apply the symbolic meanings of the stonemasons' tools to discern ways — obvious upon further reflection but often overlooked — to improve themselves and become useful and productive members of their communities. [12]

Although Freemasonry's rituals have remained nearly unchanged and are remarkably similar throughout the country, each American grand lodge has its own particular traditions and unique characteristics. While Freemasonry is one universal language, it is one spoken in a myriad of local dialects. For consistency and convenience, many of the ritual quotations and symbols appearing in this book were first published by William Preston — and his American "successor" Thomas Smith Webb — and are similar to those used in Freemasonry today.

OPPOSITE:

MASONIC CHART OF SYMBOLS

Most of the symbols and iconography from Freemasonry's three initiation degrees appear in this 1860s lithograph. The Entered Apprentice degree is at the bottom; the second degree of Fellowcraft is in the center, and the image of King Solomon's Temple with the emblems of the third degree of Master Mason are at the top.

J. H. Bufford & Sons, Boston, 1866. National Heritage Museum, gift of John H. Van Gorden, 86.52b.

Freemasonry's Governance

"The Grand Lodge consists of, and is form'd by the Masters and Wardens of all the regular particular Lodges upon record, with the Grand Master at the head, and his Deputy on his left-hand, and the Grand Wardens in their proper places."

— JAMES ANDERSON, 1723[13]

The source for the supposed secrets of Freemasonry is an inheritance from medieval operative stonemasons. Just as medieval craftsmen sought to control their profession by not divulging trade secrets, Freemasons seek to maintain the quality of their lodges by regulating their rituals. One of the prime responsibilities of Masonic grand lodges is to maintain the symbolic language and the quality of ritual taught in its subordinate lodges. If a grand lodge or lodge fails these responsibilities, then the credibility of all its brothers suffers in the same way poorly trained workmen jeopardize the soundness of a building.

The fraternity's jurisprudence and governance are derived from stonemasons' regulations or "charges" written in the 15th and 16th centuries.[14] It was not until 1723, however, that *The Constitutions of the Free-Masons* — a seminal work in the codification and establishment of Masonic governance — was published by James Anderson, a Scottish Presbyterian minister and member of the Royal Society.

According to his own accounts, Anderson was commissioned to write the book by the Duke of Montagu, who was the Grand Master of the first grand lodge in London. Anderson included several key elements that shaped Freemasonry's future development. The grand lodge in London accepted, endorsed and promulgated Anderson's *Constitutions.* Although it has been frequently revised, it remains the foundation for the governance of most Masonic grand lodges. Anderson's work limited Freemasonry's purpose and established enduring precedents. The most important points are that a Mason must be an adult male of good morals and reputation, cannot be an atheist, and must be a loyal and law-abiding citizen. Furthermore, Anderson's work established the idea that a lodge of Masons must be chartered by a grand lodge before it can be considered legal and must perform only the ritual work approved by its grand lodge. He also insisted that all lodge officers are to be chosen according to personal merit, not seniority, wealth or social status.[15]

No matter what one's achievements, credentials or titles may be in public life, all Masons assume the equal title of "brother" in a Masonic lodge. Personal or public identities are not relinquished outside the lodge.

Introduction

This is the first and most important Masonic book ever published. Prior to its publication, Freemasonry consisted of a few loosely affiliated British clubs. Through James Anderson's work, Freemasons everywhere had the information they needed to build a united and regulated fraternity. The frontispiece shows the Grand Master, the Duke of Montagu, handing the Constitutions to his successor, the Duke of Wharton. Also shown are symbols of logic — the 47th problem of Euclid, the architectural columns, and Apollo, the Greek god of art and knowledge, driving his sun chariot.

Frontispiece, The Constitutions of the Free-Masons. National Heritage Museum.

Quite the opposite, the fraternity's purpose is to improve the inner man within the security of the lodge so that he might better live his public roles.

Contrary to some accusations, Freemasonry is not on a crusade to control the world or its members. For most of its existence, the fraternity did not actively seek new members. Only in recent years has there been an effort by Freemasonry to promote itself. It is viewed as a craft in the same way that the term is used to identify stonemasons, metalworkers or carpenters. As a voluntary organization, Freemasonry can make no demands on members' time or commitment beyond what those members are willing to demand of themselves. Only the members who choose to actively participate assume leadership positions in their lodges. Indeed, many members attend the regular meetings of their lodge infrequently, if at all. It is not uncommon for brothers to attend meetings of their lodge only on special occasions. But an active brother will serve through a progression of offices that culminates in his becoming the Master, or presiding officer, of his lodge. Through diligence and talent, he may later preside as the Grand Master of his grand lodge.

As a self-improvement organization, Freemasonry has long described its mission to "make good men better."[16] It does not seek to "make bad men good." Men are denied admission if the members of a particular lodge feel that an applicant has a bad reputation or is found to have a history of immoral or illegal actions. This is done through an investigative process and a secret ballot. One negative vote (a so-called "black ball") is sufficient to deny the applicant admission. While this system can be harsh in its application, it is also one of the secrets of Freemasonry's longevity. By denying any ability to "save," rehabilitate or reform bad men, Freemasonry has avoided many serious conflicts with religious, medical or governmental authority. Of course, Freemasonry is an institution comprised of fallible individuals — volunteers at that — and as such the application process occasionally fails to function in the manner in which it is intended. The result is that from time to time misguided and reprobate men have been able to gain admission and, in some instances, even assume a leadership position within a lodge. For members who stray from the principles of the craft, there is a due process for expulsion from the fraternity.[17]

Defining Freemasonry

"By Speculative Masonry we learn to subdue the passions, act upon the square, keep a tongue of good report, maintain secrecy, and practise charity."

— WILLIAM PRESTON, 1772 [18]

Freemasonry's rituals, symbols and constitutions have led many Masons and non-Masons to attempt to define the craft. To the extent that it is a unique institution, it is not easily defined. Traditionally, Masons have defined the fraternity as "a peculiar system of morality, veiled in allegory and illustrated by symbols."[20] While this is essentially true, it is more than a system. Freemasonry is an institution and a collection of distinct communities of men and as such it only exists when men voluntarily come together. The definition, therefore, has varied from Mason to Mason and lodge to lodge over the course of American history.

One basic way to view Freemasonry is to see it as a voluntary association akin to the Elks, Rotary, Boy Scouts or other community club. Unlike these clubs, however, a prospective member cannot even attend a lodge meeting before seeking admission. Furthermore, he does not become a member until he takes upon himself various obligations. The importance of maintaining the obligations are emphasized by references to severe "ancient" penalties. He must first pass through a series of three initiation rituals before he is a full member. And in many jurisdictions, a man must prove he has memorized and understood the lessons and symbols of one degree before receiving the next.

Before the 1920s, Freemasonry was often called a "secret society." Since that time, this terminology has increasingly assumed sinister connotations, and Masons now attempt to counter this definition and the conspiratorial image it conveys by referring to the fraternity as "a society with secrets." In fact, the society has not had secrets to hide since the 1720s, when its rituals were first exposed in London newspapers. As Benjamin Franklin, himself a leading Freemason in Philadelphia, commented in the 1730s, "Their grand secret is that they have no secret at all." [21] The craft's origin, symbolism, purposes and rituals still strike some people as "weird" and "spooky," despite the fact that there are lodges in nearly every town, tens of thousands of published books on the craft, millions of members, and a growing number of Internet sites. [22] The feelings are largely due to a lack of response from the fraternity in the face of the overactive imagination of conspiracy theorists, the sensationalism of modern journalists and the rigid views of certain well-meaning, but ill-informed, religiously minded individuals.

When scholars attempt to make sense of the fraternity, some dismiss Freemasonry as a patriarchal cult or "old boys" club, where hypocrisy and ambition overrule true fraternity or equality. Its rituals and symbolism are often mistakenly equated to the sophomoric pranks of college fraternities, and its membership is erroneously identified through such television characters as *The Honeymooners'* Ralph Cramden and Ed Norton. [23] Other academics, who have given the fraternity serious attention, have discovered in Freemasonry sources for American gender, class, ethnicity, race and intergenerational phenomena. [24] Still others have sought ways to understand the genuine love and pride generations of American men have felt when they "meet upon the level, act upon the plumb, and part upon the square" — whether in the lodge or on the street. [25] While these scholars have much to say about Freemasonry that is valuable, most of them are not members, have never attended a meeting and have not actually witnessed the rituals performed. This limits their ability to fully understand the craft.

Since the 1730s, the Roman Catholic Church and certain Protestant denominations have, at various times, labeled Freemasonry dangerous. [26] The craft's combination of prayer, initiation rituals, obligations, symbolism, morality and charity has caused them to see the fraternity as a rival, parallel or false religion. Some believe Freemasonry is a religion, because lodge meetings begin and end with a prayer, a holy book (in America most frequently the Bible) is open in the center of the lodge room during meetings, and a man swears to be good to his word by placing his hand on the holy book he holds sacred. [27]

When challenged by these positions, Freemasonry replies that its use of the non-sectarian title "Grand Architect of the Universe," for example, allows those of different faiths to come together in harmony. While each Mason must profess a belief in God, Freemasonry also believes that the relationship between the individual and God is personal, private and sacred.

Anderson's 1723 *Constitutions* charges members to "leave their particular opinions [on religion] to themselves" so that they will not have to suffer religious zealots or "stupid atheists."[28] Masons stress that the fraternity only encourages men to be more devout in their chosen faith. These explanations do not diminish the spiritual dimensions of the fraternity nor do they prevent some men from professing that attending lodge meetings fulfills their spiritual needs.

American politicians, especially after the French Revolution and during the Napoleonic era, began to suspect and accuse the fraternity of conspiratorial tendencies. These attacks reached their most violent stage during the anti-Masonic hysteria of the 1820s and 1830s. Ever since, the idea of private groups of men bound together by rituals and oaths has troubled certain Americans and political leaders.[29] Freemasonry has endeavored to rebut such attacks by pointing to not only the constitutional right of peaceable assembly but also Anderson's *Constitutions,* which forbids the discussion of politics in the lodge and charges brothers to be "peaceable subjects to the civil powers."[30]

The fact that Freemasonry means different things to so many different people has been one of its greatest strengths. Its definitional elusiveness continues to attract new members while remaining the source of inspiration for its varied detractors and critics. Its supporters and critics notwithstanding, Freemasonry is an important part of many lives, entire families, and communities.

In the course of one lodge meeting, Freemasonry is a spiritual organization when the chaplain leads the brethren in prayer and asks for the blessing of Deity. It is a guild when the Master of the lodge teaches the new Mason the symbolic uses of stonemasons' tools. It becomes a school of instruction when the new brother learns about the importance of the seven liberal arts and sciences. At other moments, it is an amateur theater company when the ritual is performed. The lodge becomes a men's social club when meeting for dinner and fellowship. It becomes a charitable group when relief is provided to distressed brothers, their families or the local community. It is also a business association when members with similar interests share ideas. The lodge resembles a family when fathers and sons, strangers and friends bond as "brothers," and it is a community league when volunteers are needed for a project.

Yet at other times Freemasonry's constitutions, tenets and symbolism have emanated from the lodge as Masons have carried the principles into their communities. Just as *Robert's Rules of Order* caused the birth of infinite committees, so Freemasonry sparked the creation of thousands of American voluntary organizations. Masons and non-Masons have adapted

Masonic rituals and symbols to create new fraternities. These groups teach morality and inspire "brotherly love" within diverse communities, such as the B'nai B'rith did among Jewish-Americans, the Order of AHEPA did among Greek-Americans, and the Knights of Columbus did among the country's Roman Catholics. Other Masons used Masonic relief to develop mutual benefit associations and life insurance companies or build hospitals, orphanages, and retirement homes, such as the Benevolent Protective Order of Elks. Still others, dropping the rituals and symbols, formed so-cial, business, educational and community service clubs, such as Lions International.[31]

All these things cannot adequately explain why Freemasonry has spread around the world and found especially fertile soil in American society. But it does reveal the great desire of men like Harry Truman who join a Masonic lodge to improve themselves, care for each other and build their communi-ties. From an obscure past, a fraternity of millions of men has given billions of dollars and untold hours establishing, building and adorning their lodges for the betterment of an unknown future.

Freemasonry is a symbol of man's search for wisdom, brotherhood and charity. This universal search is ancient and is renewed every time a lodge of Masons initiates a new brother. Through rituals, symbols and obligations, a volunteer becomes a part of a community, as he begins his own individual search. Freemasonry refers to this as a journey in search of light. This book continues that search for light by telling the story of American Freemasons.

By the Glory of the Grand Architect of the Univer[se]

LUX EX TENEBRIS.

Unitas Concordia Fratrum.

At the East where Shines the Great Light, and where reigns Silence, Concord and Peace:
The 29th of the Ninth Month called Kislew 7767. A.M.5520. equal to 20th Dec. 1767.

[...]ue of a full Power and Authority committed to me by the Most Illustrious, Most Respectable and Most Sublime B[...] [G]rand Inspector of all Lodges relative to the Superior Degrees of Masonry, from Secret Master to the 29th Degree; and co[...] [Cou]ncil of Princes of Masons in the Island of Jamaica &c. &c. &c. We Hen: And:n Francken Depy. Inspr. Genl. of all [...] in the West Indies and North America; have duly examined and found [wor]thy our dear Brethren William Gamble, Francis Joseph [...] [T]homas Lynott and Richard Cartwright and find them well qualified [in] the Mysteries of Masonry to the 14th Degree, known by us [...] Masonry, by the name of Perfection of Masonry Now Know Ye that in consequence of such Power We have Consti[...] [t]o Constitute our said Worthy Brethren William Gamble, Francis Joseph Von Pfister, Thomas Swords, Thomas Lynott and Ric[...] [Lodge of Pe]rfection, by the name of INEFFABLE: to be held at the City of Albany in the Province of New York [...] [W]e appoint (pro tempore) Our worthy Brother William Gamble to officiate as Master; with power to Appoint his O[...] [Ma]ster shall be appointed by Virtue of an Instrument in Writing und[er] our hand and Seal for that purpose, to proceed to Initiate [...] [14th] Degree of said higher Degrees, as they shall be found worthy, to the 14th. Degree or Perfection, having a due care and reg[...] [...] One Degree at a time to Regulate themselves according to their well calculated Laws and Regulations, to be approved of an [...] [...u]nder; taking especial care to admit none who have not been or are Officers of a Regular Constituted Lodge, and that their nu[...] [mem]bers in all, who shall be residents in this Province, but with a pow[e]r to keep said number up, provided Death, Absence from the [...] [...] Leagues shall render it impracticable for any particular Member or Members to give due attendance. That in case of [...] [s]ince, We Authorize the said Members of said Lodge of Perfection named the Ineffable; to choose every year th[...] [...]s Officers) by a Majority of Votes. Further that said Lodge of Perfection, at all times shall pay due Obedience to our [...] [...]s of the Grand Council of Princes of Masons (if any established in this Province) and transmit quarterly to [...] [...] and their Qualities, with every Transaction of note; and in case they do find and should conclude on any Articles for the [...] [...t]icles are to be sent us by Petition, and if found Beneficial, shall be granted under our hand and Seal. And Further that [...] [...] Ineffable shall fully conform and behave themselves to this our Constitution and Patent to which I ha[ve] [...] Arms, with the Grand Seal of the Perfection of Masonry, in the [...] [whe]re the greatest of Treasures are deposited the beholding of which [...] [w]ith Comfort, Joy and Acknowledgment of all that's Good and Great [...] [fo]r the B:B: at New York, the Day and Year above written

Hen:y And:ew Francken
Sovn. Prince of Masons. Depty. gr. I[nsp.]

Establishing

Freemasonry

1600-1835

CHAPTER I

Enlightenment

Freemasonry in Britain and Europe, 1600–1800

"The supports of a Lodge are three great pillars, called Wisdom, Strength and Beauty. It is necessary there should be Wisdom to contrive, Strength to support, and Beauty to adorn all great and important undertakings."

— MASONIC RITUAL, 1730[1]

FREEMASONRY, which is often called "the craft," is founded upon architectural metaphors. Complex symbols and tenets reveal a confluence of many sources. From its perceived origins in medieval Europe up to the present day, Freemasonry's history reflects the continual use of new techniques and tools to illustrate its tenets. Since the founding of the first grand lodge in London in 1717, Freemasonry has spread from England throughout the world and now includes people of all faiths, races, talents and classes.[2]

Judeo-Christian teachings, stonemasons' regulations and the Enlightenment philosophy have each had a profound effect on the creation and development of Freemasonry. The Masonic fraternity borrows the concept of wisdom and the tenet of brotherly love from Judeo-Christian teachings. The concept of strength and the tenet of relief come from the stonemasons' guilds. Freemasonry owes its beauty and the tenet of truth to the Enlightenment.

OPPOSITE: SCRIPTORIUM OF A MONASTERY

Between the fall of Rome in 476 and the Renaissance of the 1500s, European monastic and rabbinical communities preserved and copied ancient Latin, Greek and Hebrew texts. The principles of philosophy, art and science were perpetuated through their libraries and schools.

Interior of a Convent (a Scriptorium), 1500s. Bridgeman-Giraudon / Art Resource, New York, Museo Lazaro Galdiano, Madrid, Spain.

Judeo-Christian Traditions

"Speculative Masonry is so much interwoven with religion, as to lay us under the strongest obligations to pay to the Deity that rational homage, which at once constitutes the duty and happiness of mankind."

— WILLIAM PRESTON, 1772[3]

A product of Western civilization, Freemasonry is grounded on Judeo-Christian foundations. When four London Masonic lodges formally organized in 1717, English society was beginning to recover from religious, sectarian and political strife. Some two centuries had passed since Henry VIII's fateful decision to break with the Church of Rome, and the intervening years had witnessed warfare and bloodshed. Seeking a means to reestablish unity, Freemasons sought to avoid theological and political differences by subscribing to a viewpoint that supported a universal affirmation of man's dependence on God, the existence of an afterlife, and the wisdom conveyed through Holy Scripture and evident in the designs of nature. To join a Masonic lodge, a man was obliged to respect "that religion in which all men agree, leaving their particular opinions to themselves."[4]

The first generation of European Freemasons established an important precedent by allowing Jews and Christians of many denominations to enter the lodge and become fraternal brothers.[5] From the fraternity's founding in Protestant England, its principle of universal religious toleration expanded as the organization grew. Because of its spirituality, Freemasonry is frequently described as "a brotherhood of man under the Fatherhood of God."[6] The spiritual aspect allowed men "to meet on the level" of equality, "act on the plumb" of character and "part on the square" of virtue.

Stonemasons' Guilds

"A Lodge is a Place where Masons assemble and work: Hence that Assembly, or duly organized Society of Masons, is called a Lodge, and every Brother ought to belong to one, and to be subject to its By-Laws and the General Regulations."

— JAMES ANDERSON, 1723[7]

During the medieval age, stonemasons' guilds were organized locally to regulate the work of their members. Guilds were comprised of "laborers," who wrought the stone; "foremen," who supervised the work, and "architects," who were the master overseers. Guilds oversaw a craftsman's prog-

ress from apprentice to master, maintained the quality and ownership of the craft, and provided assistance to the brothers in time of need. A stonemason's "lodge" was located at the job site and was the place where masons gathered, received instruction and stored their tools.[8]

Unlike most craftsmen, stonemasons were intimately connected to both the religious and secular powers. They worked closely with bishops and priests to build cathedrals, churches and chapels that glorified God, amplified the Holy Mysteries of the Mass and proclaimed the majesty of the Church. Kings, barons and other nobility entrusted stonemasons to build palaces and castles that beautified their courts, protected their realms and magnified their power.

To maintain their craft and satisfy both spiritual and temporal masters, stonemasons created several means to regulate themselves. Organized guilds in the 1300s drew up long lists of rules or "charges" that articulated their mythical history, established their local authority, and required the members to be faithful Christians and loyal subjects of the king.[9] In addition to these written charges were deeper traditions. Illiterate stonemasons probably used words, hand signs and grips to identify each other and retain their trade secrets. These secret signs supposedly prevented unworthy men from gaining admission into the lodges or receiving guild assistance. Masons used the secret words and grips to secure work and establish seniority as they traveled to distant job sites.

Stonemasons' guilds declined with the waning of castle and cathedral building in the late 1500s. Local guilds increasingly competed for work. Masons, particularly in Scotland, sought the protection and patronage of the aristocracy. The acceptance of influential gentlemen into the lodge generated broader public interest in Masonry, which led more non-stonemasons to seek membership.[10] With the passage of time, these "accepted" members came to dominate. In the mid-1600s, "accepted" brothers in England, such as Elias Ashmole, found broader purposes for the semi-organized guild system with its "ancient" rules and signs of recognition. The Free and Accepted Masons reinterpreted guild rules by restricting membership to only able-bodied men who were loyal to the crown and faithful to God.[11] By 1717, a systematic and rational Masonic organizational movement was underway.

The Enlightenment

"The Greater Pythagoras, prov'd the Author of the 47th Proposition of Euclid's first Book, which if duly Observ'd, is the Foundation of all Masonry, sacred, civil, and military."

— JAMES ANDERSON, 1723 [12]

The British Enlightenment of the 17th and 18th centuries influenced Freemasonry's use of symbolic rituals, appreciation for beauty and emphasis on the pursuit of truth. During the religious and political wars that spread throughout Western Europe in the wake of the Protestant Reformation, intellectuals, artists, scientists and theologians were often forced to relocate in search of safety. Within cosmopolitan communities, public taverns and coffeehouses became popular places for cultured gentlemen to gather for intelligent and social discourse. For example, the Royal Society, founded about 1660, attracted such prominent men as Robert Boyle, Sir Isaac Newton, and Elias Ashmole. These men and many others slowly accumulated, organized and transformed disparate elements of knowledge into a system of scientific principles. Distinguished by its commitment to rational thought and scientific method, a new generation believed it could discover ways to gain personal improvement, bring order to society and understand the whole universe.[13]

In their search for knowledge, they found inspiration and confirmation from their intellectual predecessors. Saint Thomas Aquinas, Galileo Galilei and Sir Francis Bacon, among others, had all sought harmony from the Bible, classical philosophies and the laws of nature. The Enlightenment's

47TH PROBLEM
OF EUCLID

OPPOSITE:
NATURAL PHILOSOPHERS
Surrounded by animal specimens, maps, instruments, and books, Enlightenment-era natural philosophers, or scientists, discuss the orbits of the planets.

Philosopher demonstrating orrery to students, Frontispiece, A New Universal History of Arts and Sciences, *1759, London. American Philosophical Society Library.*

Establishing Freemasonry

philosophers continued this work while seeking deeper meaning from ancient civilizations. They studied Greek and Roman architecture and King Solomon's Temple in search of keys to unlock the lost truths of ancient civilizations.[14]

King Solomon's Temple

"And if we consider the [Temple's] 1,453 Columns of Parian Marble, with twice as many Pilasters, both having glorious Capitals of several Orders, and about 2,246 Windows, besides those in the Pavement, with the unspeakable and costly Decoration of it within; . . . we must conclude its Prospect to transcend our Imagination; and that it was justly esteem'd by far the finest Piece of Masonry upon Earth before or since."

— JAMES ANDERSON, 1723[15]

The three disparate elements — religion (wisdom), stonemasons (strength) and Enlightenment (beauty) — provided a framework for Freemasonry to develop in the early 1700s. The biblical story of King Solomon's Temple, described in 1 Kings and 2 Chronicles, united these elements. Within a lodge, men of differing faiths accepted the Temple as a symbol from which respect and brotherly love could grow.

To Jews, the Temple was a culmination of their covenant with God; to Christians it was a reflection of the coming City of God. The Temple — as

SOLOMON'S TEMPLE

Vignettes along the bottom show various details from the Temple's interior and furnishings. Engraver John Senex (1690–1740) was Junior Grand Warden of the first grand lodge in London and published James Anderson's *Constitutions of the Free-Masons* in 1723.

Front View of the Temple of Solomon, John Senex, London, England, 1725. National Heritage Museum, gift of Union Lodge, AF&AM, Dorchester, MA, 75.46.16.

Establishing Freemasonry

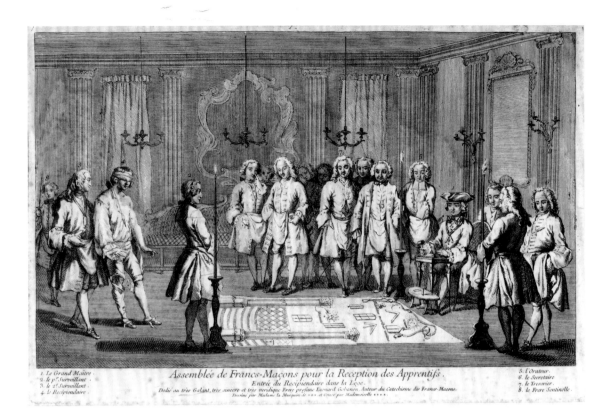

Assemblée de Francs-Maçons pour la Reception des Apprentifs.
Entrée du Recipiendaire dans la Loge.

1. Le Grand Maître.
2. le p.ᵉ Surveillant.
3. le 2.ᵉ Surveillant.
4. le Recipiendaire.

5. l'Orateur.
6. le Secretaire.
7. le Tresorier.
8. le Frere Sentinelle.

the house of the God of Abraham, Moses and Jesus — became a theologically neutral symbol for Freemasonry's spirituality and brotherly love to which all believers in a Supreme Being could relate.

Built in an ancient time and place, the Temple was also open to mythological interpretation. According to the scriptural passages, Solomon prayed for, and received, wisdom from God to build the Temple.[16]

The natural philosophers of the Enlightenment became increasingly enamored with Solomon's Temple. The Bible's detailed description combined with the accounts of the ancient historian Josephus made it worthy of serious contemplation. Built in Jerusalem around 966 B C, the Temple stood for nearly 400 years before its destruction by the Babylonians. As the house of God, the Temple became the subject of many moral and scientific treatises. Some natural philosophers believed the Temple's architecture and ornaments held mathematical and geometrical keys to understanding the nature of God and His creation.[17]

Early Scottish Freemasons used the Temple as a symbol to unify their initiation ceremonies.[18] The first degree (Entered Apprentice) symbolically begins on the Temple's "checkered pavement" where the candidate receives instruction on the morals, virtues and tenets of the fraternity. In

FRENCH FREEMASONS
AT WORK

In this scene, a blind-folded initiate (left) is conducted before the lodge to receive instruction in the symbols of the craft. Seated (right) is the lodge Master surrounded by his officers. Placed between them is a chart of symbols — called a tracing board — that guides the lecture.

Assemblée de Francs-Maçons pour la Reception des Apprentiss, engraved by C. Crepy, printed by Jacques Chevreau, Paris, ca. 1744. National Heritage Museum, gift of Charles R. Yeaton, 84.69.

the second degree (Fellowcraft), he symbolically climbs up to the Temple's "middle chamber" and is educated in architecture, the liberal arts and sciences, and intellectual improvement. The third degree (Master Mason) begins in the uncompleted and unconsecrated Holy of Holies, where the candidate assumes the role of the Temple's master builder, Hiram Abiff. Within the third degree, a member is charged with building God's Temple in his heart and employing the tenets of brotherly love, relief and truth within his community.[19]

The innovative use of an architectural metaphor centered on the Temple made the Masonic rituals interesting to contemporaries while developing an exclusive jargon among members. Performing the rituals improved members' intellectual capacities and taught them the art of memory.[20] The continuation of stonemasons' relief and the development of other charitable work gave Freemasons an important legitimate mission. The adoption of enlightened philosophies restricted membership to the culturally refined. Thus the early Accepted Freemasons transformed a tradesmen's guild into a fraternity for moral edification, intellectual recitations, benevolent service and gentlemanly socialization.

Modern and Ancient Freemasonry, 1717–1813

"And now the freeborn British Nations, disentangled from foreign and civil wars, and enjoying the good fruits of Peace and Liberty, having of late much indulg'd their happy genius for Masonry of every sort, and reviv'd the drooping lodges of London, this fair Metropolis flourisheth . . ."

— JAMES ANDERSON, 1723[21]

British society in the early 1700s experienced a period of extraordinary growth. Great Britain had survived a civil war, regicide, and the Glorious Revolution in the previous century. A new dynasty was founded when George of Hanover ascended the throne in 1714. During the next hundred years, Britain would be severely tested by France as it developed into a global military and economic superpower. London became the center of a colonial empire that stretched around the world, and thousands ventured into the city to seek their fortune and acceptance in its highest societies.[22]

The first generation of Freemasons thrived in this new cosmopolitan society. The four London lodges that organized a grand lodge in 1717 took steps to coordinate the craft and separate themselves from stonemasons' guilds. With the oldest stonemason presiding, the members elected

Anthony Sayer — an "accepted" Mason and gentleman — as their first Grand Master.[23] John Theophilus Desaguliers, a Huguenot minister and fellow of the Royal Society, served as Grand Master in 1719. He was followed by the Duke of Montagu in 1721. To distinguish themselves from "operative" masons, the Freemasons called their fraternity the "Royal Art," the "Gentle Art" or "Speculative Masonry," and they eventually chose decorated aprons to replace plain leather ones.[24] Most importantly they sought evidence to prove their ancient lineage, articulate their noble philosophy and govern their craft.

James Anderson, a Presbyterian minister and member of the Royal Society, was chosen to create the first published record of the organization. Born in Scotland and probably made a Freemason there, Anderson later moved to London. In 1723, he published *The Constitutions of the Free-masons* as the official record of the grand lodge. It is the first documented Masonic book ever printed. Its contrived history — more mythology, supposition and speculation than fact — attempted to trace Freemasonry from Adam in the Garden of Eden through Ancient Greece and Rome to the 1700s. The book set forth the regulations of the grand lodge and issued "charges" to brothers on how to act toward one another and toward society as a whole. Anderson included songs that were sung during lodge meetings and banquets.[25]

Freemasons in London soon attracted public attention. As early as 1726, descriptions of their activities and ceremonies were printed in newspapers. The most popular and important account was Samuel Pritchard's 1730 pamphlet, *Masonry Dissect'd.* Pritchard's work and other exposures led some Englishmen to dismiss the club as foolish.[26] Many more men, however, started their own quasi-Masonic clubs or sought membership in a lodge. The four lodges that formed the grand lodge in London did not necessarily own the fraternity. Nor did they have power over all the older "occasional" lodges or new Masonic-like clubs in the city, let alone across the kingdom.

As a consequence of Freemasonry's popularity, the first grand lodge came in conflict with other newly created grand lodges. In 1725 the Grand Lodge of Ireland was formed in Dublin, and in 1736 the Grand Lodge of Scotland was organized in Edinburgh. Through the rest of the century,

BRITANNIA AND MASONRY

Britannia is shown with the "coat of arms" and tools of English Freemasonry. In the distance is London with the great dome of St. Paul's Cathedral and London Bridge. The sun shines upon the many ships on the River Thames carrying English goods and the concept of Freemasonry to every point on the globe.

Frontispiece, The Constitutions of the Ancient and Honourable Fraternity of Free and Accepted Masons, 1756, London. National Heritage Museum.

as many as four other grand lodges were established at various times in England.[27]

The most serious challenge to the first grand lodge came from Irish Masons living in London. Many were merchants, artisans and other individuals of "lesser classes," who were regularly denied admittance into London lodges. Questioning the authority of the grand lodge that rejected them, they organized their own grand lodge in 1751. The primary leader and Grand Secretary was Laurence Dermott, an Irish journeyman painter and later a successful wine merchant. In 1756, he published *Ahiman Rezon: or A Help to a Brother,* in which he claimed the first grand lodge had fallen away from original Masonic usages, which his grand lodge was preserving. By labeling the first grand lodge as "Modern" and proclaiming his grand lodge, though younger, as "Ancient," he trumped the Masonic legitimacy of the more aristocratic grand lodge.[28]

The "Ancient" lodges attracted less-affluent and less-educated men, who sought the means to ascend the English social ladder. Instead of emphasizing Freemasonry's social aspects, they broadened their relief efforts as they accepted a greater variety of men.[29] Ancient Freemasonry became a pathway to extend a man's business contacts, confirm his honor and integrity, improve his manners and knowledge, and further his aspirations of becoming an affluent and respected gentleman.

The Ancient Grand Lodge challenged the Moderns in two other important ways. The Ancients willingly issued charters and warrants to any organized group of Masons who petitioned. Lodges soon formed within British regiments and among communities of merchants and traders in the expanding British colonies. By 1780, the Ancient Grand Lodge had issued hundreds of warrants to form lodges in India, North and South America.[30] The Ancients were also innovative with the rituals and symbols. Unlike the Moderns, who only worked three degrees, the Ancients conferred an additional degree, the Royal Arch, which extended the story of Solomon's Temple to the rebuilding of the Temple after the return of the Jews from the Babylonian exile. Loosely based on scriptural passages from Ezra, the drama of the Royal Arch degree referred to a lost crypt discovered by workmen while they were preparing the Temple mount for new construction. The origin of the Royal Arch degree is as obscure as the roots of the first three degrees.[31]

The rivalry between the Modern and Ancient Grand Lodges continued into the early 1800s. Yet some brothers from the Moderns partook of the Royal Arch degree. On the other hand, the Ancients followed the Moderns' tradition of noble patronage by electing the Duke of Athol as Grand Master in 1775.

Eventually the Modern and Ancient Grand Lodges agreed to unify. The pressure for unification came from several sources. First, some men

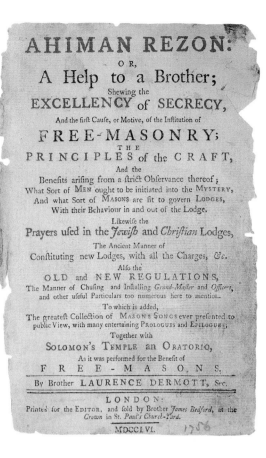

AHIMAN REZON

Written by Laurence Demott (1720–1791), this first edition of the Ancient Grand Lodge Constitutions specifies the qualifications a man must have before he may become a Freemason or govern a lodge. It also contains a history of the craft, songs for use in the lodge and "Prayers used in Jewish and Christian Lodges."

Frontispiece, Ahiman Rezon: Or, a Help to a Brother, London, 1756. National Heritage Museum.

belonged to both Modern and Ancient lodges and wished to end the organizational feud. Second, the conflict between the grand lodges caused irritation within aristocratic circles. Lastly, Irish, Scottish, and foreign grand lodges all desired a resolution to the confusion over legitimacy, prerogatives, rituals and regulations. Peace was at last achieved and harmony prevailed in 1813, when HRH The Duke of Kent (Grand Master of the Ancient Grand Lodge), installed his brother, HRH The Duke of Sussex (Grand Master of the Modern Grand Lodge), as Grand Master of the new United Grand Lodge of England. Installation of a new Grand Master, however, was the easiest part of the unification. Reconciliation of the old rituals, ceremonies and bylaws of the grand lodges took many years.[32]

William Preston

"By the proper use of talents, the wisdom of precepts and the force of example, the mind is improved and the brethren are united in social harmony; while the happiness, which originates in the lodge, disperses its influence to the wide circle of the world."

— WILLIAM PRESTON, 1796[33]

While "Ancients" and "Moderns" were bickering over prerogatives, William Preston toiled to bring deeper meaning to the fraternity. The son of a lawyer, Preston was born in Edinburgh in 1742. At the age of 18, he moved to London, where he served as a printer's apprentice and proofreader for the owner of *The London Chronicle.* Later, Preston became managing editor of the newspaper and supervised the printing of both Edward Gibbon's *Decline and Fall of the Roman Empire* and Adam Smith's *Wealth of Nations* in 1776.[34]

Preston became a Freemason in 1763 in "Ancient" Lodge No. 111, but he also joined a lodge associated with the "Modern" Grand Lodge and became Deputy Grand Secretary.[35] When he was elected Master of his original lodge in 1767, he decided to improve his understanding of the craft by studying Masonic rituals and visiting other lodges. After several years of collecting rituals, he organized this disparate material into his own Masonic lecture system, which was designed for delivery by lodge Masters to newly initiated men.[36] Published in 1772, Preston's *Freemasonry Illustrated* was the first rational and systematic attempt to codify and give deeper meaning to Masonic rituals. Although Preston perpetuated James Anderson's mythological Masonic history, his lectures forcefully interpreted Freemasonry as a means for self-improvement and social equality.[37]

Just as Samuel Johnson's 1755 *English Dictionary* sought standardization for spelling and pronunciation, Preston's system sought to standardize Masonic lodge work. Preston's work was increasingly adopted by English Freemasonry between the 1770s and 1790s, but in the 1800s it was amalgamated into other rituals and ceremonies. During this crucial period, however, *Freemasonry Illustrated* was exported and widely read. It profoundly affected the development of the craft, particularly in America. Preston's work is arguably the second most important Masonic book for the development of American Freemasonry, surpassed only by Anderson's *Constitutions.*

European Freemasonry, 1730–1790

"Our ancestors, the Crusaders, gathered together from all parts of Christendom in the Holy Land, desired thus to reunite into one sole Fraternity the individuals of all nations. . . . The word Freemason must therefore not be taken in a literal, gross and material sense, as if our founders had been simple workers in stone, or merely curious geniuses who wished to perfect the arts."

— CHEVALIER ANDREW MICHAEL RAMSAY, 1737[38]

Freemasonry on the Continent developed in different directions from its British parent. Whereas the British stonemasons and middle-class Freemasons sought honor and royal patronage, European commoners were attracted to the Masonic ideals of liberty and equality, while aristocrats sought Freemasonry's chivalric and mystical past.

British Freemasonry arrived on the Continent primarily through merchants and immigrants. As early as 1724, there may have been a lodge in France. Documented lodges existed in Spain, Italy, the Netherlands, Germany and Russia by 1735.[39] Middle-class Europeans, like their British contemporaries, joined the fraternity for many of the same reasons: self-improvement, social and business activities, and participation in an exclusive club. They also viewed the craft as an enlightening conduit for liberty, constitutional government, religious tolerance and free enterprise.[40] These growing sentiments, perpetuated in the lodge, brought the craft to the attention of the Roman Catholic Church. In 1738, Pope Clement XII issued *In eminenti,* the first of many subsequent bulls against Freemasonry. It accused Freemasonry of propagating the "evils" of British democracy by periodically electing lodge officers, teaching that authority derived from individual merit rather than from God and promoting the concept

WILLIAM PRESTON

The first great organizer of English Masonic ritualistic work and author of *Illustrations of Masonry,* William Preston (1742–1818) is shown here wearing the jewel of a Past Master of a lodge.

John Russell, England, ca. 1790. Copyright, reproduced with permission of the United Grand Lodge of England.

Within Scottish Rite Freemasonry, each of the 33 degrees has its own regalia and symbolic signs. Shown here are French watercolors of the 4th degree of Secret Master, the 14th degree of Perfection, the 18th degree of Rose Croix and the 32nd degree of Prince of the Royal Secret. Despite such lofty titles and ornate aprons, each man is shown wearing a sword indicating that he is also a gentleman.

ca. 1815. The Masonic Museum "Prince Frederick," The Hague, Netherlands.

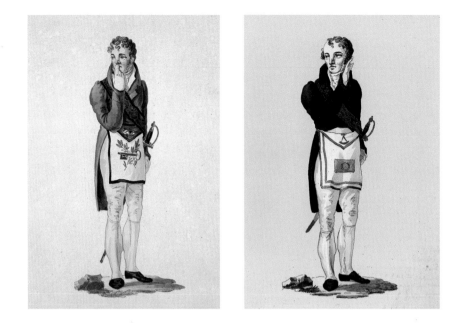

of human equality rather than the hierarchical order that Clement XII argued was ordained by God.[41]

The radicalism of Freemasonry's ideas was seen as dangerous to the authority of the Church and, by monarchs across Europe, as subversive of the divine right of kings. Masonic lodges were raided and Masons were arrested. One raid of a Paris lodge in the 1740s netted "a lapidary (or jeweler), a minor official of the poultry market, a gardener, a tapestry merchant, worse still, an actor in the Comedie Italienne, and perhaps most remarkable of all, 'a Negro who serves as a trumpeter in the King's Guard.'"[42] Similar raids and arrests occurred throughout Europe. All sought to crush the practice of elections and the development of civil society and self-government.

Although some European monarchies joined the Church's denouncement of Freemasonry, aristocrats became increasingly enamored with the craft's mythical past and mystical elements. One Scottish Mason in particular, Chevalier Andrew Michael Ramsay (1680?-1743), unexpectedly initiated a new system of Masonic history and rituals. Where his fellow Scots — James Anderson and William Preston — sought Masonic regulation and order, Ramsay's actions were to cause more confusion and chaos. The son of a baker, Ramsay became a soldier after attending the University of Edinburgh. In 1702, he fought in Flanders under the Duke of Marlborough. Remaining on the Continent, Ramsay converted to Catholicism and was made a knight of the Order of St. Lazarus. Highly intelligent and talented, Chevalier Ramsay was accepted into the Scottish community that

had fled to France following the deposition of the Catholic James II from the British throne. He tutored the two sons of James Stuart, the "Old Pretender" to the British throne, and wrote books on religion and mysticism. He also published a popular novel, *The Travels of Cyrus.* Ramsay probably became a Freemason during a visit to London between 1728 and 1730 and remained a Mason until his death in 1743.[43]

In a speech purportedly given in Paris in 1737, Chevalier Ramsay claimed that Freemasonry was derived not from stonemasons but from the Knights Templar of the Crusades. According to Ramsay, the Knights Templar, which had been outlawed in the early 1300s, had preserved the secrets that had led them into conflict with the Church and the king of France by hiding them within a guild of Scottish stonemasons. Furthermore, the manner in which they hid these secrets had kept them from being understood by ignorant stonemasons and unfaithful Christians.[44] Ramsay's widely circulated "speech" gave birth to dozens of quasi-Masonic orders. Catholic European aristocrats, who never would have acknowledged a British workingmen's guild, soon rushed to join. Within these "regenerated" orders, scores of new rituals and ceremonies were performed. The newly created higher degrees, or *hauts grades,* surpassed the third degree of Master Mason and the Royal Arch degree and were numbered to the 99th degree and beyond. Some of these rituals were organized into systems or rites. Unlike British Freemasonry, however, these degrees were restricted to the nobility within mystical chivalric orders to preserve esoteric knowledge and maintain hierarchy. They were not intended to create a more equi-

Dutchman Henry A. Francken (172?–95) visited Albany in 1767 and organized a Scottish Rite Lodge of Perfection. This patent is the first documented evidence of Scottish Rite Freemasonry in North America.

Patent of the Ineffable and Sublime Grand Lodge of Perfection, Albany, NY, 1767. Scottish Rite Valley of Albany and the Supreme Council, 33°, Northern Masonic Jurisdiction, Lexington, MA.

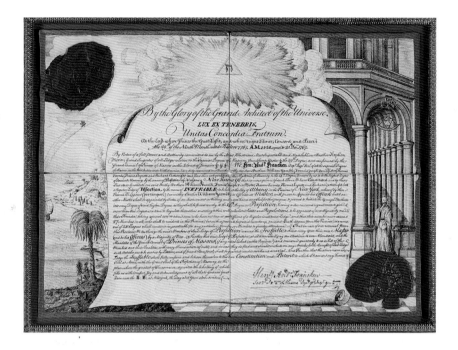

table society by improving the welfare of common people.[45] Despite attempts by British grand lodges to curtail such "irregular" and "clandestine" activities, Europeans of all nationalities throughout the 1700s freely used Masonic tenets and rituals for political, intellectual and mystical purposes.[46]

The most important of these Continental degrees, created in France, were called the *Ecossais,* or Scottish, named after the mythical Scottish knights of Chevalier Ramsay's speech. The origin of these degrees is widely debated, as is much of Freemasonry's formative history.[47] Some of the first members of the *Ecossais* believed the ceremonies had truly survived from the Knights Templar and other Crusaders; others claimed that King Frederick the Great of Prussia (1712–86) was "Most Puissant Sovereign Grand Commander" of the *Ecossais* and had later authorized its Grand Constitutions.[48] It is known, however, that in 1761 a Bordeaux merchant, Stephen Morin, was given a patent by the "Grand East of Paris" to spread the *Ecossais* degrees to the Americas.

The systems of both the British stonemasons (forerunner to the York Rite) and the French aristocrats (forerunner to the Scottish Rite) spread to North America in the 1700s and influenced the development of American community life and voluntary associations.

CHAPTER 2

Peaceable Citizens

Freemasonry in Colonial and Revolutionary America, 1730–1800

"A vast concourse of People attended to see this Procession [of Free-masons], insomuch that almost all occupations ceas'd, the Streets were crowded; Windows, Balconys and Battlements of Churches and Houses were full of Spectators, who were highly pleased with an Appearance of so many Gentlemen, who in their Countenances express'd Complaisancy, Delight and Love, in the Company of one another, which (they say) is the Cement and Connection of the Fraternity."

— BOSTON GAZETTE, JULY 2, 1739

FREEMASONRY WAS BROUGHT from Great Britain to the American colonies before the 1717 formation of the first grand lodge. The first recorded Mason in America was John Skene, who became a member of Old Aberdeen Lodge in Scotland. He emigrated from Scotland and settled in 1682 near what is now Burlington, New Jersey. Skene went on to serve as deputy governor of West Jersey from 1685 until his death in 1690.[1] The first American-born Mason is believed to have been Jonathan Belcher (1681-1757). Belcher, who was probably made a Mason when he was in London in 1704, was appointed the royal governor of Massachusetts and New Hampshire in 1730.[2]

The expansion of British immigration to and trade with the colonies played a key role in establishing American colonial Masonic lodges. While Masonic historians have sought to determine which American lodge is the oldest, Pennsylvania, Massachusetts and Georgia hold important distinctions. Pennsylvania's preeminence derives from a 1730 edition of Benjamin Franklin's *Pennsylvania Gazette* that reported, "there are several lodges of Free Masons erected in this province."[3] Franklin became a Mason in a lodge at Philadelphia's Tun Tavern in 1731. The first chartered lodge, however, was Boston's St. John's Lodge, which appeared on the 1733 regis-

ter of the first, or "Modern," grand lodge as No. 126.[4] Georgia's distinction is associated with its founder, James Oglethorpe (1696-1785), who was made a Mason in England before he founded the Savannah settlement in 1732. Two years later he organized Solomon's Lodge, which is considered today to be among the oldest continuously operating Masonic lodges in the country and which claims among its members two brothers, Moses and Daniel Nunis, who were the first Jewish-American Masons.[5]

To be sure, some early Masonic lodges were formed in the American colonies without official recognition from British grand lodges. Some colonial Masons claimed that their lodges predated the establishment of the first grand lodge in 1717 and thus claimed that they had no need for recognition from England. Just as the British Crown assigned colonial governors, so too the British grand lodges appointed provincial grand masters and other officials to charter and regulate lodges and determine the legitimacy of existing lodges. Freemasonry, however, remained a voluntary association. While some American Masons attempted to enforce Anderson's *Constitutions* and other regulations, others could not be prevented from freely using — in some cases abusing — the fraternity.[6]

Four American Masons

"As to the Freemasons, . . . they are in general a very harmless sort of People, and have no principles or practices that are inconsistent with religion and good manners."

— BENJAMIN FRANKLIN, APRIL 13, 1738[7]

By the late 1740s, Masonic lodges operated in most major communities along America's eastern seacoast and attracted some of the most affluent and respected men of the colonies. The relationship between American Freemasonry and American society during the mid-1700s can be seen through the lives and communities of four important American Masons: Benjamin Franklin, George Washington, Paul Revere and Prince Hall. Why these men joined a lodge, what they believed the fraternity's purpose to be, and how they used the craft all demonstrate a "transformation from a hierarchical society of superiors and inferiors to a republican society of independent citizens."[8] These men helped to mold the character of American Freemasonry into the fraternity that became the cornerstone for future voluntary associations.

Born into a humble yet respectable artisan family in Boston, Benjamin Franklin (1706-90) was a printer, scientist, inventor, politician, diplomat

and sage. His migration from Boston to Philadelphia and quick rise to the highest social, intellectual and political circles remains a model for the American dream. As part of this ascent, Franklin joined a Masonic lodge in Philadelphia comprised of the most influential men in the Pennsylvania colony and published the first Masonic book in America in 1734. Franklin quickly became a leading Mason in Philadelphia. He was elected Provincial Grand Master of the Grand Lodge of Pennsylvania in 1734, and in 1755 participated in the dedication of America's first Masonic Hall in Philadelphia.[9] After serving a term in that office, Franklin apparently lost interest in the fraternity until 1776, when he was sent to France during the American Revolution as a Commissioner of the Continental Congress.

In the view of historian Steven C. Bullock, Franklin and the emerging urban upper class he sought to enter saw Freemasonry in the 1730s and 1740s as "a means both to build elite solidarity and to emphasize their elevation above common people."[10] Philadelphia Masons became less interested in the spiritual and intellectual elements of the ritual and more concerned with the honorable and paternalistic virtues of the craft. Like the English aristocracy, Franklin and his peers viewed the fraternity as a means to create and endow city institutions that would earn them public honor and social respect. Franklin also established a library, a fire company, a college (later known as the University of Pennsylvania), an insurance company and a hospital. While Freemasonry never played the central role in this cosmopolitan community, it served as one of several means for Franklin and his fellow Masons to ascend socially to higher levels of colonial and even English society.[11]

Unlike Franklin, George Washington (1732–99) was born into a leading Virginia family. While Franklin focused on creating new community institutions, Washington preferred to maintain and strengthen those established by his forefathers. As a young man, Washington began his career surveying and acquiring land. He became a Mason at an early age in a lodge at Fredericksburg, Virginia, in 1752. He served as an officer in the militia and fought the French in western Pennsylvania during the French and Indian Wars. In 1758, he was elected to Virginia's House of Burgesses. Washington married the wealthy widow, Martha Custis, and settled down as a respected landowner, retired soldier, representative in the House of Burgesses and member of the vestry of his church.

Washington's Masonic membership, like his public titles, was part of a range of necessary duties expected from a man of his social status and political influence. The fact that he probably did not attend any Masonic meetings between 1755 and 1777 [12] does not diminish his regard for the fraternity any more than his sporadic attendance at his church could be considered to reveal a lack of personal faith. [13]

Within Washington's Southern society, family lineage and public obligations were paramount. Masonic membership was restricted to the colony's most honorable and respected gentlemen. While emphasis within the lodge room might be devoted to improving a man and creating equality among its members, that same Masonic brotherhood was, in practice, not extended to society as a whole. Lodge members may have wished to create a more tolerant and benevolent society among their class, but they were not directly concerned with allowing lower-

LODGE MASTER'S CHAIR

This chair used by a lodge Master incorporates numerous Masonic symbols — the compasses, square, Bible, and Corinthian pillars. It was made by Benjamin Bucktrout (?–1813) and was probably used by Peyton Randolph (1721–75) while he was Provincial Grand Master of Virginia in the 1770s. Randolph was president of the First and Second Continental Congresses in 1774 and 1775. During the Revolution, the chair was moved to Unanimity Lodge No. 7, Edenton, North Carolina. It was returned to Williamsburg in 1983.

Benjamin Bucktrout, Williamsburg, VA, ca. 1770. Colonial Williamsburg Foundation.

Establishing Freemasonry

class men to join the fraternity to improve themselves any more than they were directly concerned
with universal male suffrage.[14]

Poorer and socially less prominent than either Franklin or Washington, Paul Revere (1735–
1818) spent his entire life in Massachusetts. The
family circumstances of this son of an artisan limited his prospects in the society of colonial Boston.
Revere was recognized as a highly talented silver-
smith and a trustworthy businessman. His desire
to improve his standing in the community led him
to participate in many social clubs and political
committees.[15] Revere became a Mason in 1760 in
Boston's Lodge of St. Andrew, a lodge that was
chartered by the "Ancients" from Scotland. He
served first as the lodge Secretary and went on to
become Master. In 1794, he rose to become Grand
Master of the Massachusetts Grand Lodge that
several years earlier had united the "Ancients"
and "Moderns." During his three-year term as Grand Master, Revere chartered at least 23 new lodges, nearly doubling the number of lodges in Massachusetts. He also had the honor during his term of laying the ceremonial
cornerstone for the new Massachusetts state house in 1795.[16]

Unlike Franklin or Washington, Revere considered his participation
in the Masonic community to be a means of establishing himself in Boston
society both as an individual and as a businessman. Hard work, thrift and
industriousness were highly valued among New England's leading colonial families. Paul Revere saw Freemasonry as a step toward both self-
improvement and social advancement. He and other men like him learned
the art of rhetoric and public speaking through the steady practice of the
recitation of the Masonic rituals and lectures. They learned business and
political skills by organizing and supervising meetings, and they acquired
manners and civility by socializing and contemplating Masonic symbolism.
They mingled with higher levels of society by participating in Masonic social and public celebrations. To Revere and his middle-class community,
the fraternity provided the skills and status they sought to associate with
Franklin's and Washington's society and the membership of the more elite
St. John's Lodge.[17]

Like Franklin and Washington, Revere's community used the fraternity
to separate itself from the "common" folk. Freemasonry was not extended
to men in Boston's lower classes. While the craft declared a universal brother-

**MASONIC MEETING
NOTICE**

The lodge Secretary
sends out the meeting
notices to the brethren
and accounts for their
absences. In the 1700s,
many Masons missed
meetings due to the
rigors of travel, disease
and other misfortunes.
As the Secretary of the
Lodge of St. Andrew,
Paul Revere sent this
summons by order of
the lodge Master Moses
Deshon, an auctioneer
by trade. As an engraver,
Revere made the sum-
mons for the lodge.

*Paul Revere, Boston, ca.
1768. National Heritage
Museum, purchased
with assistance from
the Lodge of St. Andrew
and the Kane Lodge
Foundation, A2002/43/1.*

AFRICAN LODGE NO. 459 CHARTER

This charter was issued by the (Modern) Grand Lodge of England and is the founding document for all regular Prince Hall lodges in the world. Issued in 1784, it was received by Prince Hall in 1787 through the assistance of Captain James Scott, a Freemason and brother-in-law of John Hancock. In 1869, Grand Master S.T. Kendall crawled into a burning building to save the charter. Its edge, however, was severely singed.

1784, photographed by Nowlan Photography and Videography. Prince Hall Grand Lodge of Massachusetts, F&AM.

hood of equals, its members often denied access to individuals they did not view as their social equals. This paradox was demonstrated when Prince Hall (1735?–1807) became a Mason in 1775. Little is known about Prince Hall's life, but he was probably born into slavery, received his freedom from William Hall in 1770, and established a leather dressing shop in Boston. He was active in his church and supported a school and a benevolent society in his African-American community. A clergyman would later call Prince Hall "the leading African in Boston."[18]

On March 6, 1775, during the British embargo and occupation of Boston, Hall and 14 other black men were initiated into the craft by Lodge No. 441, a British military lodge attached to the 38th Regiment of Foot.[19] Prince Hall and his Masonic brothers later formed their own lodge, which continued to meet throughout the American Revolution. By 1784, these black Masons received a charter from the "Modern" Grand Lodge in England to meet as African Lodge No. 459.[20] Prince Hall served as the first Master of the lodge. Hall went on to charter other African-American lodges in Philadelphia and Rhode Island.[21] Among the members in Philadelphia were Absalom Jones, the first black Episcopal minister in America; Richard Allen, the first bishop of the African Methodist Episcopal Church, and most of the founders of the Free African Society.[22] After the death of Prince Hall in 1807, African-American Masons chose to call their organization "Prince Hall Freemasonry" in honor of their distinguished founder.

Like Paul Revere and his middle-class whites, Prince Hall and his colleagues used their affiliation with the fraternity to improve themselves while providing relief and charity to their community. But freed Africans found broader purposes in an organization that proclaimed a universal brotherhood. At the time of the American Revolution, Boston's entire African-American population numbered approximately 600.[23] This segregated community included kidnapped African slaves as well as free men, like Prince Hall, who owned property and voted in state elections. Prince Hall's Masonic lodge was a means to designate the "better sort" among Boston's black population and to allow its members to claim a brotherly association with other Masons.[24] Most importantly, within a society that viewed them with a considerable amount of prejudice, the lodge served as a legitimate and acceptable means for Africans to meet, organize, educate and help each other without white involvement or permission.

The American Revolution

"You agree to be a peaceable citizen, and cheerfully to conform to the laws of the country in which you reside."

— CHARGE TO A MASTER OF A LODGE, 1775[25]

The commencement of the American Revolution in 1775 transformed colonial Masonic lodges no less than it transformed the communities in which they existed. Freemasons from different lodges served within the Sons of Liberty. Robert Newman — a "Modern" member of St. John's Lodge — hung lanterns in the Old North Church steeple that started Paul Revere — an "Ancient" member of the Lodge of St. Andrew — on his ride to Lexington to warn fellow Mason John Hancock and others of the British army's march on Concord. Several months later, General Joseph Warren, presiding Grand Master of the "Ancients" Grand Lodge in Massachusetts, was killed at the Battle of Bunker Hill. The unfolding events caused American colonists to choose sides. Not all Masons supported the revolutionary movement. Owing to the turbulence of the times, it is not surprising that many of the nearly 100 lodges in the colonies suspended meetings. Among lodges, however, those with large memberships consisting of loyalists disbanded

JOSEPH WARREN'S FUNERAL PROCESSION

After the British army evacuated Boston in April 1776, Freemasons found Grand Master Joseph Warren's body buried on the Bunker Hill battlefield. Paul Revere identified Warren's remains by the dental work Revere had made for him. Freemasons carried Joseph Warren's body through Boston to the Granary Burial Grounds, where a Christian service was performed. In 1825, his remains were buried for a third time in the Warren family tomb in St. Paul's Church, Boston.

Diccionario Enciclopedico de la Masoneria, ca. 1844. Courtesy of the Archives of the Supreme Council, 33°, Southern Jurisdiction, Washington, DC.

Stonemasons drew their plans on tracing boards to instruct the workers. In the 1700s, Freemasonry's three initiations included lectures that explained the history and symbols of the craft. Tracing boards were used in the ritualistic ceremonies as an instructional aid. They were originally rolled out on floors and called "master's carpets," but later versions developed into a decorative art form that hung on the walls of lodge rooms. A New York City lodge used this Fellowcraft degree tracing board during the 1770s. Later, fleeing Loyalist members of the lodge took this and an Entered Apprentice degree tracing board to Nova Scotia.

ca. 1770. Grand Lodge of Nova Scotia, AF&AM.

or relocated to Canada, while lodges with more "rebellious" memberships were more likely to be among those who remained active.[26]

The various American colonies had to decide how to respond to the battles at Lexington and Concord. Among the delegates from the colonies who met as a Continental Congress in Philadelphia in 1776 to consider and vote on a Declaration of Independence, nine of the 56 signers are known to have been Masons.[27] Some Masonic historians have claimed a higher number, yet it is still significant that men from different colonies,

Establishing Freemasonry

such as John Hancock of Massachusetts, Richard Stockton of New Jersey and George Walton of Georgia, could recognize each other as fraternal brothers.

As acts of rebellion became a war for independence, George Washington received command of the Continental Army. One of Washington's greatest challenges was to unite colonial regiments comprised of men with varied levels of skill and bravery. Freemasonry became an important means of meeting this challenge. Taking the tradition from British regiments, the American regiments formed military lodges.[28] The best known of these lodges was American Union Lodge. Organized within a Connecticut regiment during the siege of Boston and chartered by a Massachusetts provincial grand lodge, the traveling lodge operated throughout the war.[29]

The officers of the regimental lodges invited brother Masons from different colonies to their meetings and social gatherings. The craft served as a point of introduction among strangers. Freemasonry's solemn obligations also reinforced loyalty to each other and to the Americans' cause. Fraternal loyalty was especially significant when foreign officers who were Freemasons — such as Lafayette, DeKalb, and Von Steuben — joined the patriots' cause.[30] On the other hand, the treasonous actions of another prominent Freemason, General Benedict Arnold, caused his name to be anathema among American Masons.[31] Lodge meetings, especially during winter encampments, provided social activities and fellowship that boosted morale while offering charity to wounded and imprisoned brothers or to the families of fellow Masons who were killed.[32] Washington participated in lodge meetings and attended Masonic celebrations and commemorations.

Freemasonry's fraternal spirit appealed to Continental Army officers. Its orderly rituals and hierarchy helped unite them as friends and brothers. Military rank during this period was usually granted according to a man's social status. Since many of the highest-class colonists remained loyal to the Crown, service in the Continental Army and membership in the Masonic fraternity elevated aspiring gentlemen. This accorded them an important separation from the common soldiers and extended their personal affiliations and connections. By the war's end, hundreds of officers had become Masons in the ten or more regimental lodges, and at least 33 of the Continental Army's 78 generals were Freemasons.[33]

While George Washington commanded the Continental Army, Benjamin Franklin, Paul Revere and Prince Hall all found their own way to serve the revolutionary cause. Franklin was sent to Paris to convince France to aid the rebellion. While there, he renewed his interest in Freemasonry and joined the preeminent French lodge, Loge des Neufs Soeurs. He served as its Master and participated in the Masonic initiation of Voltaire in 1778.

CHIEF JOSEPH BRANT (THAYENDANEGEA)

A Mohawk Indian and principal chief of the Six Nations, Joseph Brant (1742-1807) is the first known Native American to become a Freemason. He joined Hiram's Cliftonian Lodge No. 447, London, in 1776. During the War for Independence, Brant remained loyal to the British Crown but was credited with saving the lives of several colonists, including brother Masons. After the war, he moved to Ontario with his tribe and in 1798 became the first Master of his local lodge. His son and successor, John (Ahyouwaighs) (1794-1832), was also a Freemason.

Life of Joseph Brant (Thayendanegea), *Albany, NY, 1865. National Heritage Museum, gift of Lloyd M. Brinkman.*

Along with securing French support, Franklin also met the young aristocrat and brother Mason, Marquis de Lafayette, and assisted him on his journey back to America in 1780. Paul Revere remained in Massachusetts, where he served as an artillery officer, made gunpowder, and cast cannons for the Continental Army. Little is known about Prince Hall's activities during the war, but he did make leather drumheads for a Massachusetts regiment and organized petitions to the Massachusetts legislature seeking to abolish slavery.[34]

Freemasonry's revolutionary honor and prestige also came with a price. The rebellion was propagated by secret, extralegal organizations, such as the Sons of Liberty. Many well-known Freemasons were deeply involved in fomenting the American rebellion. Because Masonic lodges met in private and used secret recognition signs and words, many citizens could not distinguish between Freemasonry and the Sons of Liberty. The 1773 Boston Tea Party added to this conjecture, since both the Sons of Liberty and the Lodge of St. Andrew met at the Green Dragon Tavern the night of the tea party.[35] After the signing of the Declaration of Independence, erstwhile secret rebel groups went public, while Freemasonry remained private, and men with membership in both groups became beloved patriots. As the violent French Revolution engulfed Europe in the 1790s, Freemasonry's reputation as a conspiratorial organization took on a different hue among Americans, while the memory of the Founding Fathers' Masonic affiliations diminished. By the 1820s, Freemasonry was perceived as a dangerous international secret society whose members masked their malevolent plots behind the facades of false charity and General Washington's reputation.[36]

The United States

"[I present you] a lamb-skin, or white leather apron, which is an emblem of innocence, and the badge of a Mason; more ancient than the golden fleece or Roman eagle; more honourable than the star and garter, or any other order which might be conferred at the time of his initiation or anytime thereafter, by king, prince, potentate, or any other person, except it be a Mason . . ."

— THOMAS SMITH WEBB, 1802 [37]

The movement toward American independence that had begun in revolution led eventually to the ratification of the U.S. Constitution in 1789. Masons played a prominent role in this process. Nine of the 48 signers of the Articles of Confederation were Freemasons, as were 13 of the 39 signers

MASSACHUSETTS
MASONIC APRON

Traditionally made from
lambskin, aprons are
"the badge of a Mason"
and symbolize purity.
The hand-drawn design
on this apron includes
three pillars with the
allegorical figures of
Minerva (wisdom),
Hercules (strength),
and Venus (beauty) sup-
porting a mosaic pave-
ment, upon which
King Solomon's Temple
rests. Richard Harris
of Marblehead, Massa-
chusetts, owned this
apron. He was Master
of Philanthropic Lodge
in Marblehead from
1778–91. During the
American Revolution,
Harris served in the
same artillery regiment
as Paul Revere.

*ca. 1780. National Heri-
tage Museum, gift of
Dr. Phillip James Jones,
83.45.*

of the Constitution.[38] Several Freemasons accepted major positions in all branches of government for the new nation. George Washington received the presidential oath of office on a Bible borrowed from New York City's St. John's Lodge No. 1.[39] Freemason John A.C. Muhlenberg was elected the first Speaker of the U.S. House of Representatives, and Freemasons John J. Blair and William Cushing were among the first justices of the U.S. Supreme Court.[40]

Freemasonry was in harmony with the ideals of the new American republic. The fraternity's principles and symbols became incorporated into early American culture. Masonic symbols began to appear on household utensils and furniture. Each symbol expressed a significant virtue for maintaining a free and equal civil society. The square represented honesty; the level, equality; the plumb, rectitude; and the compasses, moderation.[41]

Freemasonry's prestige and social acceptance reached a pinnacle when
the cornerstone for the U.S. Capitol was laid in 1793. Wearing Masonic regalia, President Washington led a procession to the top of Capitol Hill. He
was accompanied by stonemasons, military units, government officials,
brother Masons, and common citizens. During the Masonic ceremony, the
stone was tried by the plumb, level and square and was symbolically blessed
with corn (representing plenty), wine (happiness), and oil (peace). Using
a Masonic trowel, Washington spread the symbolic cement of the brotherly love that would both unite the building into one common mass and
bring all Americans together as one common people.[42]

While the American people sought a more perfect union with the establishment of the United States, American Masons also sought to rebuild
the fraternity. Prior to 1775, Ancient and Modern grand lodges co-existed
in each state, and Masonic lodges — like the colonies themselves — served
as neutral space, where both the elite and artisans could prosper. But since
most members of the elite were loyalists who had left the colonies, the revolutionaries assumed control of the colonial government and Freemasonry.
American independence from the British Crown brought Masonic independence from British grand lodges. Like the American Anglican Church,
Freemasonry had to restructure its governance and establish an autono-
mous leadership yet remain in concord with the "mother country." Weakened by the loss of loyal members, Modern grand lodges were essentially

Establishing Freemasonry

forced to merge with the more dominant Ancients. By 1792, most states were left with only one recognized grand lodge, although the Ancients and Moderns in South Carolina did not unite until 1817. This transition caused the customs of the Modern lodges to be usurped by the Ancients. American Masonic lodges were no longer primarily social clubs but were remodeled as "Temples for Virtue and Republicanism" designed to create "a natural aristocracy based on equality."[43]

Between the years 1775 and 1800, the rituals and customs of the "Ancient" Grand Lodge system became dominant among the independent state grand lodges. In Pennsylvania, the transformation was so complete and the tension between the "Ancients" and "Moderns" was so strong that when Benjamin Franklin died in 1790, Freemasons were conspicuously absent at his otherwise well-attended funeral. The "Ancient" Grand Lodge of Pennsylvania simply did not recognize the older "Modern" Franklin as a brother, even though he had been a Provincial Grand Master and a Master of a preeminent French lodge. On the other hand, George Washington's funeral procession included 56 brothers from three lodges, and special memorial tributes to him were common as lodges across the country draped lodge room altars in black. Washington became America's most notable Freemason despite the fact that he had been initiated in a lodge that was not chartered at the time, his Masonic involvement had been sporadic, and he never officially presided as Master of a lodge.[44]

U.S. CAPITOL TROWEL
President George Washington used this silver and ivory trowel to lay the cornerstone of the U.S. Capitol on Sept. 18, 1793. Later Freemasons used it to lay the cornerstones of the Supreme Court building, the Washington National Monument, the Smithsonian Institution, the National Cathedral, and numerous other civic and Masonic buildings.

John Duffey, Alexandria, VA, 1793. Copyright, Alexandria-Washington Lodge No. 22, AF&AM, Alexandria, VA.

Peaceable Citizens: Freemasonry in Colonial and Revolutionary America

Federal America vs. State Grand Lodges

". . . give the right hand of affection and fellowship to whom it justly belongs; let their colour and complexion be what it will; let their nation be what it may, for they are your brethren, and it is your indispensable duty so to do; let them as Masons deny this, and we and the world know what to think of them be they ever so grand."

— PRINCE HALL, 1797[45]

American Freemasonry became independent of England and developed its own important distinctions. First, the fraternity's emphasis, reflecting the dominance of the Ancients' influence, was on equality, enterprise and other republican virtues that attracted broader classes of men into the lodge. While the Society of the Cincinnati restricted its membership to

Continental Army and Navy officers and their male heirs, Freemasonry allowed any man of good character to join.[46] Second, while the federal government asserted its power to impose the rule of constitutional law during such uprisings as the Shay's Rebellion of 1787 and the Whiskey Rebellion of 1794, Freemasonry never had any national authority to outlaw or disband rival organizations. Instead, grand lodges, organized along state lines, turned inward, each improvising its own constitutions to define and protect its jurisdictional authority. Lastly, the Ancients' "higher" Royal Arch degrees and the French "Scottish Rite" degrees set a precedent and encouraged acceptance of additional rituals within the United States.

The Masonic fraternity, therefore, became an American folkway that evolved with and adapted to changing and expanding communities. Masons continued to adjust the fraternity to meet their personal needs and to respond to societal forces. For example, the "newer" Ancients superseded the "older" Moderns, and Lafayette was embraced as a Masonic hero, although the legitimacy of his Masonic initiation was unclear. Meanwhile, Prince Hall and his African-American brethren were shunned, even though they held a Masonic lodge charter from London.[47]

Freemasonry's success in 18th-century America was due mainly to the fact that its tenets and virtues were in harmony with the Enlightenment culture of the age. But its revolutionary reputation and lack of national unity dangerously weakened the craft's foundation. Nevertheless, the fraternity's prestige and influence continued to rise after the death of Franklin, Washington, Revere and Hall. This growing social profile, however, would lead younger Americans to question the fraternity's purpose and its influence on America's fledgling republic.

AMERICAN PLATE

This earthenware plate features a blindfolded figure of Justice wearing a Masonic apron and holding an oval shield of George Washington. On the right, Freedom looks down upon a prosperous farm. Around the edge are the names of the first 15 states with flowers and fruit. In the 1820s, these images symbolized the hope of peace, unity and plenty in America.

James and Ralph Clews, Cobridge, England, ca. 1820. National Heritage Museum, 75.26.

CHAPTER 3

Act Honorably

Freemasonry and Federalist America, 1800–1835

"... my wishes that bounteous Providence will continue to bless and preserve our country in Peace ... and my attachment to the Society ... will dispose me always to contribute my best endeavours to promote the honor and interest of the Craft."

— GEORGE WASHINGTON, LETTER TO PAUL REVERE, 1797[1]

FOLLOWING GEORGE WASHINGTON'S DEATH in 1799, Freemasonry continued to flourish as the United States grew. The Louisiana Purchase of 1803 extended the nation's territory westward to the Rocky Mountains. The War of 1812 with Great Britain confirmed America's independence and strengthened national unity. Between 1800 and 1826, eight new states joined the union, and the nation's population more than doubled from five million to nearly eleven million. Yankee clippers carried American furs and tobacco abroad and returned with silk, tea and fine porcelains. On America's inland rivers, keelboats and steamboats connected Pittsburgh with St. Louis and New Orleans, and thousands of American families migrated westward to Ohio and Michigan in search of better land. In the South, slavery spread into Alabama and Mississippi as cotton and sugar crops became the foundation of the southern economy.

GEORGE WASHINGTON

This pastel portrait was commissioned by Washington's lodge in Alexandria, Virginia. At the age of 62, General Washington sat for the artist. He is shown wearing the Past Master's jewel with sash and apron. The lodge instructed the artist to give a genuine likeness of their friend and brother showing him with all the scars and blemishes that come with age.

George Washington in Masonic Regalia, William Joseph Williams, 1794. Copyright, Alexandria-Washington Lodge No. 22, AF&AM, Alexandria, VA.

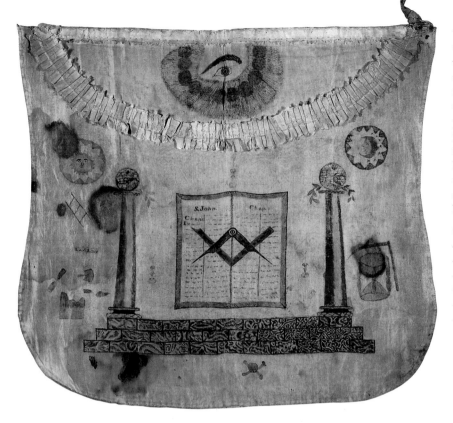

APRON

Owned by Capt. Meri-
wether Lewis (1774–
1809), this apron is
representative of highly
ornate aprons of the
period. The explorer
purportedly had the
apron with him when
he committed suicide
in 1809 and the red spots
are believed to be his
blood.

*ca. 1795. The Grand
Lodge, AF&AM, of
Montana, Montana
Masonic Foundation
and the Montana
Masonic Museum,
Helena, MT.*

During this period of rapid national growth, Freemasons played a promi-
nent role in nearly every segment of American society. John Marshall, a
Past Grand Master of Virginia, was appointed Chief Justice of the Supreme
Court in 1801. Masonic brothers Meriwether Lewis and William Clark set
off from St. Louis in 1804 on a two-year voyage of discovery to the Pacific
Coast. Masons Stephen Decatur and Winfield Scott were among those who
fought in the War of 1812. Stephen Austin became the "Father of Texas."
Governor DeWitt Clinton, who was also Grand Master of New York, helped
to build the Erie Canal in the 1820s. Andrew Jackson was the first president
who had previously served as a Masonic Grand Master of his home state.[2]

Beneath America's youthful vitality, the nation remained divided along
many lines. Among the issues that caused the formation of political, social
and regional factions were state sovereignty, universal male suffrage, tariffs, international treaties and the national bank. Perhaps the most divisive
was the issue of slavery. The Mason-Dixon line separated the northern
free and southern slave states. The Missouri Compromise of 1820 admitted
into the union the states of Maine and Missouri to maintain the balance
of congressional representation between free and slave states.[3]

Throughout America's federalist period, Freemasonry remained an important means for men to meet across social divides. Between the 1790s and 1820s, Freemasonry, wedded to republican virtues and sectarian toleration, found a societal niche as the "civic religion" of the United States. Its symbols of virtue and equality adorned furniture and furnishings in many American homes.[4] Masonic lodges were called upon to lay cornerstones of public buildings and to participate in patriotic holiday parades. Citizens viewed the fraternity's local lodges and its limited centralized power as excellent reflections of American republicanism and Jeffersonian democracy. Between 1800 and 1822, the number of Masons increased from 16,000 to a conservative estimate of 80,000, or approximately five percent of the eligible male population. In 1800, there were 347 local lodges nationwide, and by 1825, there were 500 lodges in New York alone.[6] Free African-Americans also expanded Prince Hall Freemasonry and took the craft with them when they went to Africa to assist in founding the nation of Liberia.[7]

As a voluntary association, Freemasonry conformed to the customs of a community. In contrast to the need for a courthouse, church or school, a Masonic lodge was formed only when Masons happened to gather. Government, religion and education worked for social order through the law, the Bible or children's primers. Freemasonry encouraged private harmony between lodge brethren. The honors a man earned in Freemasonry never superseded his public achievements. Elected officials, clergy, successful businessmen and farmers were always held in higher esteem than Masters of lodges or Grand Masters of state grand lodges. As the nation grew and became increasingly divided, Freemasonry's future ultimately depended on the high reputation and rational action of its members.

Scipio Lodge No. 110 - F. & A. M. Corner Stone laid 1819, Aurora, N. Y.

MASONIC LODGE HALL

Governor and presiding Grand Master DeWitt Clinton (1769–1828) laid the cornerstone for this hall in western New York in 1819. Cayuga Lake can be seen in the distance.

Scipio Lodge No. 110, F&AM, Aurora, NY, Henry Morgan, ca. 1910. National Heritage Museum, A96/066/2555.

New Masonic Rites

"The whole are here digested and arranged in such order [as] . . . that they will be easily understood; and by a due attention to the several divisions, the mode of working, as well in arrangement as matter, will become universally the same. This desirable object will add much to the happiness and satisfaction of all good Masons, and redound to the honour of the whole fraternity."

— THOMAS SMITH WEBB, 1797[8]

In the last third of the 1700s, many additional Masonic degrees were being offered throughout the United States. By 1800, the Royal Arch acquired additional degrees, and new British rituals were added, including those of the Royal and Select Masters and the Knights Templar. This new Masonic activity led to the establishment of separate Masonic bodies that met in chapters, councils and commanderies.[9] Prince Hall Masons also began to offer the same degrees and established Royal Arch chapters of their own in the 1820s.[10] Individual American Masons accepted the new degrees because of their mystique, the precedent of the Ancient Grand Lodge's higher degree, and the enjoyment of performing something new.

With such diversity in rituals and ceremonies, a new generation of Masons at the turn of the 19th century desired institutional order and ritual uniformity. Two groups of Masons — one centered in New England and the other at Charleston, South Carolina — profoundly shaped the fraternity's future. The New England group focused on the British degree system and established the York Rite, while the Charleston group used the continental European degree system to bring order to the Scottish Rite. Like America's developing political parties, these two groups became so dominant by the 1850s that other rites did not prosper.

The leader of the New England group was Thomas Smith Webb (1771–1819), originally from Boston. He learned French and Latin at an early age and worked as a printer and bookbinder. After becoming a Mason in Rising Sun Lodge in Keene, New Hampshire, in 1790, Webb moved to Albany and opened a bookstore. While in Albany, he helped to form Temple

MARK MASTER MEDAL

Each member of a Royal Arch chapter selects a personal mark to identify himself. Morgan Nelson owned this gold medal and chose the all-seeing eye as his mark. He was a member of Union Mark Chapter in Baltimore in 1818.

1818. National Heritage Museum, 86.29.

THOMAS SMITH WEBB

Webb (1771–1819), who organized and founded the General Grand Royal Arch Chapter of the United States, was Grand Master of Rhode Island in 1813. His 1797 *Freemasons Monitor* expanded upon William Preston's Masonic lectures in America and established the foundation for the York Rite degrees.

Middleton, Strobridge & Co., Cincinnati, OH, ca. 1850. National Heritage Museum, A2002/118/9.

This engraving became the pattern for most American Masonic symbols charts or "tracing boards" in the 19th century. Stonemasons' tools and basic British Masonic symbols, such as the checkered pavement and twin pillars, are combined with emblems developed by Thomas Smith Webb. They include the hourglass, a sword pointing to the heart, and the anchor and ark. The ladder (left) represents Jacob's Ladder.

Master's Carpet, The True Masonic Chart or Hieroglyphic Monitor, *Jeremy Cross, engraving by Amos Doolittle, New Haven, CT, 1820. National Heritage Museum, gift of Stanley F. Maxwell.*

MASTERS CARPET

Lodge to confer the Royal Arch degrees. Webb later moved to Providence, Rhode Island, where he helped organize the General Grand Chapter and the Knights Templar Grand Encampment.[11]

If William Preston had brought order and deeper meaning to English Masonic rituals in the 1770s, it was Thomas Smith Webb who became the "father of the American Masonic rituals" with the publication of his 1797 book, *Freemason's Monitor or Illustrations of Masonry.* Webb's book sought to unify Preston's three craft degrees with the additional degrees of the Royal Arch, Royal & Select Masters and Knights Templar. He created one integrated system that he termed the York Rite. Armed with his seminal work, Webb traveled throughout the country teaching his revised rituals and organizing local, state and national York Rite governing bodies. By the time of Webb's death in 1819, more than 16,000 copies of his *Monitor* had been sold through eight editions, and numerous state grand lodges had accepted it for their official ritual work and endorsed his York Rite structure.[12]

Jeremy Cross (1783-1861) and Amos Doolittle (1754-1832) supported Webb's work. Born in New Hampshire, Cross spent much of his professional life traveling with Webb organizing York Rite bodies before settling in New Haven, Connecticut. After Webb's death, Cross published in 1820 *A True Masonic Chart and Hieroglyphic Monitor,* which was his own version of the Preston/Webb rituals. The well-known engraver Amos Doolittle worked with Cross to illustrate the volume.[13] While the Preston/Webb system became the standard ritual work for most American lodges, Doolittle's engravings became the standard for American Masonic symbolism.[14]

The Scottish Rite system evolved from an earlier set of degrees that originated in France. The degrees became known as the *Ecossais* through the reported assertions made by Chevalier Andrew Ramsay in 1737 in Paris. By the 1760s, Stephen Morin, a French Mason, carried the degrees to the West Indies and authorized Dutchman Henry Francken to confer them to American colonists. The earliest evidence of Francken's work is from 1767, when he issued patents to Masons in Albany, New York. The recipients of patents multiplied rapidly throughout the colonies, and Masons received the rituals by purchasing them. The result was a period of proliferating Masonic confusion.

Eventually, eleven men, meeting at Charleston, South Carolina, in 1801, organized to regulate the "Scottish" degrees and to bring "order out of chaos."[15] The result of their efforts was the formation of a Supreme Council to govern and regulate the 33 degrees of Scottish Rite Freemasonry. The four principal leaders of the group were Col. John Mitchell (1741-1816), Dr. Frederick Dalcho (1770-1836), Alexandre de Grasse-Tilly (1765-1845)

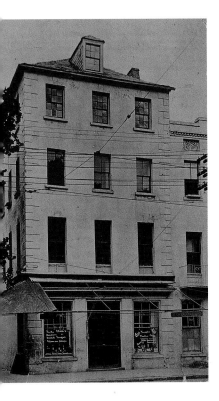

SHEPHEARD'S TAVERN

In this building in 1801, eleven Freemasons of diverse faiths and nationalities formed the first Supreme Council of the Ancient and Accepted Scottish Rite of Freemasonry.

ca. 1870. Courtesy of the Archives of the Supreme Council, 33°, Southern Jurisdiction, Washington, DC.

and Emanuel de la Motta (1760–1821). Mitchell served in the Continental Army and knew George Washington. Dalcho was a medical doctor, co-editor of the *Charleston Courier,* and an ordained Episcopal priest. A wealthy son of a famous French admiral, de Grasse-Tilly fought in Santo Domingo against a slave uprising in 1793 and returned to France in 1804. And de la Motta was a prominent Sephardic rabbi in Savannah, Georgia, and Charleston.[16] Together the eleven men created the office of Sovereign Grand Commander to head the Council and named Col. Mitchell to that position.

The Supreme Council claimed jurisdictional authority of the Scottish Rite degrees throughout the world; however, several groups in New York claimed similar authority. One was headed by Antoine Bideaud, and another by Joseph Cerneau. In Charleston, Mitchell assigned de la Motta the task of investigating the New York situation. When Cerneau refused to submit to an inspection and Bideaud fully cooperated, de la Motta declared Bideaud's group legitimate. To prevent further "clandestine" Scottish Rite activities and to help suppress Cerneau's rituals, the Charleston Supreme Council agreed to charter the Bideaud group as a Supreme Council for the Northern Jurisdiction of the United States in 1813.[17] The territorial jurisdiction for this group was limited to 15 states, bounded roughly north of the Mason-Dixon line and east of the Mississippi River. The 1801 Supreme Council, to be known as the Southern Jurisdiction, continued to administer the Scottish Rite degrees in the southern and western states. It also claimed authority over any other additional states that joined the union.[18] The agreement between the two Supreme Councils, however, did not prevent Cerneau from perpetuating his Scottish Rite degrees for years to come.

Scottish Rite Masons were also confronted with their own set of three initial degrees that differed markedly from those described by Preston and Webb. To gain acceptance from the firmly established grand lodges, the Supreme Councils conceded that they would not confer the three craft degrees and would only admit to their ranks Master Masons of recognized lodges. The Scottish Rite as well as the York Rite also acknowledged the supreme Masonic authority of a Grand Master within his state. In return, Grand Masters agreed not to interfere with the internal affairs of the Scottish and York Rites. A general agreement was reached that the third degree was the most important lesson and that the additional degrees in the two Rites provided only an elaboration of the truths contained in the craft degrees.[19]

Establishing Freemasonry

ROSE CROIX APRON

The Rose Croix degrees within the Scottish Rite affirm the immortality of the soul and supreme virtue of charity. This silk embroidered apron shows the principal symbols of these degrees including the pelican that legend says feeds her young from her own breast.

ca. 1830. National Heritage Museum, Supreme Council Collection, 74.001.48.

Masonic Capstone

"The greatest and best men in all ages have been encouragers and promoters of the art, and have never deemed it derogatory from their dignity, to level themselves with the fraternity, extend their privileges, and patronize their assemblies."

— THOMAS SMITH WEBB, 1808[20]

The spread of lodges across America and the development of national York and Scottish Rite systems encouraged a group of Masons to reconsider the idea of a national Masonic governing body. A group of Masons in 1799 had attempted to create a General Grand Lodge of the United States and offered George Washington's name as the first national Grand Master. The idea never materialized because of Washington's reluctance and his death later that year. In 1822, some grand lodge representatives assembled in the U.S. Capitol's Senate chambers. They were joined by several congressmen who were Masons, including Senator Henry Clay of Kentucky. Their desire was to establish a General Grand Lodge of the United States that could coordi-

Growing membership
in the craft and the wide
circulation of Cross'
True Masonic Chart
expanded Masonic sym-
bolism into the sphere
of decorative and fine
art. Affluent Masons
used the craft's symbols
to adorn their fine furniture, portraits and table
settings. Less affluent
brothers demonstrated
their affiliation by in-
corporating Masonic
symbols on their handi-
crafts, jewelry and
common utensils.

*Portrait by John S.
Angell, ca. 1820,
probably of Arnold
Steere, Woonsocket,
RI, photographed by
Briggs Photography.
National Heritage
Museum, 99.009. Mug,
ca. 1810–20. National
Heritage Museum,
76.50.2. Flask, 1815–25.
National Heritage
Museum, gift of Russell
Ward Nadeau, 94.008.1.
Fire Bucket [opposite],
1799. National Heritage
Museum, 81.48.*

nate efforts to prevent the spread of "irregular" or unchartered lodges, curtail the immigration of other foreign rituals, and prevent the malpractice of Masonic ritual "peddlers."[21] Despite such august leadership and high purposes, the convention failed. The grand lodge delegates reflected divisions similar to those that existed within America. Grand lodges, like states and Americans in general, were deeply concerned about decisions being made by men "a great distance from the scene of action, where the parties were but little known."[22] In the decades to follow, further calls for a national grand lodge were ignored.

Masonic honor and prestige were on display during General Lafayette's triumphal return to the United States in 1824 as "the nation's guest." His tour began in New York, moved on to New England, and took him through southern states. He traveled up the Mississippi and the Ohio Rivers before returning to the East and New England again. Every stop brought parades of bands, militias and veterans of the Revolution. There were grand receptions and balls held in his honor. Local Freemasons awaited him at every stop. Lafayette was often presented with a Masonic apron, asked to attend a lodge meeting and invited to use the lodge hall for overnight accommodations.[23] His Masonic membership inspired men to seek admission to Masonic lodges, while his fame as an aristocrat who had survived the French Revolution served to heighten the honor and mystique of the craft.

Returning to Boston in 1825, Lafayette visited with the members of St. John's Lodge and was the guest of honor at the Masonic cornerstone-laying ceremony for the Bunker Hill monument, erected on the 50th anniversary of the battle. This first great monument built in America was admired by all Americans. Bunker Hill had particular significance for Freemasons, because General Joseph Warren, a Masonic Grand Master, was killed during the battle. In 1794, members of Charlestown's King Solomon's Lodge had dedicated a monument to Warren on the hill and later donated part of the land for the second monument in 1825.[24]

Soon after the Bunker Hill ceremony, Lafayette imparted final farewells to his Revolutionary comrades and Masonic brothers and returned to France. His tour had demonstrated his love for the United States and his high esteem for Freemasonry. Americans and Freemasons alike had returned the affection with equal vigor. Yet such ostentatious displays for a European aristocrat troubled certain citizens and reminded them of Washington's warning "against the insidious wiles of foreign influence."[25] The zeal with which American Freemasons embraced Lafayette heightened suspicion of the craft as an international order with secrets and a radical revolutionary past. As Lafayette sailed toward home, Freemasonry had reached a pinnacle of honor and seemed to be in perfect harmony with the

American community. Within three years, however, a small band of misguided and overzealous Masons in a western New York town would spark a scandal that would engulf the fraternity and would nearly destroy America's Masonic lodges.

The Anti-Masonic Period, 1827–1835

"It [Freemasonry] is wrong — essentially wrong — a seed of evil, which can never produce any good. It may perish in the ground — it may never rise to bear fruit; but whatever fruit it does bear, must be rank poison — It can never prove a blessing, but by its barrenness."

— JOHN QUINCY ADAMS, 1832 [26]

The coincidental deaths of John Adams and Thomas Jefferson on July 4, 1826, signaled the symbolic end of the Spirit of '76 and the passing of America's Revolutionary War generation. Two years later, the nation marked its entry into the age of industry with the first commercial railroad. Freemasons were on hand for the ceremony of laying a foundation stone for the Baltimore & Ohio line. The revolutionary and republican generation had securely established the country, but the nation was changing again.

During this transformation, younger generations of Americans questioned Freemasonry's prominence and the extent of its involvement in public and private arenas. Political factions formed into national parties, and a new Protestant revival, identified by historians as the "Second Great Awakening," swept across the nation in the 1820s. These two social phenomena fueled a blaze of public denunciation of the craft. The flint and steel that sparked the assault on the fraternity were its secret oaths, religious neutrality and internationalism. The anti-Masonic period of the 1820s and 1830s severely damaged the fraternity in the South and nearly destroyed it in the North.

Freemasonry's troubles erupted in western New York in 1826, when a man named William Morgan boasted that he would publish an exposure of all the Masonic rituals and recognition signs. Probably a Freemason, Morgan had served in the army during the War of 1812 and was a restless, jack-of-all-trades drifter.[27] While Masonic exposures were nothing new and had been printed as early as the 1720s, Morgan's book promised something radically different. Morgan planned to illustrate the secret words and recognition signs that had not been previously published and intimated that he would also include the secrets of the York Rite degrees.[28]

Hearing of Morgan's promised exposé, some Freemasons living in the

ANTI-MASONIC
ACCUSATION

William Morgan's disap-
pearance from Batavia,
NY, in 1827, evoked
many rumors and theo-
ries. Members of the
Anti-Masonic political
party believed Free-
masons drowned him
in Lake Ontario. Others
said they saw him in
Canada, Arizona and
even Turkey. Whatever
the story, Morgan never
returned to Batavia.

*William Morgan's
Drowning, from* Anti-
Masonic Almanac for
the Year 1833, *Edward
Giddins, Utica, NY,
1831. National Heritage
Museum.*

Batavia area threatened Morgan. There were several unsuccessful attempts
to burn the printing house. There were also harassing attempts to press
charges against Morgan for minor offenses. Morgan was acquitted on one
charge and released on bail for a second. A group of men then kidnapped
Morgan, who was never seen again. A public outcry ensued, and several
Masons were eventually brought to trial. The accused claimed to have released Morgan and sent him into Canada with money. There were also sen-
sational newspaper reports that his kidnappers had drowned him in Lake
Ontario. What actually happened remains a mystery, but most likely he
was killed by his abductors either accidentally or in a fit of passion.[29]

In spite of Morgan's disappearance, his partner, David C. Miller, published *Illustrations of Masonry, By One of the Fraternity who has Devoted
Thirty Years to the Subject.* "The Morgan affair" gathered public notoriety throughout 1827–28, as numerous investigations and trials of Morgan's kidnappers could neither solve the mystery of Morgan's disappearance nor satisfy the public's demand for justice.[30]

The Morgan affair, combined with a grieving widow and the publication of the missing man's book, brought national scrutiny to Freemasonry.
To many citizens, the once affluent, morally upright association now appeared sinister. Some had long feared that Freemasons had played a major role in the bloody French Revolution and reinterpreted the adherence
to a "universal brotherhood of man" to mean a worldwide conspiracy.[31]
Others saw the Morgan affair as a precursor to an overthrow of democracy
by ruthless men. These fears increased as widely circulated anti-Masonic

tracts reported the names of prominent Masons and a list of lodges operating in nearly every town.

As controversy over the Morgan affair grew, Christian religious leaders turned to criticizing the exposed secret rituals and obligations. Baptist ministers preaching in western New York were the first and most vocal group and were soon followed by other denominations. Local pastors of New England churches viewed the fraternity as a frivolous distraction from prayer and sober work. They also feared that Freemasons were "believers in natural religion," a practice that would corrupt members of their congregations. Other clergymen accused the fraternity of distorting biblical passages for its rituals, lectures and passwords to make Freemasonry appear sacred. Many American Christians were horrified to learn of the blood-curdling symbolic penalties for breaking the secret obligations. The symbolic death, burial and "raising" of the central figure of the Masonic ritual in the third degree were interpreted as a blasphemous mimicry and mockery of the resurrection of Jesus.[32]

Newspapers, anti-Masonic sermons and pamphlets sensationalized the Morgan affair. People who had little knowledge of and no interest in Freemasonry were increasingly alarmed. At a time when women were gaining increased respect as the moral authority within the nation, they were alarmed by accounts of men meeting secretly to perform strange initiation rituals. With news of the events surrounding Morgan's disappearance, women were also concerned about the spread of secretly plotted criminal acts. The people of the newly founded republic felt alienated upon learning of Masonic officers bearing such undemocratic titles as "Worshipful Master" or "High Priest."[33] Many families feared their Masonic kin were practicing deviltry behind doors that none but Masons could pass.

MASONIC INITIATION
As depicted by anti-Masons, this allegorical ceremony of a candidate receiving the Masonic third degree was considered blasphemous.

Richardson's Monitor of Free-Masonry, *Jabez Richardson, New York, 1860. National Heritage Museum, gift of the Maxwell family.*

Establishing Freemasonry

Anti-Masonic groups attacked Freemasonry not only for its supposedly irreligious activities but also for its perceived political power. Almost immediately after Morgan's disappearance, New York political operative Thurlow Weed saw a golden opportunity to challenge older factions entrenched in state and national offices. Weed and others funded the printing of anti-Masonic tracts, almanacs and books. Some gave anti-Masonic speeches and demanded that Masons renounce their membership. Anti-Masonic leaders and a growing number of citizens were convinced that a nefarious Masonic conspiracy existed when it became known that Masons had tampered with witnesses and that some of the judges and jurors who acquitted Morgan's kidnappers were Freemasons.[34] The perception of a cabal endeavoring to cover up crimes was considered a clear and dangerous threat to the open form of government and the proper functioning of American democracy. In a speech to the Anti-Masonic Convention in LeRoy, New York, in 1828, William Wadsworth proclaimed:

> This institution threatens not only danger to government and the cause of justice, but strikes at the basis of all morality and religion. . . . To the bosom of Free Masonry, every revolution and conspiracy which has agitated Europe for the last fifty years may be distinctly traced, and the secret workings of this all-pervading order can be clearly seen.[35]

Local, county and state public officials who were Masons came under suspicion.[36] Many governors and federal officials, including DeWitt Clinton, Andrew Jackson and Chief Justice John Marshall, were placed in awkward political situations because of their previous service as Masonic Grand Masters.

Throughout 1828–29, the anti-Masonic movement spread with considerable speed across New York and other northern states. Anti-Masonic legislators attempted to pass laws banning the fraternity and exposing its membership. One such resolution was even read in the U.S. House of Representatives, but it was never acted upon. Although not a Mason, John Quincy Adams remained publicly neutral toward Freemasonry during his term as president; however, after his defeat by Andrew Jackson in 1828, Adams wrote vigorous denunciations of the craft. The movement seemed to be more effective at the state and local levels, especially in rural areas. Laws aimed at destroying Freemasonry were passed in Connecticut, Vermont and New York. The legislation, however, was never enforced and had little impact.[37]

William H. Seward of New York was influential in organizing local committees in 1830 that led to the formation of a national Anti-Masonic

ANTIMASONIC APRON

BLACKNESS of DARKNESS

VIRTUES OF MASONRY
AND VICES OF ANTI-
MASONRY

Engravings like this
one on an anti-Masonic
apron were used to stir
public opinion and
influence politicians and
religious leaders. On the
left is a hydra of anti-
Masonry breathing the
corruptible smoke of
persecution, slander and
ignorance. On the right
is the Masonic pyramid
of "Perfect Union" with
the steps of equal rights,
charity and patriotism.

*Anti-Masonic apron,
produced by William
Cammeyer Jr., Albany,
NY, ca. 1831. Library of
Congress, Prints and
Photographs Division
LC-USZ C4-8077.*

Party. This action was significant for several reasons. It was the first attempt to create a third political party to compete with the dominant Democrats and the National Republicans. By 1831, the Anti-Masonic Party was sufficiently organized to hold the country's first national convention to nominate a full slate. The party's candidate for president, William Wirt, had been Attorney General in the administrations of Thomas Jefferson and John Quincy Adams and was a repentant Freemason who became a vocal critic of his erstwhile fraternity. In the 1832 election, Wirt carried only Vermont and finished a distant third.[38] The winner was incumbent Andrew Jackson, a Past Grand Master of Tennessee. Running second was Henry Clay, a Past Grand Master of Kentucky. For the 1836 election, the Anti-Masonic Party failed to nominate a candidate, and its efforts dwindled. Most of its members joined the new Whig Party or turned their public agitation toward the prohibition of alcohol or the abolition of slavery. Protestant leaders also lost interest in attacking Freemasonry.[39] A greater perceived enemy, the Roman Catholic Church, was growing rapidly with each boatload of European immigrants, a process that only accelerated in the 1840s.

While limited in politics by its one-issue agenda, the Anti-Masonic Party nearly succeeded in killing the fraternity in America. The 500 lodges active in New York in 1825 were reduced to 75 by 1835. For a time, all lodges stopped working in Vermont; the Grand Lodge of Rhode Island did not charter a new lodge for nearly 30 years, and the total number of Masons throughout the nation — possibly as high as 100,000 in 1826 — was reduced to as few as 40,000 by 1835. Fledgling grand lodges in Illinois and Michigan were destroyed and those in Pennsylvania, Massachusetts and Ohio struggled for survival.[40] Fearing violence from anti-Masons, lodges were forced underground. Many truly came to meet in secret and curtailed their annual parades and banquets. Individual brothers were denied church membership, kept off juries or shunned by family, friends and neighbors.[41] The York Rite was hit even harder, while the Scottish Rite nearly disappeared. The Scottish Rite Supreme Councils were kept alive only by a few

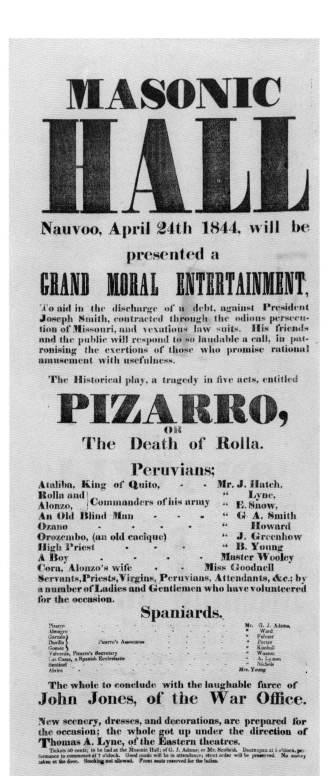

Freemason Joseph Smith (1805–44) founded the Church of Jesus Christ of Latter Day Saints, known also as the Mormon Church. He and other members of his church conducted Masonic lodge meetings in Nauvoo, Illinois, between 1841 and 1844. When the state of Missouri sued him for militant activities in the 1830s, members of the church, along with brother Freemasons, staged a fund-raising play to help pay his legal debts. Just two months after the play, Smith and his brother Hyrum were murdered in Carthage, Illinois.

1844. Missouri Historical Society, St. Louis.

committed leaders in the Southern and Northern Jurisdictions.[42] Fearing damage to their social and family relationships, many quit the fraternity, but dedicated Masons remained unshaken in their commitment to Masonic ideals.

During the anti-Masonic period, Freemasonry's response to its attackers was hindered by the lack of a national Masonic authority. State Grand Masters could speak only for their own jurisdiction and had little ability to investigate the actions of the Grand Lodge of New York or to coordinate their actions with other Grand Masters to present a unified defense of a fraternity under attack. On the local level, lodges relied on the voluntary participation of its members, and many, if not most, Masons became reluctant to attend meetings. Who could determine if Morgan had acted out of greed or altruism? On whose authority did his kidnappers act? Or were they rogue elements who had separate scores to settle with the cantankerous Morgan? Grand Masters and lodge Masters had no more power to judge their members than any other private citizen did. If a brother under suspicion refused to attend a lodge meeting for questioning or judgment, then Masonic leaders could, in reality, do nothing more than expel him from the fraternity.

Meanwhile, the Prince Hall Grand Lodge of Masons in Massachusetts issued its own "declaration of independence" in the Boston *Advertiser* in 1827: "We have come to the conclusion that with what knowledge we possess of Masonry, and as people of color by ourselves, we are, and ought by rights, to be free and independent of other lodges."[44] Following the lead of this grand lodge, the Prince Hall Grand Lodge of Pennsylvania was formed and helped spread a network of African-American brothers and lodges. While mainstream Freemasonry declined, Prince Hall Masonry grew. By 1850, lodges had formed in free African-American communities of New York, New Jersey, the District of Columbia, Delaware, Ohio and even New Orleans and Virginia. At the same time, Prince Hall Masons accomplished something that other Masons were unable to achieve. Delegates meeting in Boston in 1847 agreed to form a national grand lodge. The attempt was short-lived, because state-based grand lodges continued to assert their sovereignty. After the Civil War, Prince Hall grand lodges grew to such strength that a national grand lodge became a hindrance and was formally dissolved in 1877.[45]

The Morgan affair and the Anti-Masonic Party affected the fraternity in other profound ways. First, Freemasonry in America sought to reduce the charges against it and minimize the number of critics by moving away from the serious spiritual and philosophical discussion that religious leaders found most objectionable and began to turn toward basic self-

Establishing Freemasonry

improvement, charity and sociability. Secondly, Masons downplayed their European origins and demonstrated their loyalty to the republic through their patriotic idolization of George Washington. Finally, fear of another conflagration caused the policies and governance of the fraternity to become pronouncedly Protestant and conservative in the decades ahead.

The Morgan affair and the Anti-Masonic Party also had an effect on America. The events nurtured the deep American fear of sinister conspiracies against the government. The anti-Masonic literature of the period formed the basis for all future attacks on the fraternity, and its style and arguments were easily adapted to other "secret" or "anti-American" organizations as time went by.[46] The party itself was the first viable third party to challenge America's two-party system. Its one-issue platform and moderate success established a legacy for a host of future political parties, including not only the Whigs and Republicans but also "one-issue" or "limited issue" groups like the Free Soil, Progressive, Dixiecrat and Reform Parties.

But perhaps the most unforeseen result was the creation of new fraternal organizations on the heels of the dissemination of Masonic rituals and accounts of Masonic meetings. The Odd Fellows fraternity, which had arrived from England, and American-born organizations, such as the Improved Order of Red Men, actually grew during the period. Contriving and performing "secret" rituals that included mystical symbols and passwords became a popular pastime and a genre within 19th-century American society. By 1900, college fraternities and thousands of ethnic, veterans, labor and religious organizations — not the least of which was the Church of Latter Day Saints[47] — incorporated elements derived from Masonic models to build the nation. Through the craft's revival, especially after the Civil War, Freemasonry once again became the preeminent American fraternal association, but the anti-Masonic agitation of the 1820s and 1830s did leave lasting scars. Try as it might, the Masonic fraternity would never regain the public prestige and reclaim the honor it held in the eyes of the nation prior to William Morgan's disappearance.

PART TWO

Building Freemasonry and American Community

1835-1920

CHAPTER 4

The Foundation of Every Virtue

Masonic Self-Improvement, 1835–1870

"Among laws that rule human societies there is one which seems to be more precise and clear than all others. If men are to remain civilized or to become so, the art of associating together must grow and improve in the same ratio in which the equality of conditions is increased."

— ALEXIS DE TOCQUEVILLE, 1835[1]

WHEN FRENCH WRITER ALEXIS DE TOCQUEVILLE toured the United States in 1831–32, he saw a country rich in material resources, filled with opportunities and populated by a wide variety of energetic and optimistic people. But he also saw a fragile republic that confronted many internal divisions and external threats to its survival. The country's growth, population and wealth revealed stark divisions between race, religion and class that challenged the very definitions of liberty and freedom. Tocqueville strongly believed, however, that if America's democratic instincts and volunteer spirit were directed toward overcoming its problems, then the weak nation might become a world power. Throughout the last decades of the 19th century, American Freemasons were to play a vital role in seeking solutions to these problems.

Between the 1840 publication of Tocqueville's *Democracy in America* and 1920, the United States went through a series of transformations. In the 1860s, the Union was severely tested by the Civil War. Brother fought brother over the issues of slavery, freedom, property rights and governmental authority. After the war, Americans built national systems not only to heal divisiveness but also to make money. These systems were challenged continually during America's Gilded Age (1870–1900), as the country became more diverse. Conflicts ensued between industrial capitalists, skilled laborers and unskilled immigrants that forever changed the relationship

AMERICA AND HER
PRESIDENTS

Surrounded by the first
16 presidents, the United
States is depicted as a
young woman holding
a staff with a liberty
cap and shield and sup-
ported by a bald eagle.
In the background is the
steamship of commerce
and the newly expanded
U.S. Capitol with its
planned dome.

*Presidents of the United
States, drawn and
lithographed by A.
Feusier, published by F.
Bouclet, probably
France, ca. 1861.
National Heritage
Museum, 79.34.1.*

between men and their work. Large cities and major corporations began
to dominate rural markets and threaten small-town life. The persistence
of poverty, disease and corruption angered Americans into forming new
political organizations to reform government and regulate business during
the progressive era at the turn of the century. The emerging American
middle classes sought a balance between the demands of work, family, religious and community duties and the pleasures of spending their new wealth
on material possessions and enjoying leisure activities. By 1920, all these
societal tensions and more were unleashed, as America faced an accelerated
transformation during the Roaring Twenties.

Throughout this period, Freemasonry also matured. As a voluntary

The Foundation of Every Virtue: Masonic Self-Improvement

The windows came from the Whitehall, New York, Masonic temple, home of Phoenix Lodge No. 96, chartered soon after the anti-Masonic hysteria of the 1830s. Members may have chosen the name "Phoenix" as a symbol of the lodge's rebirth in 1844. The windows were installed in 1908, after the temple was renovated.

Windows, 1908. National Heritage Museum, 2000.060.2a, b. Masonic temple, Whitehall, NY, O.J. Benjamin, Whitehall, NY, ca. 1920. National Heritage Museum, A96/066/2933.

MASONIC TEMPLE, WHITEHALL, N. Y.

self-improvement association, it found a societal niche under political and religious authority and between the public and private spheres. Masonic lodges taught democratic principles and moral virtues to their members while forbidding the discussion at lodge meetings of political ideology and religious dogma. Lodges reflected the character of the communities in which they worked. Local Masons, in turn, adapted the fraternity to meet the needs of their families and communities. Through Freemasonry's organizations, Americans of different regions, classes, political opinions and religious creeds worked together, in their own unique way, to address the larger issues of American society. Thus between 1835 and 1920, Freemasons built their lodges and taught Tocqueville's "art of association" to millions of citizens. The Masonic craft would indeed develop and improve among Americans "at the same ratio in which equality of conditions . . . increased." [2]

Part Two of this book explores the reasons why successive generations of men joined Freemasonry and similar voluntary organizations. Of the many reasons for Freemasonry's rebirth after the anti-Masonic period, four are examined here: self-improvement teachings (Chapter 4), dramatic initiation rituals (Chapter 5), health and death benefits (Chapter 6), and social activities (Chapter 7). By successfully applying the fraternity's three tenets of brotherly love, relief and truth, Masonic membership in America increased to more than ten percent of the adult male population in 1920.[3] But Freemasonry's rituals, moral legacies and "ancient" history came in sudden conflict with Americans born after 1890 (Chapter 8). The World War I generation, less interested in contemplating and revering the virtues of the past, preferred to live for the moment and work for the future. Part Three will examine how Freemasons reinterpreted the three tenets in an effort to maintain their prestige and a large membership.

The Morgan affair and the Anti-Masonic Party of the 1820s and 1830s had toppled Freemasonry from its pedestal of social prestige and perceived political power and destroyed many of its lodges. Scared by the accusations, a significant number of men dropped their membership, and many lodges were forced to close. New generations of Masons, employing the tenets and inspired by the fraternal spirit, rebuilt Freemasonry. With approval of Masonic leaders, new organizations and "appendant bodies" were accepted into the Masonic structure. By 1920, Masons had built libraries, colleges, orphanages, charity funds and other philanthropic institutions. They had also created new Masonic-related organizations for women and children as well as groups for fun and sociability.

Conversely, when Freemasonry's structure proved to be too restrictive for some, Masons left their lodges to form new fraternal organizations. In 1842, Masons who were not content with promoting total abstinence from alcohol within Masonic lodges helped form the Sons of Temperance. Similarly, the limits of religious neutrality caused Jewish Masons to help organize B'nai B'rith in 1843.[5] After the Civil War, many more groups were created by Freemasons. Oliver Kelley started the Patrons of Husbandry (the Grange) for rural families; John Upchurch created the Ancient Order of United Workmen for skilled craftsmen; General John Logan organized the Grand Army of the Republic for Union veterans, and in 1917, Melvin Jones created Lions International for business and community service.

Other Americans borrowed heavily from Freemasonry to create their

"As an individual, you are charged to practise the domestic and public virtues. . . . Be especially careful to maintain, in their fullest splendor, those truly Masonic ornaments — Brotherly Love, Relief and Truth."

— CHARGE TO AN ENTERED APPRENTICE, 1861[4]

own "ancient" history and rituals for new organizations. Beginning with the ritual-based fraternities of the Order of Odd Fellows in 1819 and the Improved Order of Red Men in 1834, Americans adapted the Masonic model to perpetuate specific purposes. Irish immigrants organized the Ancient Order of Hibernians in 1836. With the influx of the new immigrants, white native-born Protestants responded with "patriotic" organizations, such as the United Order of American Mechanics in 1844. Many of these bore striking similarities to Freemasonry.

After the Civil War, Freemasonry became the model for countless organizations as America entered into "a golden age of fraternalism." Along with Prince Hall Freemasonry, African-Americans built dozens of other national fraternal organizations, such as the Order of Saint Luke in 1867. Rev. Michael McGivney established the Knights of Columbus for Catholic men in 1882. Combining Masonic principles with community service, Paul Harris began Rotary International in 1905.[6] Freemasonry achieved a new preeminence among American voluntary associations, as it strove to remain within its social niche and attract prominent and innovative men.

The Masonic Form of Self-improvement

"Truth is a divine attribute, and the foundation of every virtue. To be good and true is the first lesson we are taught in Masonry. On this theme we contemplate, and by its dictates endeavour to regulate our conduct."

— WILLIAM PRESTON, 1788[7]

The radical changes taking place in the United States between the election of President Andrew Jackson in 1828 and the end of the Civil War in 1865 also brought a blaze of new political, social, moral and religious organizations. Founded before 1840 were the American Temperance Society, American Peace Society, General Union for Promoting the Christian Observance of the Sabbath, American Lyceum Association, American Anti-Slavery Society, American Home Missionary Society, and American Sunday School Union.[8] The prominence of these organizations became so acute that one contemporary commented:

> Matters have come to such a pass, that a peaceable man can hardly venture to eat or drink, or to go to bed or to get up, to correct his children or to kiss his wife, without obtaining the permission and direction of some moral . . . society.[9]

Some of these societies had a pronounced Masonic influence. Such temperance organizations as the Templars of Honor and Temperance and the Order of Good Templars performed initiation rituals, wore regalia aprons

SONS OF TEMPERANCE.
Love, Purity and Fidelity.

DAUGHTERS OF TEMPERANCE.
Virtue, Love and Temperance.

SONS AND DAUGHTERS OF TEMPERANCE

After the anti-Masonic period of the 1820s and 1830s, many new fraternal organizations used Freemasonry as a model. Instead of oaths to guard secrets, the Sons and Daughters of Temperance vowed not to drink alcohol. They wore decorated collars rather than aprons and perpetuated the tenets of fidelity, moderation and love.

Nathaniel Currier, New York, ca. 1850. National Heritage Museum, 91.016.1, 2.

TEMPLARS OF HONOR
AND TEMPERANCE JEWEL

These badges or "jewels"
were worn on the left
breast to identify mem-
bers of a fraternity. The
silver jewel has an altar
with an open book at
the top, the "temple of
honor" in the center and
a medallion of the order
suspended from the
ribbon. This jewel is
engraved with the
owner's name, "C.F.
Adams."

*ca. 1855. National
Heritage Museum,
79.3.3a-b.*

and sashes and took oaths agreeing not to drink liquor or reveal the organization's secrets. The most prominent of these, the Sons of Temperance,
grew to 6,000 lodges with 245,000 members within eight years of their
founding in 1842. In the 1850s, it temporarily surpassed Freemasonry as
America's largest fraternal association.[10]

Freemasonry's revival after the anti-Masonic period lies in part in its
ability to respond to a national fear of moral failing and the belief in men's
inherent vice and women's inherent virtue. Always claiming the fraternity
to be dedicated to moral and spiritual improvement, Masons reinterpreted
the rituals and symbols to suit the new society. Downplaying its "foreign"
aristocratic history, Freemasonry followed the trend in America of pay-
ing homage to the distinguished Founding Fathers. Freemasons chose to
emphasize the ritual's biblical passages that taught fraternal and moral
virtues instead of dwelling on the esoteric mystical elements of Masonic
symbolism.[11]

State grand lodges took several other steps to ease public concerns.
They banned alcohol and reemphasized the prohibition of political and
sectarian discussions in all lodge meetings. They promoted the building
of separate lodge halls away from taverns. These "temples" retained Federalist neoclassical architecture while focusing membership activities on
more constructive pursuits. Clergymen were recruited to join the craft
and serve as lodge chaplains. Masons were encouraged to join in community
celebrations, but by order of the grand lodges the unique decorated aprons
were replaced by plainer and more uniform ones.[12]

One of the reasons for the fraternity's revival in the 1840s and 1850s
was its intellectual heritage and Enlightenment lineage. Westward expansion offered new opportunities, yet hazards awaited along the rivers and
trails of the West. This jumbled and turbulent life gave settlers a strong
urge to bring order to the frontier. As they improved the land, replaced
log cabins with framed houses, and founded towns, they sought to improve
their manners and minds. Through Freemasonry's rituals and lectures,
generations of pioneers learned about classical civilization and Enlightenment philosophy, while practicing etiquette and proper diction.

But the information conveyed in the three degrees or in the higher
degrees of the York and Scottish Rites was not true knowledge. It simply
referred men to other knowledge contained within Holy Scripture and the
seven liberal arts and sciences. Freemasonry did not claim to have or im-
part the truth. It only encouraged its brethren to seek it. Memorizing Freemasonry's rituals and lectures strengthened a man's intellectual capac-
ity, and reciting them in lodge reinforced their principles to brothers in
attendance.

Building Freemasonry and American Community

FLIGHT OF WINDING STAIRS

During the Fellowcraft degree, the candidate is escorted up a symbolic flight of winding stairs, consisting of three, five and seven steps. Each step represents a principal officer of the lodge, an order in classical architecture or one of the liberal arts and sciences. Originally taught through "tracing board" charts or paintings, American lodges in the late 1800s began employing magic lanterns and sets of hand-painted glass slides, like this one, to heighten the dramatic appeal of the lessons.

ca. 1900. National Heritage Museum, gift of Ashlar Lodge No. 639, F&AM, Maple Heights, OH, 87.9.3.

"The Rough Ashlar is a stone as taken from the quarry in its rude and natural state. The Perfect Ashlar is a stone made ready by the hands of the workmen. . . . By the Rough Ashlar we are reminded of our rude and imperfect state by nature; by the Perfect Ashlar of that state of perfection at which we hope to arrive, by a virtuous education, our own endeavors and the blessing of God."

— THOMAS SMITH WEBB, 1805[13]

Better-educated men who went West took the fraternity with them and used it as a seedbed for other civic organizations as settlements grew into towns, county seats and state capitals. Several Masonic grand lodges, such as Florida, Kansas and Minnesota, even predate the state governments. Employing the tenet of truth by promoting knowledge, Masonic grand lodges in Missouri, Kentucky, Ohio, Georgia and Arkansas all attempted to establish colleges before 1861. Many other local and grand lodges began libraries not only to hold their archives but also, in the spirit of Benjamin Franklin, to acquire and lend books to improve the brethren's knowledge.[14]

The cornerstone of the Missouri Masonic College was laid in 1847. This was one of many colleges established by state grand lodges before the Civil War. Despite having 175 students, the Missouri college went bankrupt in 1859 and was closed. After the Civil War, the grand lodge donated the building to the Central Female College of Missouri.

Lexington, MO, ca. 1860. Lexington Historical Association, Lexington, MO.

The Grand Lodge of Iowa built a headquarters and library in Cedar Rapids in 1884. The postcard shows the original building in the foreground and a 1913 red brick addition to house a growing collection of books.

Curtis Teich & Co., Chicago, ca. 1915. National Heritage Museum, A96/066/BL10.

Masonic Library and Museum, Cedar Rapids, Iowa

One such educated Mason was Theodore S. Parvin (1817–1901). Born in New Jersey, Parvin graduated from Woodward College and was made a Mason in Nova Caesarea Harmony Lodge No. 2 in Cincinnati. In 1838, he moved to the Iowa territorial capital at Burlington and joined Des Moines Lodge No. 1. There he worked as the private secretary of Robert Lucas, the territorial governor and a Mason. Parvin served as a district attorney, trustee and professor at the University of Iowa, and founder of the Iowa

State Historical Society. In 1845, the newly formed Grand Lodge of Iowa budgeted five dollars to begin a Masonic library; Parvin became the Grand Secretary and librarian. Both the Iowa state archives and the grand lodge library are a credit to Parvin's efforts. He served as Grand Secretary until his death in 1901 and lived to see the grand lodge library grow to over 22,000 volumes.[15]

Prince Hall Freemasonry also spread westward through the free states. After its 1827 "declaration of independence" from other Masons, Prince Hall grand lodges were formed in Maryland in 1845, New Jersey in 1848, Ohio in 1849 and California in 1855.[16] Like other pioneers of the era, Pennsylvania Mason Richard Gleaves traveled to Ohio in 1847 to help establish Prince Hall lodges. In Cincinnati, there were more than 2,000 free blacks who owned property and supported six private schools for their children. Within a year, Gleaves reorganized one lodge, secured the charter for another and served as the first Grand Master of the Prince Hall Grand Lodge of Ohio. After the Civil War, Gleaves and his fellow Ohio Masons spread the fraternity to southern and western states.[17]

Assisting Gleaves in the formation of Ohio Prince Hall Masonry was another noted African-American, Martin Delaney. This "Father of Black Nationalism" was a doctor, explorer, close friend of Frederick Douglass, and the first black U.S. Army major during the Civil War. Delaney served as an officer in several Masonic lodges as he edited the abolitionist newspapers, *The Mystery* and *The North Star*.[18] Among his publications was his 1853 treatise on Freemasonry in which he argued:

> . . . But to deny to black men the privileges of Masonry, is to deny to a child the lineage of its own parentage. From whence sprung Masonry but from Ethiopia, Egypt, and Assyria, all settled and peopled by the children of Ham? Does anyone doubt the wisdom of Ethiopia? I have but to reply that in the days of King Solomon's renown and splendor she was capable of sending her daughters to prove him with hard questions. If this be true, what must be her sons![19]

Through the endeavors of Masons and the self-regulation of grand lodges, Freemasonry accepted its subordination to political power and religious authority. By simply seeking to "make

good men better," it regained an honored place in America's communities. Lodges that had closed or "gone dark" during the 1830s reorganized and new lodges were chartered. Immigration in the 1840s spurred this growth. Germans, Irish, Scots, French and others who became Masons formed their own lodges to suit their language and ethnicity. In cities such as New York, Pittsburgh, New Orleans, Chicago and San Francisco, lodges were named after Mozart, Lafayette, Robert Burns, Goethe, Voltaire or Saint Patrick. By the early 1850s, Masonic membership had recovered from anti-Masonic attacks, and in 1860, the number of American Masons had increased to more than 193,700.[20]

We Have Seen His Star in the East: Order of the Eastern Star

"Here [female relations of Master Masons] may share with the Masonic brothers in promulgating the principles of Brotherly Love, Relief, and Truth."

— ORDER OF THE EASTERN STAR, 1890 [21]

THE "FEMALE MASON"

While women cannot be Freemasons, there are many stories of individual women being "adopted" into the fraternity. The best known was Elizabeth St. Leger (1693–1773). The daughter of an Irish lord, Elizabeth was supposedly caught eavesdropping on her father's lodge meeting and after much deliberation was made a Mason. She later married Richard Aldworth and continued her honorary membership for many years.

The Honorable Mrs. Aldworth, engraved by John Cameron, published by Macoy & Sickels, New York, 1865. National Heritage Museum, 83.53.

Despite its revival as a civic self-improvement organization, Freemasonry was still considered suspect by many religious leaders, but especially by American women. As a male-only club with "secrets," Freemasonry encroached on the spiritual and moral dominion of the "private sphere." Many women viewed Freemasonry's rituals and oaths as a threat to marriage vows, family obligations and societal duties. The time men spent in the lodge, they believed, should be spent at home, in church, or in some other godly activity where they could benefit from women's influence.[22] Freemasonry's total redemption and community acceptance would only be earned if it could both prove its benevolence and allow women into its private lodges.

The first documented American woman who feared Freemasonry's secrecy was Boston's Hannah Mather Crocker. A member of one of the city's founding families, she was asked by her friends in the 1790s to investigate Freemasonry. Women feared their husbands' membership would "injure their moral and religious sentiments." After examining Freemasonry, Hannah was so taken with the craft that she began her own female lodge, called St. Anne's. This lodge was "founded on the original principles of true ancient Masonry so far as was consistent for the female character." She saw "a desire for cultivating the mind in the most useful branches of science and cherishing the love of literature." Like her contemporary and fellow Bostonian Prince Hall, Crocker claimed the same rights to Freemasonry's

Building Freemasonry and American Community

EASTERN STAR
SYMBOLS CHART

Designed by Willis D. Engle, Indianapolis, IN, ca. 1890. National Heritage Museum, gift of the Supreme Council, 33°, Northern Masonic Jurisdiction, 94.004.1.

ancient lineage of King Solomon's Temple through the Queen of Sheba. More importantly, she was adamant that Freemasonry would allow women to see that God had given women talents equal to men.[23] Although Hannah Crocker's lodge was short-lived, many 19th-century American women used the same arguments to form their own community organizations.[24]

It was not until the 1850s that Freemasons began to recognize a place for women within their fraternity. Following the lead of the Odd Fellows' creation of the Daughters of Rebekah, Freemason Rob Morris (1818–88) created the Order of the Eastern Star in 1855 as a group whose membership

ESTHER.

was open to Master Masons, their wives, widows, sisters and daughters.[25] Morris, who was president of the Masonic-supported college at La Grange, Kentucky, wrote extensively and lectured exhaustively on Freemasonry, investigated the Morgan affair, and later earned the title, "Poet Laureate of Freemasonry."[26] He justified the Eastern Star, in part, by insisting that the organization would provide Freemasons with a better means of recognition when wives or widows of Masons needed assistance.[27]

QUEEN ESTHER

The Order of the Eastern Star teaches the virtues of five biblical heroines: Jephthah's daughter, Ruth, Esther, Martha and Electra. Shown here is Esther who, during the Jewish Babylonian captivity, risked her life and begged King Xerxes to stop the persecution of her people. Esther represents the virtue of fidelity and is symbolized by the color white and the crown and scepter.

Illustration from Manual of the Order of the Eastern Star, *1868. National Heritage Museum, gift of Eugene C. Gerhart, Binghamton, NY, in memory of Charles V. Beams.*

Women who joined the Eastern Star did not, however, become Masons. The stonemasons' "ancient charges," upon which Freemasonry's laws were built, strictly banned female members.[28] Masonic leaders protested against women's desire to join fraternities. Women, they argued, were born naturally virtuous; therefore, they were in no need of the rituals' morality and teachings that were so necessary to save "corruptible" men.[29] Despite such objections, Eastern Star and the other women's groups gained wide acceptance, but Freemasonry has always classified Eastern Star as only an auxiliary body of the fraternity.

The Order of the Eastern Star had two unique features. First, local chapters could not operate without a Mason present. Jointly presiding over each chapter was a Worthy Matron and a Worthy Patron (often a husband and wife). The Worthy Patron had to be a Master Mason in good standing. The "sisters" performed the rituals, elected officers and kept the records. Second, Eastern Star conferred only one initiation degree. Unlike Masonic rituals, this degree did not convey new morals or bestow new duties on the candidates. It only affirmed women's roles as daughter, sister, wife, mother, and widow. Eastern Star's five-part ceremony taught these feminine roles and their virtues of obedience, devotion, fidelity, faith and charity through the biblical heroines of Adah, Ruth, Esther, Martha, and Electra.[30]

Although men and women could not meet as equals within the Masonic lodge, they could call each other brother and sister within the Eastern Star. In 1874, Prince Hall Masons created a parallel that included the "Queen of the South" degree, in which the Queen of Sheba challenged King Solomon to share his wisdom. By 1900, there were more than 200,000 Eastern Star sisters in the United States.[31] By allowing wives to have their own secret rituals and share in their husband's social activities, Eastern Star successfully bridged the private and public spheres.[32]

Brother against Brother: The Civil War and Freemasonry

"Justice is that standard or boundary of right, which enables us to render unto every man his just due, without distinction. This virtue is not only consistent with divine and human laws, but is the very cement and support of civil society."

— THOMAS SMITH WEBB, 1802[33]

America's voluntary associations greatly affected the character and outcome of the Civil War. Abolitionists and the new Republican Party relied on volunteers and grass roots support, but so did the Southern defenders of slavery and Northern Copperhead agitators, such as the Knights of the Golden Circle. Throughout most of the war, both armies relied on volunteer regiments mustered in local communities. Women also played greater public roles. In the North, they organized sanitation commissions and fairs to raise money to help soldiers and care for the wounded. In the Confederacy, women worked together to produce supplies and munitions for the rebel army.

The secession of eleven Southern states divided American society, split families and pitted Masonic brothers against each other. During the Civil War, tens of thousands of Masons served the Union and Confederacy. Some of the war's more famous Masons were Generals George McClellan, Joshua Lawrence Chamberlain, Lewis Armistead and George Pickett. Politicians who were Masons included Confederate Secretary of State Robert Toombs, Union Secretary of War Edwin B. Stanton and Vice President Andrew Johnson.[34] Within the armies, some 225 military lodges were formed. African-American regiments also formed military lodges, the most famous being in the Massachusetts 54th Volunteer Infantry.[35] Like their Revolutionary predecessors, these lodges became refuges from the chaos of war and a place where "the private and the general met on the level of equality, to part when the lodge was closed on the square of discipline."[36]

Freemasonry as an institution avoided serious division during the war, for it had no national governing body and each grand lodge followed the loyalty of its state. Anderson's 1723 *Constitutions* had urged Masons to be "a peaceable subject to the civil powers, wherever he resides or works."[37]

Upholding this obligation, Missouri Grand Master Marcus H. McFarland stated in 1861:

> Our fraternity embraces the whole in bonds of charity; as Masons we know no North, no South, no East, or West; yet we know our country and brotherhood everywhere. Peace and harmony are the mission of our order. Whatever individuals may feel to be their duty as citizens, let us not forget our brotherhood.[38]

Through the course of four years of fighting, countless stories are told of Masons who did not forget their fraternal obligations to each other. On many occasions, Masons greeted each other across enemy lines, Union or Confederate regimental lodges invited captured brothers to their meetings, and Masonic funeral rites were performed on battlefields for dead brothers.[39] The Masonic brotherly love that crossed America's political and social divisions inspired many men to join the fraternity. Major William McKinley, while guarding a Union army hospital in Winchester, Virginia, was impressed by the Masonic charity a doctor gave to rebel prisoners. Although an Ohio native, McKinley petitioned the local "Confederate" lodge, Hiram No. 21, and received all three degrees in 1865. McKinley, who remained an active Mason, was elected president of the United States in 1896 and 1900.[40]

After the Union victory in 1865, the American volunteer spirit was redirected into new endeavors. Between 1865 and 1870, more new voluntary associations were founded than in any other five-year period in American history. This included such national organizations as the Slovak Gymnastic Union Sokol (1865), the Benevolent and Protective Order of Elks (1867), the Knights of Labor (1869) and the P.E.O. Sisterhood (1870).[41]

War veterans also sought ways to continue the fraternal ties they had experienced as "brothers in arms." In 1866, Union soldiers, led in part by General John A. Logan (a Freemason), organized the Grand Army of the Republic (GAR) along Masonic lines.[42] The GAR's first regulations included three degrees of initiation, secret signs and grips for recognition, and loyalty oaths.

UNION SOLDIERS AT A MASONIC LODGE

Taken at the end of the Civil War, the photograph shows Union soldiers who were Freemasons gathered at the Petersburg, Virginia, Masonic temple.

Petersburg, VA, ca. 1865. National Heritage Museum, 81.17.

Building Freemasonry and American Community

In time, most of these requirements were eliminated, as the initiation of battle was deemed sufficient for member loyalty. Meeting in local "posts," veterans enjoyed the fellowship of army life without the danger and deprivation of war. In 1896, the GAR had 357,639 members, or an estimated one-half of the Union Army soldiers and sailors.[43] It moved away from simple fraternity toward greater political lobbying for health benefits for veterans and their families.[44]

Also in 1866, six ex-Confederate veterans founded the Knights of Ku Klux Klan in Pulaski, Tennessee. This local club was organized originally for fun and mischief but soon became a vigilante secret society. Its secrets and initiation rituals were derived from Freemasonry, but it also adopted elements of other southern fraternities.[45] The Klan spread sporadically across nine states, terrorizing freed blacks and white "carpetbaggers." These illegal and vicious attacks caused its first "Grand Wizard," former Confederate General Nathan Bedford Forrest (a Freemason), to order the disbandment of the organization in 1869, which curtailed the Order in many states.[46] The U.S. Congress passed new civil rights laws and created a commission to investigate the Klan activities and to arrest individual Klansmen, yet the group persisted unofficially for years. In the 1870s, Klan members played a significant role in controlling southern state governments and reestablishing white rule and segregation.[47]

While the GAR and the Klan grew, Prince Hall Freemasonry quickly spread throughout the North and South. Many African-American Masons

GAR FREEMASON

A Union veteran, identified as Theodore Tripp, is shown here in his uniform of the Grand Army of the Republic. He wears both the GAR five-pointed star pin and the jewel of a Past Master of a Masonic lodge.

Collin Cards, ca. 1880. National Heritage Museum, gift of Jacques Noel Jacobsen Jr., 98.077.2.

KU KLUX KLAN

Soon after the Civil War, men in the former Confederate states organized vigilante societies to terrorize the newly freed African-Americans. The most infamous of these groups was the KKK, which incorporated Masonic elements into the rituals.

"The Union as It Was," Thomas Nast, Harper's Weekly, *1874. Library of Congress, Prints and Photographs Division LC-USZ62-128619.*

answered the call to help establish community institutions for freed families. One such man was James W. Hood, who came to North Carolina in 1864. He was born in Philadelphia in 1831, the son of an African Union Church minister. He was probably made a Mason in Pennsylvania in 1855, a year before receiving a preaching license from Reverend William Councy, pastor of the New York African Union Church.[48]

After the Civil War, Hood was appointed assistant superintendent of public instruction in North Carolina under the Freeman's Bureau. Traveling throughout the state, he simultaneously consecrated churches, built schools and established Masonic lodges. Eventually he became the senior bishop of the North Carolina African Methodist Episcopal Zion Church and served as Grand Master of the state's Prince Hall Masons from 1870 to 1883. Between 1864 and 1873, he helped start 366 churches with more than 20,000 members and 18 Prince Hall lodges containing 478 members. As assistant superintendent of education, Bishop Hood helped as many as 49,000 black children attend school.[49]

Other Prince Hall Masons traveled throughout the reunited states organizing lodges so that by 1877, Prince Hall grand lodges existed in every former Confederate state and as far west as Colorado.[50] Individual Prince Hall Masons, such as Richard Gleaves, were elected to statewide executive offices in southern states. In the North, Prince Hall abolitionists John J. Smith and Louis Hayden were elected to the Massachusetts state legislature.[51]

Freemasonry's reconstruction and growth between 1835 and 1865 owed much to its common ancient lineage and moral truths, as it adapted to the needs of America's society. Men who would not have joined temperance, ethnic or religious improvement societies found a more inviting and convivial fraternity within a Masonic lodge. Conversely, Masons took their symbols and tenets out of the lodge to create new organizations that built America's broader communities. Other Americans used Freemasonry as the model for their distinctive organizations. Finding a respectable place in society beneath political and religious authority and between the family and work, the fraternity would continue to meet the needs of new Americans in the last decades of the 1800s to become the preeminent community voluntary association.

CHAPTER 5

Safely Lodged

Secret Rituals and Freemasonry, 1870–1900

"There is a strange and powerful attraction for some men in the mysticism of the ritual. There is a peculiar fascination in the unreality of the initiation, the allurement about fine 'team' work, a charm of the deep potency in the unrestricted, out-of-the-world atmosphere which surrounds the scenes where men are knit together by the closest ties, bound by the most solemn obligations to maintain secrecy as to the events which transpire within the walls."

— W.S. HARWOOD, 1897[1]

RESPONDING TO PRESIDENT LINCOLN'S call to "bind up the nation's wounds" after the devastation of the Civil War, Americans turned their energy toward reuniting the nation. In just 30 years, transportation and communications networks extended across the continent, huge industrial and manufacturing corporations employed millions of people and new inventions transformed everyday life. But as the United States grew in strength, it became increasingly divided along social, racial and economic lines. Eastern native-born Protestants resented the flood of mostly Roman Catholic and Jewish immigrants arriving from Europe. African-Americans were segregated by "Jim Crow" laws throughout the South. In the western territories, Indians fought a losing war against pioneers and the U.S. Army, while railroads swindled the profits and holdings of homesteaders and miners. In northern cities, wealthy industrialists exploited both native-born and immigrant workers in mills and factories. America's Gilded Age is the story of people searching for order and stability while participating in an era of growth and change.

During this period, many Americans turned toward the family and the Bible to reunite the nation and restore peace. Social harmony, it was believed, would come about when families trusted in God and committed

themselves to living a righteous life. Women assumed moral authority over the home and children, while men provided for the family and governed society. A woman who did not keep a clean house or properly care for her family lost respectability and was viewed socially as lacking in virtue. A man who failed to work or fell prey to vice lost public esteem and was viewed by others as lacking character.

Children in the Gilded Age were raised to assume these proper social roles. While girls learned to become future models and guardians of virtue, boys were trained to strengthen their personal character and seek public responsibilities. To keep them on the right paths, teenage boys and girls were restricted from each other's company and could meet only at events with adult supervision. Young women expanded their authority in education, religion and etiquette, while young men were directed toward achieving success. Upon reaching young adulthood, they formally courted and sought parental approval prior to marriage. Once in a safe home under the care of a godly wife, a good husband was properly prepared to achieve greater success and improve society.[2]

The Golden Age of Fraternity

"The plumb admonishes us to walk uprightly in our several stations before God and man, squaring our actions by the Square of virtue, ever remembering that we are travelling upon the Level of Time 'to that undiscovered country, from whose bourne no traveller returns.'"

— THOMAS SMITH WEBB, 1808 [3]

Faced with the often brutal societal transformations of the Gilded Age, Americans sought to extend the harmony of the home into the greater society. Community organizations and fraternal orders were the primary means to accomplish this goal. Some organizations, like the Women's Christian Temperance Union, sought to improve society through collective enactment and enforcement of laws and ordinances. Freemasonry and other fraternal orders sought to improve individuals by teaching moral truths through secret rituals and obligations. Of the two types of voluntary associations, fraternal organizations played the primary role during the Gilded Age. Between 1865 and 1900, more than 235 fraternal orders were founded (16 in 1896 alone) with as many as six million members. [4] Fraternal

Top Ten American Fraternal Organizations, 1896

Odd Fellows	810,000
Freemasons	750,000
Knights of Pythias	475,000
Ancient Order of United Workmen	361,000
Knights of the Maccabees	244,000
Modern Woodmen of America	204,000
Royal Arcanum	189,000
Junior Order United American Mechanics	187,000
Improved Order of Red Men	165,000
Knights of Honor	118,000
Total	3,503,000

Source: W.S. Harwood, "Secret Societies in America," North American Review, *1896.*

LODGE MASTER'S CHAIR

This chair, made for
Swan Lodge No. 358
in Ohio, is inscribed:
"Manufact'd by John
Luker" and "J. H. M.
Houston." Houston
was Master of the lodge
from 1867 to 1873.

*John Luker, Vinton
County, Ohio, 1870.
National Heritage
Museum, gift of the
estate of Charles V.
Hagler, 85.20.1.1.*

associations were so prevalent and important
that in 1897 W.S. Harwood called the period "the
golden age of fraternity."[5] The first in-depth
documentation of America's golden age of fraternities is found in Albert Stevens' 1897 edition
of *The Cyclopaedia of Fraternities.* Stevens
classified more than 600 American fraternal organizations into 12 types, ranging from mutual
assessment fraternities to social and revolutionary societies.

Writing some 100 years later, sociologist
Mary Ann Clawson reduced Stevens' catego-
ries to two distinct types. The first type was
based upon personal character or beliefs and
organized on a national level. The second type
was based upon a skill or class and organized on
a local level in the workplace. The first sought
to build a broad peaceful society through benevolence and common morality. The second sought
order and solidarity within a specific skilled profession or class.[6]

Both fraternal types, however, were united
in their use of dramatic ritual initiations to
achieve their goals. According to Stevens' estimate, American fraternal orders during the
golden age "conferred about 1,000 [different]
degrees on 200,000 'novitiates' annually, aided, in instances, by a wealth
of paraphernalia and dramatic ceremonials which rival modern stage effects."[7] Stevens, recognizing Freemasonry as the oldest and most prestigious, stated: "The Masonic fraternity is directly or indirectly the parent
organization of all modern secret societies, good, bad or indifferent."[8]

The secret rituals of Freemasonry and its imitators imparted moral
lessons and virtues considered necessary for a younger man to gain respectability and success. The fraternal lodge became a safe harbor between a
mother's care and a wife's attention. Freemasonry's simple mission to
"make good men better" became a persistent means of bringing order to
an increasingly dynamic and ever-shifting society.[9] Men who would otherwise have remained divided by class, race, creed and geography became
brothers within a fraternal family. Thus Freemasonry allowed new generations of Americans to broaden the harmony and order of the home into
the public sphere of community life.

Building Freemasonry and American Community

The Masonic Phenomenon of Dramatic Ritual

"The attentive ear receives the sound from the instructive tongue, and its [Masonry's] sacred mysteries are safely lodged in the repository of faithful breasts."

— WILLIAM PRESTON, 1772 [10]

After the Civil War, Freemasonry entered a new period of prosperity and prestige. The tenets of brotherly love, relief and truth — an integral part of colonial and early American society — were reinterpreted to conform more closely to Protestant morality and to meet the challenges of the Gilded Age. Younger generations of Masons expanded the ritual, charity and social activities as they built lodges in every corner of the nation and joined the additional Masonic bodies of the York and Scottish Rites. From 446,000 members in 1870, Freemasonry nearly doubled its membership in 30 years. By 1900, at least five percent of the American-born, adult male population belonged to the Masonic fraternity.[11] After the church and school, the Masonic lodge was often the most important institution established in a new town. Those lodges provided the stability and legitimacy for towns that were hoping to attract a railroad and other industries and to be awarded the county seat, a land grant college, or other government benefits. As towns grew into cities, Masonic lodges also grew and often divided into smaller lodges to retain the intimacy among the brethren. New city neighborhoods and suburbs often included lodge halls for closer proximity to meetings and family functions.

During this period, the fraternity attracted such diverse men as Republican President James Garfield, three-time Democratic presidential nominee William Jennings Bryan, labor organizer Samuel Gompers, industrialist George Pullman and showman Buffalo Bill Cody. Laura Ingalls Wilder joined the Order of the Eastern Star.[12]

The beauty and complexity of the rituals were the foundation upon which Masons built their impressive membership. Yet dramatic methods that taught allegorical lessons were not unique. Prior to the Civil War, moral crusade organizations had used drama to persuade people to live a good life. The popular stage performances of *Uncle Tom's Cabin, Ten Nights in a Bar Room* and other plays in the 1850s had a proven effect for the crusades of the abolitionist and temperance leaders. Even Evangelical Protestant camp meetings of the Second Great Awakening in the 1830s and 1840s contained dramatic and theatrical elements.[13]

The phenomenon of American ritual-based fraternities came also from their pure entertainment appeal and the pleasure of mystery. Nineteenth-

MASONIC LODGE ROOM

As representations of King Solomon's Temple, Masonic halls are supposed to be situated due east and west. Regardless of its true orientation, the location where the Master presides is always called the "East" (top), while the Senior Warden sits in the "West" (middle), and the Junior Warden in the "South" (bottom). No officers sit in the "North," for it is symbolically termed a place of darkness. In this lodge room, however, the North is a place of warmth from the stove.

Bristol, RI, ca. 1885. National Heritage Museum, 85.5.2,3,4.

century Americans loved biblical reenactments, minstrel shows and Shakespearean plays. People worked long hours at physical labor and relished the chance to escape into a make-believe world. They enjoyed the opportunity to don elaborate costumes, assume exotic titles and perform solemn and esoteric initiations.

Proper governance and ritual performance within a fraternal lodge required dedicated leadership. Elected officers were responsible for conducting a well-run meeting, satisfying the needs of the members and attending to correspondence and finances. They rehearsed the rituals frequently and worked in pairs to teach each other. Most rituals were printed in "secret" code, or cipher, that required long study and memorization, but the rituals were not to be simply recited from rote memory. The participants were urged to perform initiations with a profound drama that would convey the fraternity's serious purposes.

A man seeks membership in Freemasonry through a friend who is a Mason. The applicant's background is investigated before the members of the lodge vote to accept or reject him by using a white or black ball in a secret ballot. During the Gilded Age, Freemasons regularly rejected an average of 20–30 percent of the applicants per year, most often at the investigation stage.[14] While widespread prejudice offered explanation for some rejections, an applicant's drinking habits, use of profanity or social reputation was often enough to convince a lodge that it did not feel comfortable having the prospective member join the ranks as a "brother."[15]

If accepted, the candidate usually receives the three degrees over the course of three lodge meetings. In the first degree, the candidate enters the lodge room without his personal possessions and wears a special ceremonial garb. In this way, he is not judged by his outward appearance. He is also blindfolded, or "hoodwinked," and told to trust a brother to conduct him safely through the ceremonies. After he accepts the oath or obligation to abide by the rules and maintain the ancient secrets of the fraternity, the blindfold is removed, and he is instructed in the symbolism, tenets, and virtues of the craft. The second degree follows a pattern similar to the first but focuses on intellectual improvement.

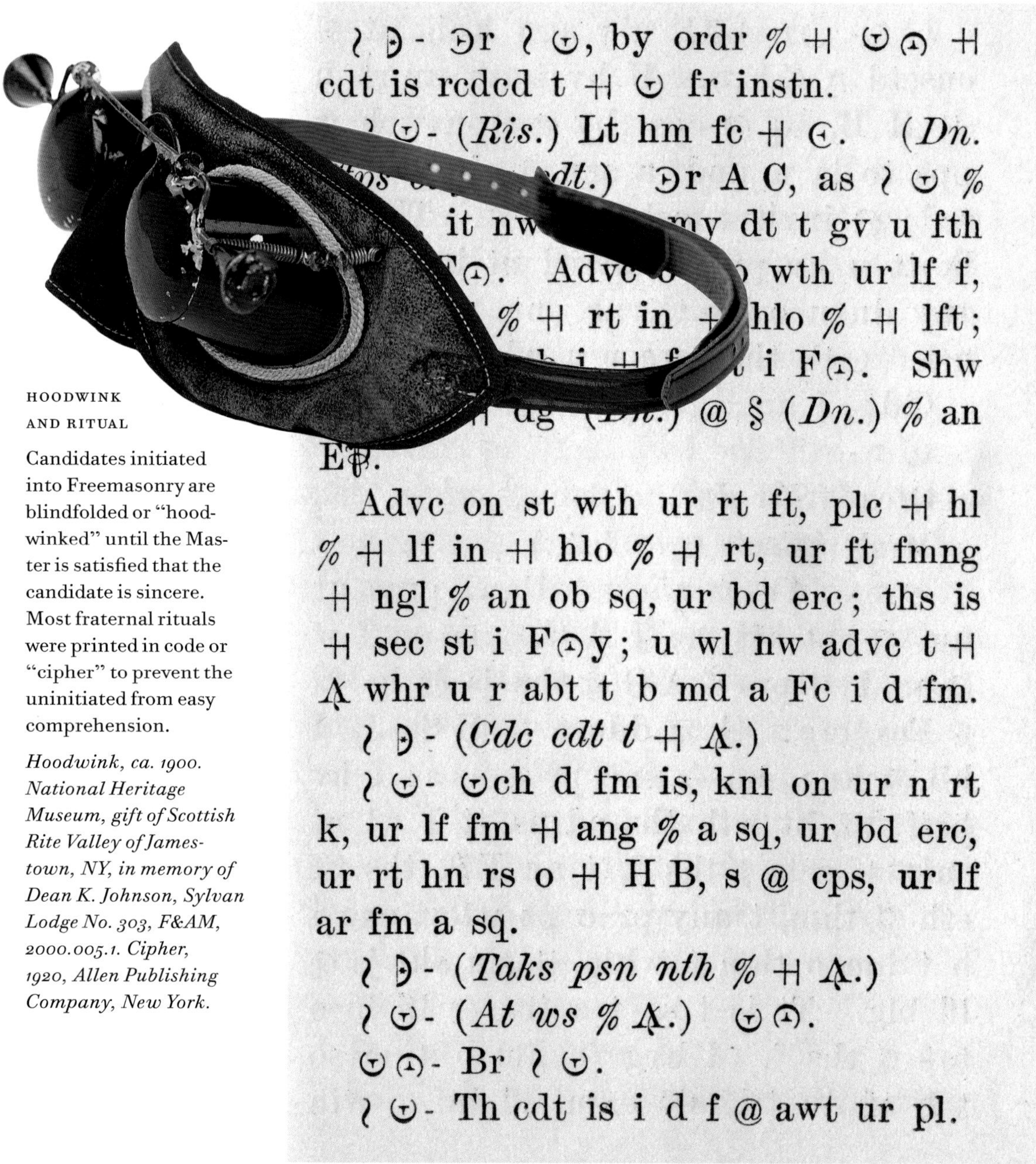

〉 Ͽ - Ͽr 〉 ☉, by ordr ％ ╫ ☉ ⊙ ╫ cdt is rcdcd t ╫ ☉ fr instn.

〉 ☉ - (*Ris.*) Lt hm fc ╫ Ͼ. (*Dn.* ~~...~~ dt.) Ͽr A C, as 〉 ☉ ％ it nw ~~...~~ my dt t gv u fth ~~...~~ ⊙. Advc ~~...~~ o wth ur lf f, ~~...~~ ％ ╫ rt in ＋ hlo ％ ╫ lft; ~~...~~ i F⊙. Shw ~~...~~ dg (*Dn.*) @ § (*Dn.*) ％ an E℞.

Advc on st wth ur rt ft, plc ╫ hl ％ ╫ lf in ╫ hlo ％ ╫ rt, ur ft fmng ╫ ngl ％ an ob sq, ur bd erc; ths is ╫ sec st i F⊙y; u wl nw advc t ╫ ⅄ whr u r abt t b md a Fc i d fm.

〉 Ͽ - (*Cdc cdt t* ╫ ⅄.)

〉 ☉ - ☉ch d fm is, knl on ur n rt k, ur lf fm ╫ ang ％ a sq, ur bd erc, ur rt hn rs o ╫ H B, s @ cps, ur lf ar fm a sq.

〉 Ͽ - (*Taks psn nth ％* ╫ ⅄.)

〉 ☉ - (*At ws ％ ⅄.*) ☉ ⊙.

☉ ⊙ - Br 〉 ☉.

〉 ☉ - Th cdt is i d f @ awt ur pl.

HOODWINK AND RITUAL

Candidates initiated into Freemasonry are blindfolded or "hood-winked" until the Master is satisfied that the candidate is sincere. Most fraternal rituals were printed in code or "cipher" to prevent the uninitiated from easy comprehension.

Hoodwink, ca. 1900. National Heritage Museum, gift of Scottish Rite Valley of James-town, NY, in memory of Dean K. Johnson, Sylvan Lodge No. 303, F&AM, 2000.005.1. Cipher, 1920, Allen Publishing Company, New York.

The initiation cycle culminates in the third degree, or sublime degree of Master Mason. Once again, the candidate agrees to accept the obligations of the degree, after which the Hiramic legend unfolds in a dramatic presentation. The candidate assumes the role of King Solomon's master builder, Hiram Abiff, who is coerced to reveal the secrets of Freemasonry. Refusing to break his sacred trust, he suffers a symbolic death at the hands of his attackers. At the completion of the ritualistic drama, the candidate is raised by the right hand of the lodge Master to become a Master Mason.[16]

Freemasonry refers to its three degree rituals as "the work of the lodge." Performing the work properly is a craft and is another reason why the Masonic fraternity is called "the craft." Freemasonry is therefore an art and science for improving individual men. It differs from all other fraternities of the golden age, because the rituals evolved slowly. They originated in Scottish stonemasons' guilds in the 1600s, were practiced through successive generations and were perfected through such men as William Preston and Thomas Smith Webb. Masons have considered the language of the rituals to rival the beauty of Shakespearean verse, its historical scope reminiscent of the work of Edward Gibbon, and its allegory equal to the tales of John Bunyon.[17] The great Shakespearean actor and Mason Edwin Booth (1833-93) reportedly once said of the Masonic rituals:

> In all my research and study, in all my close analysis of the masterpieces of Shakespeare, . . . in my earnest determination to make those plays appear real on the mimic stage, I have never, and nowhere, met the tragedy so real, so sublime, so magnificent as the legend of Hiram. It is substance without shadow — the manifest destiny of life which requires no picture and scarcely a word to make a lasting impression upon all who can understand.[18]

The York Rite

"If called upon to draw a sword, I will wield my sword in defense of innocent maidens, destitute widows, helpless orphans and the Christian religion."

— MASONIC KNIGHTS TEMPLAR

In addition to his lodge, the Master Mason also has other opportunities for participation. He can affiliate with other lodges, join his wife in the Order of the Eastern Star, or receive additional Masonic degrees in the Scottish and York Rites. The York Rite reached its zenith during the Gilded Age, while the Scottish Rite's full majesty would not come until the 1920s. The three separate bodies within the York Rite — Royal Arch chapters, Royal and Select councils and Knights Templar commanderies — are progressive. To become a Knight Templar, a Mason usually must first receive the degrees of the Royal Arch and Royal and Select Masters.

African-American Masons quickly followed the lead of their predomi-
nately white brethren and created Prince Hall Masonic Scottish and York
Rites in the 1800s. Although no official recognition existed between the
segregated branches, much of Prince Hall growth came from white Masons
either initiating blacks into the "higher" degrees or sharing the secret rituals.[19] By 1897, 25 percent of Masons (or approximately 194,000 men) belonged to the York Rite, and about 3,000 Prince Hall Masons were Knights
Templar.[20]

The popularity of the York Rite reflected American community life of
the age. Each body met in regional locations and conferred the degrees
individually. Royal Arch chapters usually drew membership from several
local lodges, and most of those members continued into the councils and
commanderies. Because the York Rite was conveniently located, a member
was able to expand his network of friends and brothers simply by traveling
to a Masonic hall in the area.

The York Rite's Knights Templar became especially important between 1870 and 1920. Despite the romantic notions of some historians to link this group to the medieval Knights Templar, there is strong evidence that Irishmen in the mid-1700s created the Masonic Knights Templar rituals.[21] These rituals spread to Boston, Philadelphia and North Carolina by the 1780s. Nearly destroyed during the anti-Masonic period, the Templars rapidly recovered after the Civil War. The Order's regeneration was due in part to the American love for military order, martial music and parades. A huge war surplus of uniforms and swords added to the appeal. In 1800, there were an estimated 500 Knights Templar in the United States. By 1898, there were 998 commanderies and 114,540 Knights, or about one out of every seven Masons.[22]

Templary differs from other parts of Freemasonry in several ways. First and foremost, it is specifically Christian in its rituals and purpose. All other Masonic organizations are open to men of all faiths that profess a belief in a Supreme Being, yet a Knight Templar pledges to defend the Christian religion. The three rituals (called orders) conferred by the Knights also differ from the rest of Freemasonry. They are based on neither biblical passages nor stonemasonry but are derived from the tales and history of the Crusades. The degrees in the craft, the Royal Arch and the Royal and Select Masters take their imagery from the building of the first and second Jerusalem Temples, while the Knights Templar emphasize the sacrifices made by the crusaders to protect Christian pilgrims to the Holy Land. Borrowing a term from the monastic orders, the Masonic Knights call their

KNIGHTS TEMPLAR

The Masonic Knights Templar are organized into local commanderies, and the meeting halls are called "asylums." Members of Columbian Commandery No. 1, New York City, are shown here in their asylum (originally the Rutgers Presbyterian Church) on 29th Street and Madison Avenue.

ca. 1895. National Heritage Museum, 2001.083.2.

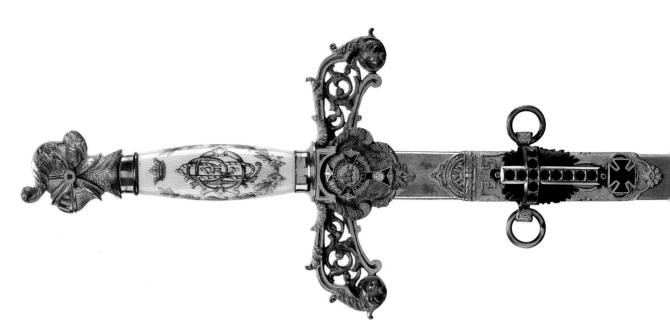

meeting halls "asylums." The medieval Knights Templar, however, were more than initiating monks. They were Christian warriors and a paramilitary organization.[23]

The three senior officers of a modern commandery of Knights Templar are the Eminent Commander, Generalissimo, and Captain General. At the meetings, the Knights practice complex drills and ceremonies with swords. Supervising the local commanderies are the statewide grand commanderies as well as the national Grand Encampment led by the Most Eminent Grand Master. Local commanderies often made "pilgrimages" to other cities to march in parades, compete in drill competitions or hold conventions that they termed "conclaves." The cost for dues, uniforms and pilgrimages kept less affluent Masons out, while its Christian requirement effectively barred observant Jewish Masons from entering the "asylums." After the Civil War, the Knights Templar became the place for Protestant Masons to exercise their faith by marching to the hymn "Onward Christian Soldiers" and by publicly challenging any anti-Masons who accused Freemasonry of being pagan, irreligious or worse.[24]

The growth of Freemasonry — especially the York Rite — after the Civil War allowed Masons to perform new and different rituals, strengthen their morals and spirituality, assume exotic and mysterious personae and titles, and expand their network of friends and social engagements. The cost of belonging to so many Masonic bodies tended to separate upper-class and more established men from younger and poorer men, who could afford the money and time to join only a Masonic lodge.

One Mason, Henry L. Palmer (1819–1909), typified the attraction and importance of Freemasonry as a community institution during the Gilded Age. Born in Mount Pleasant, Pennsylvania, and made a Mason in Albany,

New York, Palmer later moved to Wisconsin and became the president of Northwestern Mutual Life Insurance Company. Palmer was elected to the Wisconsin State Assembly and was Speaker of the House in 1853. Later he served as a state senator and a Milwaukee County judge. In his Masonic career, he was the first Master of Tracy Lodge (now Wisconsin No. 13) in Milwaukee and served for six terms; he then became Grand Master of Masons in Wisconsin (1852-53, 1871-72). In the Wisconsin York Rite, he was elected to head the state's Royal Arch Masons (1858-59), Royal and Select Masters (1863-64) and Knights Templar (1859-65). On the national level, he served as the Grand Master of the Grand Encampment of Knights Templar (1865-68). He concluded his Masonic career by being elected Sovereign Grand Commander for the Scottish Rite's Northern Masonic Jurisdiction and served for nearly 30 years (1879-1909) until a few days before his death.[25]

Palmer's personal industry and participation in Masonic activities exemplified the energy of his generation and the central role Freemasonry played in his life. He achieved great financial success and political power, served on numerous church and civic committees and rose to the highest social circles in Wisconsin. Equally devoted to the craft, he ambitiously pursued his Masonic career. At his funeral, Palmer was eulogized as a good husband and father, a devout Christian, an honest businessman, an honorable politician and a dedicated Mason. His devotion to Freemasonry was demonstrated when his body was laid to rest in Milwaukee's Forest Home Cemetery with the assistance of his Masonic brothers and Knights Templar companions.[26]

HENRY LYNDE PALMER

Successful businessman and speaker of the Wisconsin House of Representatives, Palmer also served as head of every Masonic organization in Wisconsin. He was also the only Mason to become both a national Grand Master of Knights Templar and a Sovereign Grand Commander of the Scottish Rite.

From A Portrait Gallery with Biographical Sketches of Prominent Freemasons Throughout the United States, *1892, engraved by W.T. Bather, published by John C. Yorston & Co., Brooklyn, NY. National Heritage Museum.*

Brothers All

"Stranger, we are no longer in the busy world. We have left its turmoils, strife, and selfishness. We are now in the primeval forest, amidst God's first temples. . . . Here humanity has scope and breathing-place. Here the uncrowded individual grows in strength and grandeur as the oak. Among the Neighbors of this forest you will find true brotherly love."

— MODERN WOODMEN OF AMERICA, 1904[27]

Freemasonry's popularity attracted a wide diversity of men into its lodges. Many of those men went on to create new and distinctive organizations. Published Masonic rituals were so prevalent that many other non-Masonic fraternal organizations purposely or unknowingly plagiarized them. Just

These Knights of Rocky
Hill Lodge in Portland,
Maine, are dressed in
full initiation regalia.
Shown here are the king,
guards, and wise men
prepared to conduct
a candidate through the
degrees of Page, Squire
and Knight.

*Allen L. Hubbard,
Portland, ME, ca. 1910.
National Heritage
Museum, 80.45.*

as James Fenimore Cooper's books became the model for American West-
erns, so did Masonic rituals become the source for new fraternities in America's ever-changing communities.

One such Mason was Justus Rathbone, who founded the Knights of
Pythias in 1864. He wanted to "rekindle the brotherly sentiment which
had been all but stamped out by the merciless heel of human passion."[28]
A federal government clerk during the Civil War, Rathbone based the
Knights' dramatic rituals on legends and John Banim's popular play *Damon and Pythias.*[29] The fraternity was promoted as a means to help reunite the country after the war. Organized into local units, called castles,
the Knights performed three initiation rituals that taught the tenets of
friendship, charity and benevolence. The Order grew slowly at first and
suffered from early disorganization, but by 1887 it surpassed 100,000
members, and ten years later it had more than 475,000 Knights.[30]

African-Americans were also drawn to the Order and were unofficially
initiated by white men. However, they were denied equal status and not
allowed to charter their own castles, so in 1869, they created their own
organization, called the Knights of Pythias of North and South America,
Europe, Asia and Africa. Under the leadership of Supreme Chancellor
James C. Ross, a Georgia school principal, the African-American Knights
had more than 40,000 members by 1900.[31]

Observing the Pythians' medieval chivalric pageantry was Joseph
Cullen Root, a Mason and a Knight of Pythias.[32] Inspired by a sermon
about "the woodmen clearing away the forest, from whose felling of trees
came so much of use to man," Root created a uniquely American organization, the Modern Woodmen of America, in 1882.[33] Within 15 years, the

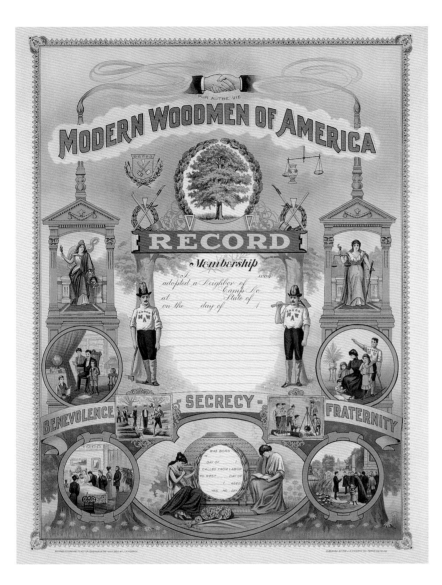

WOODMEN MEMBERSHIP
CERTIFICATE

The symbols, emblems
and emblems and motto of the Modern
Woodmen of America
appear on this certifi-
cate. A brother could
fill out his membership
record and frame the
lithograph for his home.

*J. M. Vickroy, Terre
Haute, IN, 1902.
National Heritage
Museum, gift of John
Reps, A97/016/0019.*

MWA counted more than 210,000 "neighbors" in 4,180 local "camps."[34]
Like Freemasonry, it had a series of three initiation rituals and used tools
— such as the axe, wedge and beetle — as symbols of virtues. Along with
the initiation rituals, secret handshakes and passwords, the MWA incorporated an insurance plan and policy that aided its members and spurred
its growth.[35]

The popularity of fraternities with dramatic rituals based on myths or
folklore caused religious denominations to become concerned. In particular, the Roman Catholic church hierarchy in America felt threatened
by such anti-Catholic organizations as the Order of United American Me-

In 1899, the Knights of Columbus added a fourth degree for members who had served the order, Church or community with distinction. Members of the degree provided honor guards for religious and civic ceremonies and parades. Shown here is the first team of fourth degree knights that taught or "exemplified" the degree to other knights.

First Fourth Degree Exemplification Team, ca. 1899. Knights of Columbus Supreme Council photograph archives.

chanics and worried that parishioners would be led astray by such "secret societies" as Freemasonry, the Odd Fellows and others.[36]

To counter Catholic membership in non-sectarian Orders, Rev. Michael J. McGivney of St. Mary's Church in New Haven, Connecticut, created the Knights of Columbus in 1882. Unlike other Catholic fraternal orders of the time, this organization was not based on European history or ethnicity but on broad American assimilation.[37] Under the leadership of Father McGivney, the organization venerated Christopher Columbus and achieved three important distinctions. It placed the fraternity within the church structure and mission. It proclaimed a legitimate Catholic presence in America long before the Protestant arrivals at Jamestown and Plymouth. It united American Catholic men of many ethnic affiliations under its banner. The initiation rituals were adapted from Freemasonry's three-degree system, all under the supervision of a parish priest. Within 25 years, the Knights of Columbus grew across the country to nearly 230,000 members and 1,300 local councils.[38]

As America's golden age of fraternities flourished, competition arose among the hundreds of new voluntary associations. Fraternal leaders realized that their rituals were important products and their organization's growth would be tied to presenting new and exciting ceremonies. Soon most fraternal organizations established committees to review the rituals, and some, like the Improved Order of Red Men, offered competition and cash prizes to their members, encouraging them to improve old rituals or write new ones.[39] Since Freemasonry was bound by a mythical past, built by revered Americans and divided by so many state grand lodges, the rituals were considered by most Masons to be untouchable. Instead, Masons boasted that their work was not contrived, but pure. It was not written by one individual, nor was it edited by a committee or "test-marketed" before being conveyed. Freemasons' pride proved to be double-edged. While many men became Masons because of the fraternity's ancient prestige and affluent reputation, others rejected it, because it was considered elitist and refused to evolve with the modern world.[40] Throughout the Gilded Age and into the 20th century, leaders of other voluntary organizations diversified their "products," changed their mission, and even dropped the rituals altogether. Freemasonry, however, remained basically the same but welcomed new organizations that required affiliation with the fraternity.

RED MEN BALLOT BOX

Rather than voting with white and black balls, the Improved Order of Red Men used white and black "twigs." Each member cast a secret ballot in "twig boxes" such as this one. One black twig was sufficient to prevent a man from joining a local tribe.

ca. 1880. National Heritage Museum, Supreme Council collection, 74.1.59.

Fathers and Sons

"In Youth, as Entered Apprentices, we ought industriously to occupy our minds in the attainment of useful Knowledge; in Manhood, as Fellow Crafts, we should apply that knowledge to the discharge of our respective duties to God, our neighbors and ourselves; so that in age, as Master Masons, we may enjoy the happy reflection consequent on a well-spent life, and die in the hope of a glorious immortality."

— THOMAS SMITH WEBB, 1808[41]

The rituals of American fraternities were designed to unite strangers through a shared experience. They were based on biblical stories or old myths and emphasized man's dependence on his brothers and a patriarchal God to save him from ruin. They also reinforced accepted truths and the bonds of generational continuity. Through the process of initiation, a man became a member of a universal brotherhood, while he was encouraged to strengthen his character and develop strong moral convictions.[42]

The need for this additional spirituality came in response to the growing cruelty of industrialization and the emergence of a liberal Protestant theology.[43] There was also a growing awareness after the Civil War that fathers and sons were becoming disconnected. As men moved away from small shops and farms and into factories and offices, boys were being raised more often by their mothers and increasingly educated by women in both the public and Sunday schools. Fathers less frequently taught their sons a

trade and inadequately prepared them for manhood. The fraternal lodge, however, became a vital means for fathers and sons to bond. In the lodge and through Freemasonry's rituals, a young man literally learned "the craft of living" from his father's lodge and was "raised" into adulthood by community, business and religious leaders who were brothers of the lodge.[44]

As the Gilded Age progressed, Americans used fraternal lodge networks to extend the order of their private lives to cope with an increasingly chaotic society. The nation's population burgeoned from 35 million to more than 83 million between 1870 and 1905. Fifteen years later, the majority of Americans found themselves no longer living in a rural setting but in the city. The vast industrial complexes destroyed the dignity of the craftsman, while powerful corporations crushed the ideal of the self-made independent man. The national economic depression of 1873 followed by the 1877 railroad strikes and riots caused Americans to lose confidence in their business and government leaders. To survive in this new age, it seemed that men had to either organize for mutual protection or sacrifice their souls to gain personal success. In search of moral answers to these problems, Americans continued to rely on the strength of national fraternal orders and found solace in the brotherly love and truths taught in dramatic rituals. Freemasons — charged to practice "relief" — would begin a quest to reconcile the virtue of charity with the spoils of free enterprise.

CHAPTER 6

Relieve the Distressed

Mutual Benefit in the Industrial Age, 1870–1900

*"The habit of forming associations becomes possible to understand
practically all the important economic and social developments merely
by examining the activities of voluntary organizations. . . . Associations
are created, extended and worked in the United States more quickly
and effectively than in any other country."*

— JAMES BRYCE, 1888[1]

THE UNION VICTORY in the Civil War ignited the industrial age, and Americans began systematically exploiting the continent's vast natural resources. After the 1862 Homestead Act, farmers and ranchers filed more than 600,000 claims for 80 million acres to feed the nation. Miners and lumberjacks harvested raw materials, more than 12 million immigrants supplied labor, and great cities were built to meet the demands of insatiable factories and mills. Industrialists and capitalists controlled industry. Andrew Carnegie made steel, George Pullman built railroad cars, Phillip Armour processed and sold meat, and John D. Rockefeller refined oil. On Wall Street, J.P. Morgan dominated them all.

The control of the nation's economy by a few privately held industries radically changed America's traditional means of working and living. On the farm, homesteaders found their crop prices manipulated by commodity brokers and their profits lost to inflation and transportation fees. In the cities, the small unionized labor force feared mass production and fought to keep unskilled workers and mechanization out of the factories. The dangers and inequities of industrial life provoked Americans to stage 37,000 strikes involving more than seven million workers between 1881 and 1905. Many Americans found themselves frequently unemployed or working longer hours for less pay.[2]

During this period, the United States government upheld property

THE NEW MEMBER OF MONOPOLY LODGE HAS TAKEN THE "FIRST DEGREE."

GROVER CLEVELAND
ENTERS "MONOPOLY
LODGE"

This cartoon portrays
newly elected President
Grover Cleveland being
initiated among the rail-
road "robber barons."
At the left is Jay Gould
in a knight's uniform.
In the center are C.W.
Field and Russell Sage
(box hat). Seated in
"The Grand East" is
W.H. Vanderbilt.

*New Member of
Monopoly Lodge Has
Taken the First Degree,*
Puck Magazine,
*drawn by F. Opper,
lithographed by Mayer
Merkel & Ottmann
New York, 1882–1884.
National Heritage
Museum, 89.22.*

rights and practiced laissez-faire economics. From the federal level to the
local neighborhoods, wealthy men and city bosses maintained political
power. Politicians preferred to enrich themselves rather than arbitrate between labor and management. Federal and state governments turned their
attention to creating police departments, reorganizing the National Guard,
and legalizing private security forces. At the same time, city bosses, alder-
men and ward captains developed spoils systems of patronage and graft.[3]

In this turbulent and often brutal age, the average American struggled
to uphold the dignity of labor while remaining self-reliant. To earn a wage,
many workers were enslaved to relentless machines, fluctuating markets
and corrupt politicians. Even as the Gilded Age society exerted constant
pressure on families to live a strict moral life, abhor the receipt of charity
and reject radical labor ideologies, millions of Americans looked for fair
and respectable solutions to their dilemma by forming grass-roots political
parties to reform government and regulate industry. Others sought to expand the roles of labor unions by bargaining for better hours, conditions
and wages. Many others joined new ritual-based fraternal organizations
to acquire health and life insurance benefits and partake of social activities.
Through such fraternal associations, many Americans hoped to extend
family charity and harmony and help ease the friction between labor and
capital. These new mutual benefit fraternities were based upon a Masonic
foundation and often were established by individual Freemasons employing
their tenet of relief.

Masonic Charity

"To relieve the distressed is a duty incumbent on all men, but particularly on Masons, who are linked together by an indissoluble chain of sincere affection."

— WILLIAM PRESTON, 1775[4]

American industrialization challenged Freemasonry's traditional charity. From early Scottish lodges of the 1600s through development of grand lodges in the 1700s, Freemasonry always provided assistance to its brothers in need. This was based on its heritage from stonemasons' guilds, its tenet of relief and the obligation of its members "to help, aid and assist all poor and distressed brother Masons, their widows and orphans."[5] Charity helped distinguish the first Masonic lodges from other intellectual and social societies while giving them a collective purpose.[6]

Masonic charity in America during the 18th and 19th centuries focused on the needs of its members and their families. The first record of Masonic relief in America appeared in the bylaws of Boston's St. John's Lodge. The 1733 record states: "Every Member shall pay at Least two shillings pr. Qrd. [per quarter] to be applied as Charity Towards the Relief of poor Brethren."[7] The Grand Lodge of Pennsylvania created a fund financed through annual assessments of 65 cents per member and distributed more than $6,000 in

MASONIC FUNERAL, TAUNTON, MASSACHUSETTS

At the funeral procession for Alden Hathaway Blake, his brother Masons are shown wearing their aprons, and the casket and horses are decorated with Masonic emblems. Blake was a carpenter, a Civil War veteran and a member of King David's Lodge in Taunton. When approved by the family, burial services are conducted by the officers of a departed brother's lodge.

1916. National Heritage Museum, 83.18.

Building Freemasonry and American Community

relief between 1789 and 1800. This was higher than the median annual spending of other private charities in Philadelphia.[8]

At a time of economic instability, disasters and high mortality, Masonic charity provided important assistance. Some lodges appointed a member, often called an almoner, to look after sick and indigent brothers. Freemasonry's secrecy played a necessary part in this process. A man too proud to seek help from his church or kin could quietly accept it from his lodge. Private Masonic aid allowed many needy members to maintain self-respect and provided care for widows and orphans. Indeed, this may be Freemasonry's greatest secret, for no one knows how many people may have been helped by a coin, a paid bill or a load of firewood given anonymously in the name of brotherly love. Freemasons call these acts of kindness part of the "mystic tie" that binds them together as brothers.

Masonic Temple, Post & Montgomery Sts., after the fire of April 18th 1906. San Francisco, Cal.

SAN FRANCISCO
MASONIC TEMPLE

After the San Francisco earthquake and fire in 1906, Masons around the country sent money for relief.

Richard Behrendt, San Francisco, CA, 1906. National Heritage Museum, A96/066/4342.

Numerous Masonic magazines and newspapers of the 1800s often recounted stories of the "mystic tie." One such apocryphal tale appeared in the three-volume compendium, *Gems from the Quarry,* published in 1893. According to its author, George Moulton of Illinois, a California Mason and his family moved to Mississippi and tragically died from yellow fever. Only the youngest boy survived. The Masons took it upon themselves to send the boy back to his California relatives. Lacking the funds for a full fare, they placed him on a westbound train with a note pinned to the young boy's coat that read:

> This is a Master Mason's child; his father and mother are both dead, and he has no relatives to assist him. He is endeavoring to make his way to his father's lodge in the state of California and is commended to the care and attention of all Master Masons throughout the world.

As the train rolled along, various traveling Masons read the note, bought the boy meals and cared for him. The last of a series of unknown Masons delivered the boy safely to the care of the father's California brothers.[9]

Although Masonic relief developed within local lodges and among brothers, grand lodges were slower to create institutions to help solve long-

In the 1800s, Free-
masons in many Ameri-
can cities established
boards of relief to help
destitute and distressed
Freemasons and their
families. By pooling the
resources of many local
lodges, the boards
helped larger numbers
of needy people. This
ledger book records
the help given by the
Albany board of relief
to many people, both
Freemasons and those
related to Freemasons,
living and traveling
through Albany, New
York, in 1873.

*ca. 1873. National
Heritage Museum, MA,
004 1992/005.*

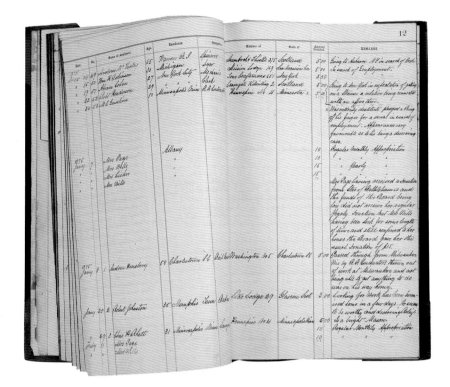

term and more complex needs. After the Civil War, they organized state
charitable institutions and national relief funds. In 1866, the Grand Lodge
of Kentucky opened America's first Masonic home in Louisville. By 1893,
eleven grand lodges had built similar facilities. Grand lodges also responded
to the needs of Masons outside their jurisdiction by sending money to help
destitute Masons affected by the Great Chicago Fire of 1871, the Johnstown
flood of 1889, the Galveston hurricane of 1900 and many other disasters.[10]

Urban lodges established charity boards of relief to cope with the
greater demands of a transitory population. Pooling the funds of several
lodges, boards convened during business hours and interviewed those in
need. An applicant first had to prove that he was a regular Mason through
secret words and grips. A deserving brother then received either cash to
continue on his journey or Masonic references to find work. The board
also distributed monthly allotments to local widows and orphans. Freemasonry's first truly national organization was born out of this loose network of relief boards. The General Masonic Relief Association of the United
States and Canada was established in 1885. The main function was to issue warning notices of traveling imposters. The association distributed
lists of scoundrels or unworthy brothers who had let their membership
lapse or had fallen below Freemasonry's proper moral code of conduct.[11]

Building Freemasonry and American Community

Freemasonry's relief was never guaranteed to its members, nor was it open to all citizens. Several institutional traditions and historical factors retarded Freemasonry's ability to expand its benevolent activities. The primary function of the lodges was to confer the three degrees and instruct members in the craft's tenets and virtues. As a self-improvement organization, Freemasonry encouraged men to live better, but it did not promise a happier or safer life by joining. It was felt that allowing a brother to claim charity by right would undermine the fraternity's purposes and disrupt the work and harmony of the private lodge.

Freemasonry's jurisprudence also restricted its charity. Both Anderson's 1723 *Constitutions* and Dermott's 1756 *Ahiman Rezon* had established the craft's "unalterable" rules or so-called "landmarks." They were based on medieval stonemasons' charges and articulated the Enlightenment philosophy of rational thought and dispassionate action. Created and codified before the Civil War and bound by honor and obligations, Freemasonry had no mechanism to address the real and often desperate needs of the industrial age.[12]

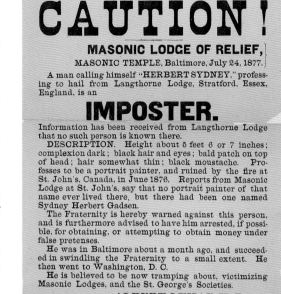

CAUTION!

MASONIC LODGE OF RELIEF,

MASONIC TEMPLE, Baltimore, July 24, 1877.

A man calling himself "HERBERT SYDNEY," professing to hail from Langthorne Lodge, Stratford, Essex, England, is an

IMPOSTER.

Information has been received from Langthorne Lodge that no such person is known there.

DESCRIPTION. Height about 5 feet 6 or 7 inches; complexion dark; black hair and eyes; bald patch on top of head; hair somewhat thin; black moustache. Professes to be a portrait painter, and ruined by the fire at St. John's, Canada, in June 1876. Reports from Masonic Lodge at St. John's, say that no portrait painter of that name ever lived there, but there had been one named Sydney Herbert Gadsen.

The Fraternity is hereby warned against this person, and is furthermore advised to have him arrested, if possible, for obtaining, or attempting to obtain money under false pretenses.

He was in Baltimore about a month ago, and succeeded in swindling the Fraternity to a small extent. He then went to Washington, D. C.

He is believed to be now tramping about, victimizing Masonic Lodges, and the St. George's Societies.

ALBERT LYMAN, M. D.,
Secretary.

Please post the above in every Lodge in your jurisdiction.

D. K. Osbourne & Co. Masonic Printers and Stationers, Baltimore, U. S.

MASONIC IMPOSTER

Local Masonic boards of relief often sent out posters to other cities warning of men posing as needy Masons, or women as worthy widows, trying to take advantage of the fraternity's charity. The poster warns of a man claiming to be "Herbert Sydney," supposedly an English Mason left destitute by a fire in Nova Scotia.

D. K. Osbourne & Co., Baltimore, MD, 1877. National Heritage Museum, A2002/118/1.

The fraternity's iconography of the late 1800s reinforced its conservatism. Many popular Masonic lithographs of the day perpetuated the traditional portrayal of George Washington as Master of a lodge. According to Masonic ritual, lodge Masters were representational of King Solomon, and Washington had assumed this persona since the 1790s. The 1860s added two American heroes to the Masonic pantheon, President Andrew Jackson and the Marquis de Lafayette. Jackson was portrayed as a lodge Senior Warden and therefore representational of Hiram, King of Tyre, Solomon's ally in the building of the Temple. Lafayette, portrayed as a lodge Junior Warden, became Solomon's master craftsman, Hiram Abiff. Masonically viewed together, Washington founded the nation with wisdom, Andrew Jackson built the country through strong action, and Lafayette beautified the nation through charity in the cause of freedom. But it was George Washington in particular that generations of American Masons admired. As president, he obeyed the Constitution and governed with moderation and conservative policies.[13]

As a voluntary association, Freemasonry promoted a universal member-

ship but was ruled by a hierarchy. While all good men could seek membership, only the well-connected and more affluent men could expect to be
elected to high office. State Grand Masters were fiercely independent as
they protected Freemasonry's ancient customs, rituals and symbolism.
Like other institutions of the day, Freemasonry's upper-class grand lodge
officers had little desire to meet the needs of every member. They proudly
helped the "worthy poor," widow and orphan, but they also feared that
too much charity would encourage pauperism or begging and would attract
to the fraternity a class of shiftless men.[14]

Subordinate to grand lodge officers and thus restricted from affect-
ing Freemasonry's relief policies were its thousands of middle-class brothers. In an age when the average American worker made between $500–700
a year, most Masons could barely afford the initiation fees that were frequently $50 and even $100 plus annual lodge dues and expenses.[15] Yet it
was these middle-class men who most needed financial insurance to protect their families. Not finding it within the Masonic lodge, they left to employ the tenet of relief in broader communities.

Freemasons in the Community of Relief

*"The Anchor and Ark are emblems of a well-grounded hope and a well-
spent life. They are emblematical of that divine ark which safely wafts us
over this tempestuous sea of troubles, and that anchor which shall safely
moor us in a peaceful harbor, where the wicked cease from troubling,
and the weary shall find rest."*

— THOMAS SMITH WEBB, 1808[16]

Between 1870 and 1900, millions of factory workers and farmers, immigrants and migrants joined a variety of mutual benefit societies in search
of some form of group health and burial insurance. These groups, largely
patterned after Freemasonry, also provided self-improvement activities,
performed secret rituals and sponsored social functions. While they provided personal relief in time of trouble and upheld traditional self-reliant
work ethics, they differed from Freemasonry in many ways.

Mutual benefit fraternities were governed through a national headquarters rather than Freemasonry's loose confederation of state grand
lodges. The founders were often salesmen, entrepreneurs and insurance
agents rather than enlightened gentlemen or affluent volunteers. Thanks
to the railroads, telegraph and centralized business structure of the Gilded
Age, a new breed of professional organizers — who called themselves "fra-

Continuing the adora-
tion of George Washing-
ton as a man, a soldier
and an American, many
Freemasons attempted
to elevate him to a
symbolic title of "Grand
Master of the United
States." Flanking him
in the lithograph are the
Marquis de Lafayette,
with the words "An
Order Whose Leading
Star is Philanthropy,"
and Andrew Jackson,
"Past Grand Master
of the Grand Lodge of
Tennessee."

*Washington as a Free-
mason, created by J. W.
Clayton, lithographed
by Gibson and Co.,
published by Payne &
Holden, Cincinnati, OH,
1865. National Heritage
Museum, gift of Armen
Amerigian, 90.19.32.*

ternalists"[17] — concentrated on meeting the demands of specific people
with particular problems.

The model for these new nationally governed fraternities was the Independent Order of Odd Fellows (IOOF), which had begun as an English
"friendly society" in the late 1700s. Thomas Wildey broke away from the
British organization in 1840 and established an independent group in
America. Sometimes referred to as the "poor man's Freemasonry," the
IOOF steadily grew to 7,371 lodges with a membership of almost 466,000
within 40 years. By 1897, it surpassed Freemasonry in membership with
11,222 subordinate lodges and more than 831,718 members. The Odd Fellows increased family involvement by adding Daughters of Rebekah lodges
with 164,649 sisters.[18]

A large part of the success of the IOOF was due to its national grand
secretary, James Ridgely, and its commandments to "visit the sick, relieve
the distressed, bury the dead and educate the orphan." During Ridgely's
tenure (1840–80), the IOOF's annual relief fund dispersed more than $25
million. By 1899, the Odd Fellows were distributing over $3.3 million in
relief annually and supporting at least 34 homes for elderly members and
orphans in 19 states.[19] These numbers outshone Freemasonry's reverence
for "ancient customs and usages" and mythological past.

John Jordan Upchurch was credited with combining Freemasonry's
rituals and tenets and the Odd Fellows' national organization. "Father"
Upchurch, as he was called, was born in North Carolina in 1822 and was

orphaned at an early age. He probably became a Freemason before the Civil War. While working as a railroad machinist in Meadville, Pennsylvania, in 1868,
he founded the Ancient Order of United Workmen
for skilled workers.[20] As America's first mutual benefit
society, the AOUW was neither a limited trade union
nor an aloof ritual-centric society. Its main purpose
was to alleviate family financial hardships due to in-
jury or death. It also provided enjoyable social activities. Using a degree system of initiation rituals and
controlled by a national headquarters, the AOUW developed an innovative system of assessed membership rate. For $1 a month a workman was guaranteed
life insurance of not less than $2,000 for his family.
Upchurch's fraternity was so successful that by 1895
its total membership was more than 318,000 in some
6,000 lodges. During its first 26 years, more than
$70 million was paid to widows and orphans.[21]

Sadly, Upchurch proved to be a better lodge brother than a businessman. He lost his authority and was eased out of the national office. Never
a stable man, he eventually moved to Steelville, Missouri, and was later
obliged to petition his fraternity for relief. The AOUW leaders made him
a beloved figurehead by bestowing him with the title of "Father" and used
his name to build membership. When he died in 1887, he received a
magnificent funeral in St. Louis, and his destitute widow was given a lifetime pension of $50 per month.[22]

As Father Upchurch was creating the Ancient Order of United Workmen, other labor organizations came on the scene in the 1860s and 1870s.
Freemasons were involved in the founding of the Sons of Vulcan (for iron-
workers), the Knights of Saint Crispin (for shoemakers), the American
Flint Glass Workers' Union and the Brotherhood of Locomotive Engineers.[23] These fraternities used secret rituals to create solidarity among
skilled tradesmen by separating themselves apart from both unskilled
workers and factory owners.

The most ambitious of these new "fraternal unions" was the Noble
Order of Knights of Labor of America, founded in 1869 by Freemason Uriah
S. Stephens. It sought to organize all workers, regardless of skill or trade.
By 1886, the Knights of Labor membership reached 711,000, as it welcomed
black and female workers. Despite such national power, Stephens' successor
and brother Mason, Terence Powderley, complained bitterly that its rank
and file often preferred ritual performance to collective bargaining.[24]

After the brutal failures of the 1886 Haymarket riot, the 1892 Homestead steel strike and the 1894 Pullman strike, the Knights of Labor membership dropped dramatically, and by 1900, it was nearly extinct.[25] Its demands for an eight-hour work day, the end of child labor and equal pay for equal work became the cornerstones of the 20th-century labor movement.

Life on the land was often not much better than life in factories or mills. To address loneliness and financial hardships of country folk, another Mason returned to the farm with a new fraternal organization. Oliver H. Kelley, a clerk in the U.S. Bureau of Agriculture, saw the need for a farmer's organization that transcended party, region and crop. With other government clerks and his niece, Caroline A. Hall, Kelley created the Patrons of Husbandry in 1867. The organization became known as the Grange. Its mission was to create direct cooperatives between agricultural producers and consumers and to provide healthy social activities for isolated farm families. Through Caroline Hall's influence, the Grange also gave women full participation.[26]

Borrowing heavily from Freemasonry's rituals, the four degrees of the Grange provided members with distinctive titles. Men proceeded from Laborer to Husbandman, and women advanced from Maid to Matron. Male Grangers held administrative offices, while female Grangers assumed protective roles of the goddesses Pomona, Flora and Ceres. A passage from its rituals extolled rural life and elevated life on the land:

> . . . to rove over the verdant fields with a higher pleasure than we should have in carpeted halls of regal courts — to inhale the fresh air of the morning as if it were the sweet breath of infancy — to brush the dew from the glittering fields as if our paths were strewed with diamonds. . . . This is to love the country, and to make it not the home of the body only, but of the soul.[27]

The Patrons of Husbandry proved extremely successful. Between 1870 and 1875, the number of local granges rose from 150 to 13,000. In February 1874 alone, the National Grange chartered 2,239 local granges, or an average of 77 per day. The Grange's cooperative stores and its support for legal action against railroad freight rates were the major reasons for the organization's success. But economic depression caused the Grange membership to decline rapidly after peaking at 858,000 members in 1875. Overtaking the Grange was the more militant Farmers' Alliance established in 1880. While the Alliance proved better suited to combat the farmers' enemies, its members insisted that initiation rituals be a part of its activities. By the mid-1890s, however, the Farmers' Alliance had become strictly a political organization and eventually failed. The Grange continues to the present day.[28]

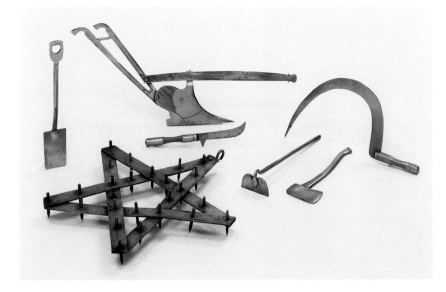

SYMBOLIC WORKING
TOOLS OF THE GRANGE

Just as Freemasonry
uses the square, level,
plumb and other tools to
convey moral principles,
so did the Patrons of
Husbandry select minia-
ture representations
of farming tools to
reinforce lessons. The
pruning knife that
removes useless growth
on trees reminds mem-
bers to curtail thoughts
and actions, the axe
teaches perseverance
and the five-pointed
harrow (used to break
up soil and cover seeds)
is emblematical of
study and observation
necessary to achieve
knowledge.

*Joseph Seymour and
Son, Syracuse, NY, 1879.
National Heritage
Museum, 80.7.2a-h.*

The rapid changes and persistent economic hardships that had motivated Masonic brothers Upchurch, Stephens and Kelley inspired many
other American "fraternalists" to begin new mutual assessment or insurance-based fraternities. With such mystical names as the Royal Arcanum
(1877), the Knights of the Maccabees (1878), the Improved Order of Hepta-
sophs (1878) and the Protected Home Circle (1886), each provided life insurance at a discount rate.[29] The pinnacle of these fraternities may have
been the Tribe of Ben-Hur. A group of insurance agents contrived the organization in 1893 and based its three initiation degrees on General Lew Wallace's 1880 best-selling novel, *Ben-Hur, A Tale of the Christ*.[30]

African-Americans, often Prince Hall Masons or members of the Grand
United Order of Odd Fellows, formed their own mutual benefit fraternities.
In some, such as the Independent Order of Saint Luke (1867), men and
women received equal status. Other national black fraternities included
the Grand United Order of Galilean Fishermen (1856), International Order
of Twelve Knights and Daughters of Tabor (1871), the Grand United Order
of True Reformers (1881) and the Colored Brotherhood and Sisterhood of
Honor (1886). Usually Christian in their rituals and often overseen by
clergy, these fraternal organizations were an important pillar in African-
American communities.[31]

Exploited by factory owners and politicians and reviled by native-born
Protestant Americans, European immigrants also organized for mutual
protection. Founded before 1900 were the Czech Catholic Union, the Polish Beneficial Association, the Sons of Norway and the National Croatian
Society of the U.S.A. Many of these groups were based on the Masonic

ETHNIC FRATERNAL
RIBBONS

While Freemasonry
considered the apron
"the badge of a Mason,"
members of immigrant
and ethnic organizations
usually wore ribbons.
Represented here are the
French, Czech, Portu-
guese, Scottish and Aus-
trian. The French ribbon
in black was reversible
and was worn at funerals
for departed members.

*1875–1910. National
Heritage Museum,
2003.023.3; 2003.005.6;
2003.005.5; 2003.022.7;
2003.023.2.*

model, and in deference to the Roman Catholic Church, they substituted
initiation rituals and secrecy with folk stories and ethnic symbols to build
pride and solidarity.[32]

All these new "extended families" or fraternities successfully amalgamated the symbolism of Freemasonry, governance of Odd Fellows and the
assessment insurance of AOUW. Strangers, friends and neighbors became
fraternal brothers and sisters as they extended their families through shared
initiations. The money from membership fees, annual dues and fundraising
events could be given as assistance and received without shame. The fraternal sector offered safety and security from the casualties of heavy industry
and volatile markets.

The Business of Fraternity

*"Cherish well the protection afforded you by this Order, for there
will surely come a time, when our hands are nerveless, and our brains
no longer active, that the protection guaranteed by your Beneficial
Certificate, and mine, will prove a blessing to those we love."*

— COURT DEGREE RITUAL OF THE TRIBE OF BEN-HUR, CA. 1900[33]

The explosion of new mutual benefit associations during the golden age
of fraternities led to intense competition for members. Like Benjamin
Franklin's enterprises or Andrew Carnegie's international steel company,
American fraternal orders diversified their services, expanded their activi-

ties and integrated their subsidiaries. Evolving out of Freemasonry's static "ancient form," mutual benefit fraternities adapted to economic realities.

Fraternal leaders sought to regulate their organizations' services and expand their market share by implementing modern business practices. They employed salesmen to travel around the country signing up policyholders, organizing local lodges and building state grand lodges. To stabilize their insurance premiums, they denied membership to men who worked in dangerous occupations (such as miners or balloonists) or disreputable trades (such as barkeepers and baseball players) and established age limits to avoid the higher mortality rates of the child and elderly. They hired doctors to screen unhealthy applicants and to legally certify health and death benefit payments. Some lodges changed the secret passwords every six months to ensure that members kept their membership dues paid in full. Finally, and against repeated protest by its members, mutual benefit leaders increased monthly rates and established reserve funds.[34] Through such self-regulation and often uncharitable policies, mutual benefit fraternities claimed more than 1.5 million members and accounted for half the total value of all American life insurance policies in force in 1895.[35]

Mutual benefit fraternal leaders focused on insurance actuarial numbers and positive cash flow and began to view their dramatic rituals as an inefficient premium rather than their primary service. Farmers, workers and shopkeepers, however, were less likely to give their cash for only a certificate promising peace of mind. Almost universally they insisted that there be something entertaining and substantial in return for their monthly assessments. They wanted the thrill of being a Heptasoph, Forester, Knight or a member of the Tribe of Ben-Hur. They wanted the prestige and practical experience of becoming the chief, king, or master workman among their lodge brethren.[36]

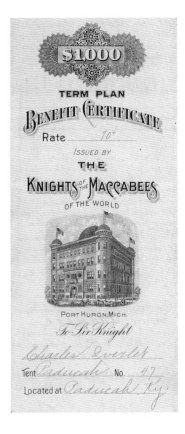

KNIGHTS OF THE MACCABEES BENEFIT CERTIFICATE

Issued to Sir Knight Charles Iverlet of Paducah Tent No. 47, Paducah, Kentucky, this certificate shows the Maccabees' headquarters and guarantees that $1,000 will be paid to the Iverlet family upon Charles' death.

Toledo Lithograph Co., Toledo, OH, 1908. National Heritage Museum, A2001/48/1.

RED MAN MARTIN DUNHAM

A member of the Improved Order of Red Men, Martin Dunham proudly wears his wampum belt, embroidered with his tribe, No. 67 of Binghamton, New York.

E.E. Conrad, Binghamton, NY, ca. 1885. National Heritage Museum, 88.42.80.

FRATERNAL RITUAL COSTUMES

Americans sometimes joined multiple fraternal organizations to participate in different dramatic rituals and enjoy the pageantry. Richly illustrated catalogs from mail-order regalia companies highlighted the finest theatrical costumes, such as these of a high priest, stonemason, king, and monk.

Cincinnati Regalia Co., ca. 1900. National Heritage Museum, gift of Grant B. Romer, 88.42.156.2, 5, 13a, 30.

MODERN WOODMEN
OF AMERICA AXE AND
DRILL TEAM

While other fraternal
marching orders carried
swords or rifles, the
Woodmen performed
with aluminum axes.
Drill teams from Wood-
men camps, like this
one from Delaware, Ken-
tucky, competed on the
state and national level
for awards and prizes.

*Parade Axe, ca. 1900.
National Heritage
Museum, gift of Modern
Woodmen of America,
Rock Island, IL, 88.15.5.
Greenwood MWA Camp,
Delaware, KY, Schroeter
Studio, Green River,
KY, ca. 1910. National
Heritage Museum,
2003.022.2.*

The love for dramatic initiations and the competition for new lodge members led to a demand for elaborate ritual costumes and props. Following the 1850s lead of the Masonic publishing and supply companies of Malonzo Drummond and Robert Macoy, manufacturers of Civil War uniforms and swords retooled to meet the new fraternal demands. In turn, fraternities revised their rituals to maximize their theatrical presentation. No longer was it respectable to perform the story of Solomon's Temple or Damon and Pythias in handmade costumes with crude props. The best lodges donned embroidered velvet costumes, used theatrical backdrops and special lighting effects to heighten the drama and the moral message of the initiation experience. Larger companies, such as M.C. Lilley & Co. and Henderson-Ames Co., distributed regalia catalogs to fraternal lodges across the country. These mail-order catalogs sold everything necessary or imaginable to furnish a lodge. While brothers could buy personal jewelry, lodges were offered package rates for whole sets of regalia and furniture according to style and quality.[37]

Regalia for marching and paramilitary units were particularly popular among the new range of fraternal products. By 1900, every major fraternity had parade units modeled after the Masonic Knights Templar. Odd Fellows joined the Patriarchs Militant, Ancient Order of United Workmen began the Select Knights, the Modern Woodmen formed the Foresters with precision ax drill teams, and the Red Men dressed not as Indians but as colonial militia. As city celebrations, pageants and holiday parades became important leisure-time events, these groups marched behind a banner

wearing impressive uniforms and performed complex parade drills. Generations of men too young to have served in the Civil War were able to enjoy
the martial camaraderie without leaving home. Fraternal leaders also
viewed parade units as good advertisements.[38]

From a historical point of view, however, the members of these paramilitary units were often the very men who suffered most from unsafe
working conditions and laissez-faire economy. Following the devastation
that resulted from the 1877 national railroad strike, states reorganized
their National Guard units and built castle-like arsenals. Corporations began forming private security forces and hiring Alan Pinkerton's agents.
Rather than fearing such developments, fraternal marching units were
often organized and led by state politicians and National Guard officers.
Bastions of the working class — the Odd Fellows' Patriarchs Militant and
the AOUW's Select Knights — justified their drills, tactics and discipline
as an important line of defense against communist agitators, anarchists,
and tramps — albeit behind the police, National Guard and regular army.[39]

Other mutual benefit fraternities expanded their services beyond assessment insurance and orphanages. The Independent Order of Saint Luke,
for example, owned a department store, built a printing plant and published a newspaper. Most importantly, it established the St. Luke Penny
Savings Bank in Richmond, Virginia, in 1903. Right Worthy Grand Secretary Maggie L. Walker may have been the first woman in America to serve
as a bank president. In an address, she stated: "Sisters, let us combine our
pennies, our nickels, our dimes and our dollars. Let us provide employment
for our girls."[40]

After the Civil War, Americans began separating by social and economic
class. Farmers and laborers, older and newer immigrant communities built
America from the bottom up. Carnegie, Rockefeller and other entrepreneurs organized international industries, while local businesses expanded
into regional and national markets. A growing class of professionals coordinated, counted, supervised and sold the products of the farm and factory.

In the 1870s and 1880s, local Masonic and fraternal lodges operated
as neutral grounds and private sanctuaries from the demands of work and
everyday life. Through the necessity of mutual protection, Americans from
all walks of life came together as fraternal families. But striving and sacrifice
also brought success and exclusivity. Affluent men began to seek special
places to spend their money, enjoy their free time and socialize. Once again
Freemasons, reveling in the tenet of brotherly love, would lead their fraternal brothers out to play.

Building Freemasonry and American Community

A MASON
Giving the Password!

CHAPTER 7

From Labor to Refreshment

Fraternal Fun, 1880–1910

"Every trade, every profession, every benevolence, every sport, every church furnishes distinctions commensurate in territorial magnitude with our great country. And still the full measure of American officialism is not attained. . . . The chief officer is Ruler, Chancellor, Commander, Seigneur, President, Potentate, with many superlative and worshipful prefixes. . . . Here then we have the great American safety-valve — we are a nation of presidents."

— WALTER B. HILL, 1892 [1]

OPPOSITE:

MASONIC QUILT

Made by the sisters of Beacon Light Eastern Star Chapter No. 75, this six-by-seven-foot quilt was presented to their sponsors, Beacon Light Lodge No. 710, Staten Island, New York. Quilts were often used to raise funds for charitable causes or to support the social activities of a lodge. Other quilts were made for use in the home.

ca. 1900. National Heritage Museum, gift of Mrs. Everett C. Carey, 74.001.43.

THE RAPID CHANGES of the Gilded Age increased competition and created friction among America's social classes. In many ways, fraternal organizations helped to ease this friction by serving ever-changing communities. As they diversified, fraternities became associated with the social class of its members and were ranked accordingly. The least affluent belonged to mutual benefit and immigrant fraternities, like the Ancient Order of United Workmen. Lower middle classes gravitated to groups that were focused on ritual, such as the Knights of Pythias, while the Odd Fellows were composed of "the great middle, industrial classes." [2] Near the top stood Freemasonry with only its York Rite Knights Templar and the Scottish Rite ranked higher. By 1900, being a Mason was almost a prerequisite for middle-class respectability.

As much a product of the industrial age as aluminum and steel, America's new middle classes changed the country. Where once Americans worked for daily wages or the fruits of the land, many now received annual salaries, company bonuses and sales commissions. Regular and reliable income allowed families to budget their expenses, save for the future and buy on credit. Safer railroads and the advent of the telephone and trolley lines encouraged the growth of the suburbs and allowed families to consume

a wider selection of food and household products. The impact of science, Marxism, pragmatic philosophy and Darwinism challenged traditional religious beliefs and the way Americans worked and played. Colleges and business schools attracted younger men in greater numbers, and corporations built new urban skyscrapers to house the staff and records to compete in national markets.

The success of America's new economy and technology contributed to a growing sense of optimism and encouraged the middle classes to look for new ways to spend their discretionary money and free time. Men joined recreational clubs, women shopped at large department stores and families enjoyed weekend outings or extended vacations. Amusement parks, sports grounds and public parks developed, and baseball became America's national pastime. Larger cities competed to build the best museums, opera houses and zoos and to host world fairs as a means of attracting businesses and tourists.[3]

The expanding middle classes made Freemasonry stronger and gave it greater national prominence. Within its 49 grand lodges, more than 11,600 local lodges initiated 51,000 new brothers in 1900 alone.[4] The big industrial states of New York, Pennsylvania and Ohio each had more than 500 local lodges, and Western lodges sprouted in towns along railroad lines.[5] The Masonic York Rite and the Order of the Eastern Star continued to thrive, and Scottish Rite leaders were developing the secret to becoming the most successful Masonic organization of the 20th century. Many, if not most, of the leading citizens in almost every segment of society were Masons. The craft's brotherhood included presidents, senators, judges, prominent clergy, businessmen, professors and inventors.[6] Freemasonry attracted popular entertainers, such as the seven Ringling Brothers and Tom Thumb, explorers, like Robert E. Peary, and military heroes, like the "Buffalo Soldiers" of the 9th and 10th Cavalry Regiments.[7]

As the new middle-class men joined Freemasonry, they replaced a departing older elite class of men. The wealthier class had effectively dominated the fraternity since colonial days, but they moved into the more exclusive downtown gentlemen's and country clubs during the Gilded Age. As the new middle class assumed leadership positions in the Masonic fraternity, they began reinterpreting the purpose of the craft. Many college-educated men became less impressed with repetitive instruction in so-called timeless intellectual and moral truths. The mythical dramatic rituals paled in comparison to the bright lights of Broadway or even local opera houses. Professional men with savings and investment accounts did not see the need for basic Masonic relief. In the late 1800s, younger Masons turned their attention to Freemasonry's social aspects.

High Society in the Lodge

"On this principle [Brotherly Love], Masonry unites men of every country, sect and opinion, and conciliates true friendship among those who might otherwise have remained at a perpetual distance."

— WILLIAM PRESTON, 1775[8]

From the early lodges of the 1700s, Freemasons formed strong personal ties between men. To avoid religious and political divisions, the craft united men through a common desire for self-improvement and mutual aid. Initiations and sociability cemented the fraternity's diverse membership. Early Masons were well known for their conviviality around the festive board, and both Anderson's 1723 *Constitutions* and Dermott's 1756 *Ahiman Rezon* included Masonic songs and toasts. Lodge officers were assigned the task of organizing fraternal fellowship and moderating a brother's indulgences.[9]

MASONIC SPITTOON

Although smoking was banned within many lodges in the 1800s, some brothers still chewed tobacco during meetings.

ca. 1890. National Heritage Museum, 99.031.1.

JOHN PHILIP SOUSA

Called "The March King," Sousa (1854–1932) was one of the most popular musicians of his generation. He joined Hiram Lodge No. 1, Washington, DC, in 1881, and was a member of many other Masonic organizations. In addition to *The Washington Post March* and *Star and Stripes Forever,* he also wrote Masonic music, including *The Nobles of the Mystic Shrine March.*

John Philip Sousa, ca. 1890. "The President's Own" United States Marine Band, Washington, DC.

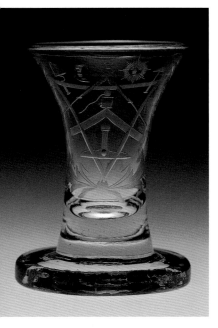

Taverns and inns usually served as the venue where these Masonic lodges met, since they were often the only building in town that could accommodate a large number of brethren and also provide the necessary food and drink. The early meetings in London of the first grand lodge in 1717 were held at the Goose and Gridiron Alehouse. Colonial American lodges followed a similar pattern.

British and American regimental lodges, with their love for drill and ceremony, developed the "table lodge" in the 1700s. Meetings were held in conjunction with a multi-course banquet during which each brother drank from a heavy-footed firing glass, called a "cannon." Before each course, the "cannons" were charged with wine and the lodge Master then presented a toast. After the toast, the brothers "fired the charge back" and slammed their glasses loudly on the table. The cupped foot of the glass resounded with a loud boom that resembled a cannon salute. The occasional table lodges today follow a similar pattern. They are not only conducted as a social occasion but also have been known to provide an opportunity to raise funds for charity or to honor old and faithful brothers.[10]

The anti-Masonic period, the evangelical revival and the early temperance movement of the 1820s and 1830s curtailed such Masonic activity. After the Civil War, lodge social life continued to gravitate toward family participation, as evidenced by the growth of the Eastern Star for women. Lodges balanced their private banquets with picnics, sleigh rides, concerts or other respectable entertainment.

During the golden age of fraternities (1865–1910), Freemasons played a highly important and visible role in community life.[11] Local Masonic lodges and state grand lodges were invited to conduct a special ceremony to lay a cornerstone for public and private buildings. For instance, significant Masonic ceremonies were held in connection with the Statue of Liberty in 1884 and the North Gate of Yellowstone National Park in 1903.[12] Parades provided an occasion for Masonic lodges to lead a long line of civic and fraternal units. Masons also enjoyed marching when they met for their annual state grand lodge sessions and for the consecration of a new Masonic building. The Masonic Knights Templar, in particular, were well known for their military parades. In the 1880s and 1890s, major cities welcomed the Knights for their triennial national conventions. Tens of thousands of citizens turned out to see as many as 20,000 Knights Templar on foot and horseback perform precision drills and to hear bands playing Christian, patriotic and Masonic marches.[13]

This Masonic beehive of activities was built by the growing upper middle-class membership. As professional men became Masons, they often brought their business associates into their lodges. This caused many older

GRAND PARADE OF THE KNIGHTS TEMPLAR   TRIENNIAL CONCLAVE, SAN FRANCISCO, AUGUST 20, 1883.

KNIGHTS TEMPLAR
PARADE

An 1883 parade com-
prised of more than
15,000 Knights was
viewed by more than
100,000 spectators.
The Templars' motto,
"In Hoc Signo Vinces"
(In this Sign Thou Shalt
Conquer) was seen
before a battle in a
vision by Constantine
the Great in 312 A.D.

*Grand Parade of the
Knights Templar,
H. S. Crocker and Co.,
San Francisco, CA,
1883. National Heritage
Museum, 85.21.3.*

lodges to become more exclusive and more expensive to join. Wealthier Masons also formed new lodges with an implicit purpose to limit member-ship according to their preferences.[14] In these lodges Masons with their wives held lavish banquets, dances, and other social events. By 1890, the younger Masons who were increasingly bored with what they perceived as repetitive rituals based on Jewish allegories or Christian morality longed for a place to play.

The Playgrounds of Freemasons

"Brethren, by order of the Worshipful Master, you are now called from labor to refreshment."

— MASONIC RITUAL, CA. 1760[15]

According to his own account, the well-known American comedian and Freemason William J. "Billy" Florence claimed that he traveled in 1870 to the edge of the "mysterious East" and found an oasis of pleasure. While attending a party hosted by a Persian diplomat in Marseilles, France, he and the other guests were initiated into a "secret" Muslim Order, called the "Bektashy." Centered in Cairo, Egypt, the Order supposedly originated in Mecca in 1698, and its ceremonies were first performed in Aleppo, Syria. Unable to stay for the initiation's second show, however, Florence obtained

the Order's rituals and laws and was invited to spread it to American Free-masons. Or so the legend of the Mystic Shrine is told.[16]

In reality the Ancient Arabic Order Nobles of the Mystic Shrine (AAONMS) was the brainchild of Dr. Walter Fleming and was cooked up over lunch at New York's Knickerbocker Cottage bistro on 6th Avenue. Attending this 1870 luncheon were twelve other Masons, including Billy Florence, just back from Europe. Among the others were Charles T. Mc-Clenachan, a lawyer and prominent Scottish Rite Mason; William S. Paterson, who was fluent in Arabic, and William Fowler, the bistro owner.[17]

At the first formal meeting in June 1871, Dr. Fleming presented his contrived initiation ritual and conveyed it to the other 12 attendees. Based on so-called ancient Muslim punishments meted out to criminals, the initiation was little more than burlesque adapted to the romantic setting of *The Arabian Nights.*[18] The new "Nobles" decided to limit membership to Freemasons who had reached the 32nd degree in the Scottish Rite or were York Rite Knights Templar. The requirement seemed odd, since Dr. Fleming was not a member of either branch until nearly a year later. Only then was Mecca Shrine Temple organized. Fleming was elected Mecca's first Potentate, while others assumed such positions as Chief Rabban, High Priest and Oriental Guide.[19]

Despite such romantic beginnings, Fleming's Shrine languished in its first years. By 1876 there were only 43 Nobles, with all but six living in New York City.[20] Yet Fleming was determined to take the Shrine nation-wide. To achieve this goal, he designated several Nobles outside the New York area as "Past Potentates" and empowered them to initiate new members and create local temples. Billy Florence used his dramatic skills and celebrity status to embellish his romantic origins of the Order and create new Shriners in the cities and towns where he performed. The ritual took on a life of its own, and its Oriental pageantry became a popular theme around which to organize a party. The Shrine adopted the red fez as its distinctive headgear. Picking up the theme, other Shriners freely concocted an odd combination of ancient Egyptian, Persian, Arab, Turkish and Islamic cultures.[21] The second Shrine Temple, chartered in Rochester, New York, in 1875, was called Damascus, and a third, called Mount Sinai, was chartered in "the oasis" of Montpelier, Vermont, in 1876.[22]

To govern the fledgling order, Dr. Fleming formed the Imperial Grand Council of the United States and chose New York City as "the Grand Orient." The members of the Council elected Fleming as the first Imperial Grand Potentate and set the fees for chartering new temples and initiating new members. Most important it upheld the policy of restricting membership to Knights Templar or 32nd degree Scottish Rite Masons.[23] With the founding of the Imperial Grand Council, Freemasons had a national organization, and the Shrine became "the golden rivet in the superstructure of Masonry."[24]

With a well-chosen theme and the ground rules set, the Shrine attracted thousands of upper-class Masons to its party. Despite the great economic upheaval of the era, 14 new Shrine temples were chartered before 1884.[25] Nine years later, there were nearly 27,000 Nobles in 64 temples across the continent, ranging from "Jerusalem" in New Orleans to "Morocco" in Jacksonville, Florida, to "Afifi" in Tacoma, Washington. There was also a Canadian Shrine temple, "Rameses" in Toronto.[26] In less than 30 years, the Shrine had more members than the Scottish Rite and more than a quarter of the members of the York Rite Knights Templars. By 1920 the Shrine, with its 445,279 Nobles, had maintained its lead over the Scottish Rite and surpassed the Knights Templar in membership.[28]

The key to the Mystic Shrine's rapid success was its pure love for fun and local freedom. Unlike other Masonic and fraternal groups, Shrine meetings, or "ceremonials," were grand initiation pageants overseen by a Potentate and his divan of officers. Candidates were initiated in a large group, and many endured burlesque tricks. The Imperial Shrine supervised and coordinated local temples but did not dictate a mission or structure to its subordinate branches. Local Shriners were free to start their own clubs under the dome of their temples. Men who enjoyed hunting, fishing or other recreational activities were encouraged to start a Shrine unit. Those who were musically inclined established choruses and various types of bands. Other parade units performed complicated drills, rode horses and camels and wore outlandish Arabic costumes. Shrine temples often hosted luncheon clubs, held evening banquets and all-day outings at parks and ballgames. Shriners did not consider themselves obliged to follow Freemasonry's "ancient customs and usages."[29] They wrote their own rules, performed their own hilarious rituals and left behind the self-improvement mission and Masonic virtues of silence and circumspection.

The Shrine became known as the "the playground for Masons," and the founders had creatively designed it to succeed. Since it never professed to be a form of Freemasonry, it sold itself simply as a private club open only to Freemasons who had completed the degrees in the York or Scottish Rite. This allowed the Shrine to be considered part of the Masonic family, like the Order of the Eastern Star, yet sufficiently independent to govern itself. By placing the Shrine at the end of the twin Masonic paths, it did not compete with the York and Scottish Rites for members but relied on the two groups as a ready pool of applicants.[30]

The Shrine's pleasures, however, were open to only a select class of

"Pleasure without intemperance, hospitality without rudeness, and jollity without coarseness should here prevail among all of the true Faith."

— IMPERIAL POTENTATE WILLIAM B. MELISH, 1892[27]

Masons. Local temples retained the black ball voting system that prevented the "wrong sort" of brothers from joining. It was not unusual in the early years for Jews, Catholics and other "foreigners" to be rejected, even though Billy Florence was a Catholic.[31] To become a Noble, a brother had to maintain his annual dues to his craft lodge, as well as the York or Scottish Rite, before he paid his Shrine membership. These fees at the time often totaled more than $300 a year and did not include the costs for banquets, travel, lodging and refreshment. In this way a further class division was made within the fraternity, since only the wealthiest Masons could afford to escape to the Mystic Shrine.

The Shrine's national Imperial Session became the highlight of all Masonic events and attracted the most affluent and fun-loving men from across the country. The 1900 Imperial Session in the nation's capital capped two decades of phenomenal growth for the organization. A grand parade of more than 3,000 nobles marched down Pennsylvania Avenue and under the White House portico, where President (and Shriner) William McKinley reviewed dozens of bands, marching units and camel and horse patrols.[32] Public notoriety of Shriners' "pilgrimages" earned them a reputation for late-night revelry and practical jokes and set the bar for 20th-century American conventioneers.

The Shrine's Masonic affiliation was a precedent that other Masons soon followed. As an open voluntary organization, Freemasonry had little power to prevent its members from forming clubs. How far any Masonic club grew beyond its home state was limited only by the energy of its members and its ability to gain acceptance. The Shrine succeeded partly because its upper-class members had the ready resources to spread it across the nation and were entrenched in grand lodge hierarchies.

In the wake of the Shrine, two other major Masonic social organizations were created. Built by less affluent men, the groups grew more slowly and

Following the popularity of the Shriners, many organizations adopted unusual fraternal hats as regalia. Seen here are a Kora Shrine Fez from Lewiston, Maine, the Odd Fellows Oriental Order of Humility and Protection, the African-American Elks, the Knights of Pythias "Dokey," the Masonic Tall Cedars of Lebanon triangular hat, and the Masonic Kolah Grotto from Newport, Rhode Island.

Manufactured between 1900–1960. National Heritage Museum, Kora, gift of Linda Barrows, 97.051.1; OOH&P, 2001.039; Elks, 2001.028.1; Koraz, 2001.033; Tall Cedars, gift of Barry R. Stocker, Past Supreme Tall Cedar, 2001.056.1; Kolah, gift of Bessie M. Johnson, SC80.2.1.

received less acceptance. LeRoy Fairchild and his Masonic brothers in Hamilton, New York, formed the Grotto in 1890. Its official name was the Mystic Order of Veiled Prophets of the Enchanted Realm, but it was nicknamed "the playhouse of the craft."[33] All Master Masons (third degree) were eligible to apply for membership in the Grotto. The initiation ritual was supposedly discovered in a secret vault of a sacred temple in Teheran, Persia. Members wore black fezzes and met in local Grottos. By 1908, there were 20 Grottos and 7,087 prophets.[34]

Another spontaneous attempt at Masonic fun was made by the introduction of the Tall Cedars of Lebanon. Begun in New Jersey in 1902, the Tall Cedars took the name and ritual themes from the trees used to build King Solomon's Temple. Rather than wearing a fez, members wore high triangular hats and met in local "forests." Like the Grotto, the Tall Cedars was open to all Master Masons, and its national leader carried the title of Grand Tall Cedar.[35] Within 20 years, it had grown to nearly 100 forests and more than 45,000 Cedars. Mostly an East Coast organization, it never planted a forest west of the Mississippi.[36] Reacting to all these intrusions into their serene oasis, some Shriners in 1911 formed a still more exclusive social group called the Royal Order of Jesters, where "Mirth is King."[37]

Animal Crackers

"Wherever Elks may roam, whatever their lot in life may be, when this hour falls upon the dial of night, the great heart of Elkdom swells and throbs. It is the golden hour of recollection, the homecoming of those who wander, the mystic roll call of those who will come no more. Living or dead, an Elk is never forgotten, never forsaken."

— ELEVEN O'CLOCK TOAST, ORDER OF ELKS, CA. 1906[38]

The popularity of the Shrine was not lost on other American fraternal organizations. Perpetually competing among themselves for new membership and retention, individual fraternal leaders quickly created Shrine-like auxiliaries. The Odd Fellows started several clubs, the first of which was the Imperial Order of Muscovites founded in 1894. They met in Kremlins and were ruled by Czars. Other fun organizations within the Odd Fellows were the Knights of Oriental Splendor, the Oriental Order of Humility and Protection, and the Ancient Mystic Order of Cabirians. Ultimately all these regional Orders merged in 1924 to form the Ancient Mystic Order of Samaritans (AMOS).[39] The Knights of Pythias created the Dramatic Order Knights of Khorassan, called "Dokeys," in 1894, and by 1920 there were more than 100,000 members.[40] Individual Knights of Columbus councils formed the International Order of Alhambra in 1904.[41] Even the Order of United Commercial Travelers got into the act by creating a Shrine-like fun group called the Ancient Mystic Order of Bagmen of Baghdad.[42]

The turn of the 20th century also brought a new breed of social fraternities in which the members would call each other animals. The first-born was the Elks in 1867, followed by the Moose (1888), the Eagles (1898), the Owls (1904) and the Orioles (1910).[43] These were among the largest and longest lived. Parallel to the mostly white Orders were the black Improved Order of the Elks (1898), the Afro-American Owls (1911) and the Improved Order of Moose (1922).[44]

Of these new orders, the most important was the Benevolent and Protective Order of Elks (BPOE). The genesis of the Elks was a joke. In 1867 Charles Algernon Sidney Vivian, an English singer and dancer, arrived in New York. With other actors, he organized a private club to dodge laws against Sunday drinking. Club initiates became unwitting victims of a practical joke, and the consequence required them to buy all the members a round of drinks.[45]

Called the "Jolly Corks," the club soon changed its purpose after a member died leaving his wife and children destitute. Several "Corks" decided to add benevolence and charity to good fellowship and, after viewing

BENEVOLENT &
PROTECTIVE ORDER
OF ELKS MEMBERSHIP
CERTIFICATE

*J. M. Vickroy, Terre
Haute, IN, 1902.
National Heritage
Museum, A97/023.*

the stuffed animals at P.T. Barnum's museum, suggested the elk as the symbol for their new order. Elks, they believed, were "fleet of foot, timorous of doing wrong, avoiding all combat except in fighting for the female and in defense of the young and helpless and weak."[46] By 1872, the BPOE had created a grand lodge, had begun chartering local lodges, and had donated money for the victims of a fire in Chicago.[47] Comprised mostly of actors and performers, the Elks spread their fraternity through the vaudeville circuits and the growing number of America's theaters.

In its early decades, the Elks were heavily influenced by Freemasonry. The Elks met in local lodges and used secret rituals, handshakes and passwords. The lodge doors were guarded by a "tyler," the members wore aprons, and they even conducted a Masonic-like "Lodge of Sorrow" for deceased members. But founded on a joke, organized for benevolent purposes and having little pretense of an ancient heritage, the Elks gradually de-emphasized the rituals and dropped most of its secrets.[48] In 1898, there were some 300 lodges with 35,000 members, and by 1923 there were 850,000 Elks throughout the United States, Panama and the American-held Pacific Islands.[49]

Operative As Well As Speculative Masonry

"Ours is an order of builders, the most ancient and honorable in the world, and it is beneath the dignity of our Lodges to eke out a comfortless existence in rented flats."

— MASONIC STANDARD, 1908[50]

As the preeminent fraternal organization in America's Gilded Age, Freemasonry remained aloof from the unbridled competition for members. Traditionally Masons did not solicit men to join, rather a man was expected to seek out a Mason and ask to join. While the Odd Fellows achieved a higher number of members and lodges than the Masonic fraternity in the 1890s, Freemasonry attracted a better quality of men. To retain a select

MASONIC FAIR,
NEW YORK

To fund new buildings, Freemasons hosted city fairs. While wives sold their handicrafts, Masons who owned business donated their products. Department stores and shops were solicited to rent display booths.

Table of the Executive Committee Masonic Fair, New York, Frank Leslie's Illustrated, *1873. Courtesy of William D. Moore.*

Building Freemasonry and American Community

membership and to proclaim an elite status, local lodges turned toward building impressive
temples. The grand lodges in New York and
Philadelphia opened new edifices in 1873. New
York secured the talents of the famous architect
Napoleon LaBrun, and the Grand Lodge of Pennsylvania selected a prominent site across the
street from Philadelphia's city hall. Although
fires destroyed temples in Boston and Baltimore,
both rebuilt new temples that were even more
ornate than the first. Cities such as Springfield,
Massachusetts (1892), Detroit (1896) and St.
Louis (1896) did not serve as the homes of grand
lodges, yet the Masons in those cities joined in
the building boom and a competition of sorts
arose among Masons in major cities across the
country.[51]

Masonic Temple,
Broad and Filbert Street,
Philadelphia, Pa.

The new temples served multipurpose functions. As well as providing space for the three
degrees of the craft lodges, they also housed specially furnished rooms for the presentation of
York and Scottish Rite degrees. The facilities included administrative and charity offices, libraries and museums, banquet halls and kitchens,
smoking rooms and women's lounges.

To erect such edifices, Masons employed a variety of fundraising methods. Mortgages were secured through the sale of bonds and contributions
from brothers. Masonic buildings were also financed through Masonic
fairs. Open to the public, these fairs ran from three days to as long as three
weeks. They provided entertainment as well as the selling of new consumer
goods from an "automobile to breakfast cereal." Organized and managed
by Masons, the fairs were staffed mostly by women, who also chaired several
committees and provided much of the handiwork and crafts that were
sold.[52]

Civic, Masonic and architectural pride united for Chicago's 1893
World's Columbian Exposition. During the fair's six-month life, more
than 27 million people visited the "White City" to view the numerous arts
and sciences exhibition, domestic and international pavilions and recreated
villages from around the world.[53] Freemasons joined in the celebration by
dedicating the tallest building in the world. Built by Burnham & Root, the
Chicago Masonic temple stood 302 feet high with 21 stories. *Scientific*

PHILADELPHIA
MASONIC TEMPLE

Begun in 1868 and com-
pleted in 1873, the Philadelphia temple is still
considered by many to
be the most beautiful in
the country. Freemason
James H. Windrim was
the architect. The cost
of construction was $1.6
million. The building
serves as the headquar-
ters for the Grand Lodge
of Pennsylvania.

*Curt Teich Company,
Chicago, ca. 1910.
National Heritage
Museum, A96/066/3537.*

MASONIC TEMPLE, CHICAGO.

American proclaimed it "A City Under One Roof" because of its central courtyard ringed with shops on the first nine floors, offices on the middle floors and Masonic lodge rooms on the top two levels.[54]

The six-month life of the fair saw many novel innovations that would shape American popular culture — the Ferris Wheel, Cracker Jacks, hamburgers, diet carbonated soda, and the elevated electric trolley. Historian Frederick Jackson Turner proclaimed at a meeting of the American Historical Association that the American frontier era was over.[55]

The fair, however, did not welcome everyone. African-Americans were barred from attending or even working on its construction.[56] Local Prince Hall Masons, however, claimed they met with representatives of the "Grand Council of Arabia" who were part of the fair's Moorish village exhibition. Through this liaison, Imperial Grand Potentate John George Jones assumed all the rights and prerogatives of the white Shriners. Jones established Palestine Temple No. 1 in Chicago in June 1893. Within seven months, there were four other temples located in Washington, DC, Baltimore, New York City and Indianapolis. To distinguish themselves from their white Nobles, Jones inserted "Egyptian" into the name of their organization. Two years later, there were 25 Prince Hall Shrine temples and a women's auxiliary, the National Grand Court, Daughters of Sphinx.[57]

Freemasons born at the beginning of the 1800s lived through a century of change for their country and their fraternity. They witnessed the birth of railroads and the troubles of the anti-Masonic period, the Civil War and the breaking of brotherly love, the great energy to rebuild a divided country and a rededication to Masonic rituals and charitable endeavors. Where once Freemasonry was the only fraternal order, by 1899 it was surrounded by its several auxiliaries and countless other fraternal offspring. Where once the lodge

Building Freemasonry and American Community

had met in a cabin, now the members were taking elevators to meet in sky-scrapers.

But Freemasonry's emphasis on the fragility of life and the necessity of strong morality was becoming anachronistic. With the coming century a tension would grow between generations. The older generation that fought in the Civil War lived according to Protestant piety and personal character and believed in separate spheres for men and women. Those of a more romantic younger generation, often the offspring of immigrants, were increasingly less pious and looked forward to an exciting new future. They were eager to learn new ideas, use new technology and were happy to enjoy frivolous leisure pursuits that included both men and women.

Within Freemasonry, this tension was keenly felt. Many older Masons resented the popularity of the Shrine and its imitators. They were concerned that young men were breezing through the sublime degree of Master Mason and either the York or Scottish Rite degrees so they could frolic on Free-masonry's "playgrounds." If younger brothers spent all their time at recess and refreshment, they asked, how could they ever learn Masonic truths and morality necessary to live a good life? How could the tenets of brotherly love, relief and truth be practiced when Masons were not at labor but play-ing in the Shrine, Grotto or Forests of Lebanon? The tension would increase as these questions were slowly drowned out in a progressive new century where younger Masons and their wives continued to play, and science and psychology increasingly supplanted religion and morality.

CHAPTER 8

Powers and Properties of Magnitudes

Tensions in the Lodge, 1900–1920

> *"[I enjoy some] little lodge, where I meet the plain, hard-working men — the men who work with their hands — and meet them on a footing of genuine equality, not false equality, of genuine equality conditioned upon each being a decent man, a fair-dealing man."*

— THEODORE ROOSEVELT, 1905 [1]

BETWEEN 1900 AND 1920, traditional American beliefs came face to face with modern realities. The older generation had built the country through hard work, moral character and free enterprise. But the new century brought a younger generation that challenged its elders and remodeled the nation through technology and regulation. Freemasonry and other fraternal organizations experienced similar conflicts. Entrenched fraternal leaders struggled to maintain control and keep their fraternities politically neutral and isolated from change, while younger members challenged organizational missions and sought to reinterpret the tenets. The way Freemasonry and the nation reacted to the changing society deeply affected the course both would take in the future.

America in the early 1900s was a dichotomy. In the preceding century, the nation had expanded from the Atlantic seaboard to the Pacific and shifted from an agricultural economy to an urban society. Yet the majority of people remained east of the Mississippi and retained strong provincial values. Between 1865 and 1900, ten states joined the Union and the nation's population doubled. After 1912, no new states were admitted for 47 years, and after 1914, immigration was restricted. Even as the United States became an international power under Presidents William McKinley and Theodore Roosevelt, Americans remained deeply isolationist. They were suspicious of foreigners and demanded that President Woodrow Wilson

1459:—The Green Room, Masonic Temple, Spokane, Wash.

During his 1912 Bull Moose Party campaign for the presidency, Roosevelt visited the newly opened Masonic temple in Spokane, Washington. The postcard shows the lodge room where Roosevelt posed as a Worshipful Master. He was a member of Matinecock Lodge No. 806, Oyster Bay, New York, and helped lay the cornerstone of the north gate of Yellowstone Park in 1903.

Roosevelt, The Master Mason, J.L. Phelps, Spokane, WA, 1912. National Heritage Museum, 2000.059.10. The Green Room, Masonic temple, Spokane, WA, John W. Graham & Co., Spokane, ca. 1910. National Heritage Museum, A96/066/1172.

MASONIC OUTING

A Mason and two friends
hold pennants from a
picnic. King Oscar
Lodge No. 855, Chicago,
was chartered in 1898
and was named after the
then king of Sweden and
Norway.

*ca. 1916. National
Heritage Museum,
A96/066/0880.*

keep the country out of the war that was raging
in Europe. The Democratic Party maintained
control over the South and the Republican Party
over the North, but by 1912 the national elec-
torate had many more choices with the introduction of the Socialist, Progressive, Temperance and Bull Moose Parties.[2]

The tensions within American society were
also felt within the privacy of the Masonic lodge.
The fraternity's top echelon was comprised of
older men whose personal success provided not
only the resources to govern but also a commitment to the status quo. Younger men were eager to work and get ahead in the fraternity but
their opportunities were often limited.

In *Freemasonry and American Culture,* historian Lynn Dumenil contends that by 1910
Freemasonry had been infected with institutional
"goal displacement."[3] Masonic leaders were
maintaining their bureaucratic and hierarchical structures, rather than focusing on their
stated goal of "making good men better." Less emphasis was placed on
teaching the basic Masonic tenets as more attention was directed toward
receiving additional degrees. Few leaders realized that the "golden age of
fraternity" was waning, because Masonic membership had surpassed 1.5
million in 1915. Larger Masonic buildings were being constructed even
though attendance at lodge meetings was decreasing. The top stagnated
as the bottom grew frustrated.[4]

The confusion felt by many Freemasons caused some to reexamine
the craft's purpose. They began to question the need for perpetual re-
minders of self-improvement and the strict adherence to initiation rituals.
They sought cheaper ways to care for their families and more enjoyable
ways to spend their leisure time. Four of the major reasons why men had
joined fraternities were being challenged. As the older generation faded,
the new breed of Masons discovered new reasons to join by reinterpreting
Freemasonry's three tenets and redirecting the fraternity toward solving
society's pernicious problems. By entering the modern world, however,
they faced a greater challenge — how to shed what they perceived as archaic
ritual while retaining the fraternal spirit.

Superficial Self-improvement

"Geometry treats the powers and properties of magnitudes in general, where length, breadth, and thickness are considered — from a point to a line, from a line to a superfice, from a superfice to a solid."

— THOMAS SMITH WEBB, 1808[5]

Freemasonry has always viewed itself as an organization devoted to the self-improvement of its members. From its earliest days, men had joined for a variety of reasons, the most important of which was a desire to improve themselves. The beneficiaries were not only the individual Masons but also the community and society as a whole. But by 1910, the growing success of public schools and universities made Freemasonry's "ancient truths" seem truly ancient. Masonic lectures highlighting the seven liberal arts and sciences and the five classical orders of architecture paled in comparison to scientific discoveries, modern psychology and the inventions of Thomas Edison.

Changes in gender roles and the new progressive era also undermined Freemasonry's self-improvement mission. Men enjoyed greater affluence in new white-collar professions, as women began working in "pink-collar" jobs, such as secretaries, store clerks and telephone operators. Upper-class women assumed a greater role in community health and welfare. Progressive politicians, prohibitionists and suffragists all argued for stronger governmental regulations to improve society.[6] In the early 1900s, Americans moved away from self-improvement and toward community improvement. A man's character became less important than his personality, and "who he knew" became more important than "what he knew."

After dining at a friend's suburban Chicago home at the turn of the century, Paul Harris joined his friend on a stroll through the neighborhood visiting various shops. As the friend greeted each tradesman by name, the congenial business relationships reminded Harris of his Vermont hometown, and he asked himself:

> . . . why not in big Chicago have a fellowship composed of just one man from each of many different occupations, without restrictions as to their politics or religion, with broad tolerance of each other's opinion? In such a fellowship could there not be mutual helpfulness?[7]

In 1905, the young lawyer Harris acted upon the idea and invited three other businessmen to his office to form a new luncheon club. It was called the Rotary Club, because its meetings rotated among the offices of the initial members. By 1912 there were 4,500 members in 38 clubs across the

"R U A MASON?"
POSTCARD

In 1901, the comedy *Are You a Mason?* opened on Broadway and featured a young Cecil B. DeMille. In 1915, John Barrymore starred in the silent film version.

A Little Mason Wearing His First Pin, Ullman Mfg. Co., New York, 1908. National Heritage Museum, A96/066/0871.

country.[8] Six years later there were 40,000 Rotarians.[9] Harris had discovered a new way for a professional man to improve himself, his business and his community without disrupting his leisure time. The quest for truth became a quest for honesty and service.

Ritual Innovations

"The Compass, therefore, as the Symbol of the Heavens, represents the spiritual, intellectual, and moral portions of this double nature of Humanity; and the Square, as the Symbol of the Earth, its material, sensual, and baser portions."

— ALBERT PIKE, 1871[10]

Freemasonry's self-improvement mission went hand in hand with its dramatic ritual. Taught through the Biblical story of King Solomon's Temple, the craft's morals and tenets resonated with the piety of the Civil War generation. By 1900, however, the ritual genre was spent and the number of new fraternal orders declined.[11] The advent of grand pageants, professional vaudeville, opera and burlesque houses supplanted the quiet mystery of initiation ceremonies. More distressing was the advent of motion pictures. Each weekly adventure flashed another blow to ritual-based fraternities. For a nickel, anyone could be transported through light and shadow to exotic places and romantic adventures. The neighborhood butcher or banker who dressed up as Solomon or an Indian chief for ritual portrayals seemed positively quaint when compared with the likes of professional actors on the screen who provided new story lines every week.

But the movies also initiated a new generation into another fraternity that cursed America for decades. The 1915 release of D.W. Griffith's *Birth of a Nation* reignited the long-smoldering Ku Klux Klan. Within six years, the Klan's estimated membership was 100,000.[12] After World War I, the Klan grew across the South and deep into the North, feeding off a fear of Jews, Roman Catholics, communists and others whom they considered to be "un-American." Although its intention was to protect the interests of native-born white Protestants, the secret brotherhood lynched African-Americans, corrupted governments and terrorized entire communities.

Nowhere would the growing popularity of theaters and movies affect American fraternities more than the Scottish Rite of Freemasonry. Throughout most of the Gilded Age, it had remained the elite mystical branch of the craft. Its local lodges, called "valleys," existed only in larger cities. To receive the 29 degrees (4th–32nd) was expensive and time consuming.

Movie posters spread the popularity of D.W. Griffith's 1915 famous movie and the infamous organization it spawned.

National Heritage Museum.

The Rite's highest degree, the 33rd, was bestowed only upon those who merited it through exceptional service to the fraternity or humanity. In 1880, the Scottish Rite had fewer than 9,000 members, while the York Rite had more than 109,500 and Freemasonry's blue lodges surpassed 537,000 members.[13] But with America's growing love for theater, the Scottish Rite found itself suddenly popular. Its French aristocratic lineage

made it mysterious and romantic. The 29 allegorical initiations provided a wide range of dramatic settings and themes to explore. The Scottish Rite was also blessed with one of the most influential American Freemasons of the 19th century. But perhaps equally important, its elder leaders passed away just as the younger members began their theatrical revolution.

During the first half of the 19th century, the Scottish Rite remained an obscure branch of American Freemasonry. From the founding of the first Supreme Council in the South in 1801 and the Northern Jurisdiction in 1813 through the anti-Masonic period of the 1820s, the Rite experienced minimal growth. Concentrated mainly in New York, South Carolina and Louisiana, the Rite consisted of little more than a collection of 32 brief initiations that conferred secret signs, words and mysterious-sounding symbols and titles. After the hysteria of the anti-Masonic period, two important men arose to rebuild the Rite — one in the Northern Jurisdiction and one in the Southern Jurisdiction. In the North, Killian Henry Van Rensselaer (1800–81) helped John James Joseph Gourgas resuscitate the fortunes of the Supreme Council by traveling extensively to create new valleys. Between 1848–63, the membership grew to more than 4,000. Van Rensselaer later served as Sovereign Grand Commander in the 1860s and guided it through a bitter schism.[14]

The dominant personality in the Scottish Rite during this period was also the fraternity's foremost philosopher. Born in Boston in 1809, Albert Pike set off for New Mexico in 1830. Later moving to Arkansas, he taught school, published a newspaper, became a lawyer and served as a captain in the Mexican War. During the Civil War, Pike reluctantly served as a Confederate general and saw his financial success and reputation nearly destroyed. In his leisure he wrote prose, poetry and philosophy, learned several ancient and modern languages and became an active Freemason.[15]

The turning point for the Scottish Rite and for Pike occurred ironically during a York Rite convention. In 1853, Albert Pike met Dr. Albert Mackey, a well-known Masonic historian and the Secretary General of the Southern Jurisdiction of the Scottish Rite.[16] Impressed with Pike's intellect and energy, Mackey conferred upon him all 29 degrees and gave him the written rituals to study and revise. Pike infused the degrees with his deep understanding of ancient mysticism, Jewish and esoteric knowledge and European chivalric traditions.[17] By 1858, Pike's revisions were accepted by the Southern Jurisdiction, and he became a member of the governing board of the Supreme Council. One year later, he was elected the Southern Jurisdiction's Sovereign Grand Commander, an office he held for life.

Perhaps Albert Pike's greatest contribution to Freemasonry was his magnum opus, *Morals and Dogma of the Ancient and Accepted Scottish*

Rite of Freemasonry, published in 1871. Complex in its narrative and infused with the author's vast knowledge of languages, cultures and religious traditions, *Morals and Dogma* reconceptualized American Freemasonry. Pike found the Scottish Rite little more than a series of allegorical initiations. He left it as a system of understanding human existence and with a philosophy that urged men to seek harmony and unity with the universe.[18]

Pike heavily influenced both the Northern and Southern Scottish Rite Jurisdictions and most of American Freemasonry. He struggled to keep Scottish Rite highly selective. During the "golden age of fraternity," Southern Jurisdiction membership rose slowly. But as Albert Pike grew older, a grass roots movement formed in the Midwest. Rather than conferring the degrees in succession, valleys began to abbreviate them so that new members could progress quickly to the 32nd degree. Pike detested this practice but was unable to stop it.[19]

With his death in 1891, a younger generation pushed their reforms further. Rather than conducting each degree upon a single initiate as Pike intended, they performed them as allegorical dramas in front of large groups of Masons. This practice was first developed in Cincinnati but was demonstrated with full effect in Chicago when the new Masonic building opened in 1893.[20]

The innovation spread to Arkansas, Kansas and Oklahoma and then throughout the country. The three Masons credited with this ritualistic revolution were Joseph S. Sosman, Charles E. Rosenbaum and Bestor G.

SCOTTISH RITE
FREEMASONS

This photograph from Little Rock, Arkansas, shows one of the first "casts" for the presentation of a Scottish Rite Masonic degree as a theatrical performance.

1899. Courtesy of the Archives of the Supreme Council, 33°, Southern Jurisdiction, Washington, DC.

Brown. Sosman, a partner in a theatrical scenery painting company, worked on the sets for the Chicago degrees. Adding to Sosman's scenery, Rosenbaum adapted Pike's degrees for theatrical presentation. Together they staged the dramatic degrees with great success in Arkansas. Membership in the Valley of Little Rock more than doubled between 1895 and 1899. In Wichita, Bestor Brown directed Rosenbaum's plays using Sosman's backdrops. Brown, a salesman for the M.C. Lilley Regalia Company, added the necessary costumes and props from his company.[21]

The dramatic degrees were so successful that Brown induced the Scottish Rite Masons of Guthrie, Oklahoma, to build a new Masonic temple with a fully equipped auditorium. At the grand opening in 1900, it boasted "$10,000 worth of robes, vestments and paraphernalia, and magnificent scenery for a stage 50 feet wide and 25 feet high."[22] Scottish Rite membership in Guthrie skyrocketed, and soon valleys throughout the country were purchasing backdrops from Sosman, scripts from Rosenbaum, and costumes and props from regalia companies.

By 1901, the presentation of Scottish Rite degrees had shifted by design, if not by default, from the lodge room floor to an auditorium stage.[23] This change had an immediate impact on Scottish Rite membership. In the Southern Jurisdiction, membership rose by 181,661 between 1900 and 1920, while in the Northern Jurisdiction, membership expanded from 26,858 to 179,410 between 1900 and 1920.[24] The Scottish Rite was no longer the "academy of the fraternity" but the "theater of the fraternity."

Expanding Mutual Benefits

"The embodiment of courage and strength, a source of inspiration to all the nobler qualities of life, the antlers of the moose are ever borne in defense of Purity, Aid and Progress."

— MOOSE INITIATION RITUAL, CA. 1915[25]

America's growing disinterest in moral self-improvement and the fading allure of ritual-centric organizations led "mutual benefit" fraternal associations to reexamine their services and social mission. Although they firmly believed in fraternal principles and the brotherly love created in the lodge, mutual benefit leaders were businessmen with a fiduciary duty. During the early decades of the 20th century, several internal and external pressures gave them an opportunity to cut costs, consolidate their services and completely retool their fraternities. Freemasonry was not affected as much by these new societal forces. Grand lodges continued to build and maintain

1001   MASONIC HOME FORT WORTH, TEXAS.

TEXAS MASONIC HOME

Begun with a donation
of 200 acres and $5,000
by Fort Worth Lodge
No. 148 in 1897, the
Home cared for widows
and orphans of Texas
Masons. In 1911, widows
moved into their own
Home in Arlington.
Since 1899, more than
1,100 children have
graduated from the
home.

*Masonic Home, Fort
Worth, TX, distributed
by S.H. Kresse Co., New
York, ca. 1907. National
Heritage Museum,
A96/066/pub20.*

their Homes for older Masons and orphans, but they generally resisted the temptation to become an insurance company.[26]

The first revision of mutual benefit fraternities was the initiation ritual. The cost for outfitting a lodge and securing a meeting hall kept insurance premiums high and created an obstacle for membership growth. Roman Catholics and other immigrants, like Greeks and Ukrainians, were often uncomfortable with involvement in any perceived "secret society" that did not fall under the authority of Church officials. Responding to these concerns, ethnic fraternities defended their communities against continued attacks from Protestant nativists. By 1915, the Jewish Anti-Defamation League had been initiated by B'nai B'rith and the Sons of Italy were founded in part to protect Italian immigrant communities.[27]

Mutual benefit orders also suffered attacks from the insurance and medical sectors. In 1886, the National Fraternal Congress (NFC) was founded as a forum to discuss management and mortuary rates. The NFC was soon pulled into politics as commercial life insurance corporations grew and federal and state governments began to regulate the industry. The NFC lobbied legislators to protect the welfare of mutual benefit organizations.[28]

The American Medical Association also challenged the fraternal system of retaining lodge doctors. In the late 1800s, "lodge practices" benefited both the doctors and the lodge members. The doctors gained patients and received fixed wages based on the number of members in the lodge. Each member was guaranteed the care and expertise of a physician for the price of his membership and annual dues. Some doctors, however, were concerned

that this approach was under-selling their skills and enslaving the profession. Between 1910 and 1920, many mutual benefit organizations evolved into insurance companies, and the lodge medical practice disappeared.[29]

As the older mutual benefit fraternities responded increasingly to pressure from the outside world, one man — an immigrant, ironworker, union member and Freemason — took charge of a dying social club and built it into one of the most well-known fraternities of the new century. James J. Davis, born in Wales in 1873, immigrated to western Pennsylvania with his family. Young Jim soon learned the highly skilled craft of an iron puddler and joined a union in 1893. By 1906, he had moved to Elwood City, Indiana, where he became a Freemason in Quincy Lodge No. 23. On his 33rd birthday, he was enrolled as the 247th member of the failing Loyal Order of Moose.[30]

Upon Davis' initiation, he was appointed Supreme Organizer of the Moose and was hired to recruit new members. For every new member he recruited, he received a portion of the dues. By offering membership and mutual benefits at cheap rates, he increased the number of lodges from two to 333, and the membership jumped from 247 to more than 80,000 — all within four years. By 1912, there were nearly 500,000 members in more than 1,000 lodges. Davis was appointed Director General. He also encouraged a women's auxiliary, which received official recognition in 1913.[31]

Davis' greatest innovation came when he decided to build an independent community for the needy children of Moose members. Founded in Illinois in 1912, Mooseheart was built on 1,000 acres of farmland along the Fox River. The town included its own post office, fire department, electrical power plant and 100 other buildings. "The School that Trains for Life" provided more than just subsistence and basic education. Children worked on a farm, or in machine, wood or printing shops, and took a number of other vocational, administrative and technical courses. Starting with eleven children, the village grew to 1,000 children by 1920 and peaked at 1,300 during the Great Depression.[32] Not satisfied with taking care of the young, Davis created Moosehaven in Jacksonville, Florida, for older members. "The City of Contentment" covered 63 acres and cared for 400 residents.[33]

His success did not go unnoticed. President Warren G. Harding appointed Davis in 1921 as the Secretary of Labor, a position he continued to hold under President Calvin Coolidge until 1928. Davis also remained active in Freemasonry. He was a member of Pittsburgh's Syria Shrine, the Scottish Rite and the Tall Cedars of Lebanon. He was selected to receive the 33rd degree in 1929. After selling out his interest in the Moose in 1930

MOOSEHEART, THE SCHOOL THAT TRAINS FOR LIFE.

MOOSEHEART PRINTING CLASS.

MOOSEHEART, ILLINOIS

Spread across 1,000 acres along Illinois' Fox River, the "Child City" has its own homes, schools, industrial arts shops, recreational fields, farm, health care center, post office, and house of worship. Shown here is where Mooseheart's newspaper was printed.

Mooseheart, The School that Trains for Life, ca. 1925. National Heritage Museum, gift of the Loyal Order of Moose, A2002/52/1.

for $600,000, Davis was elected U.S. Senator from Pennsylvania. While serving as senator between 1930 and 1944, he often returned to Mooseheart for graduations and other events. In 1947, Davis collapsed while addressing a Moose convention and died three months later.[34]

The Changing Role of Social Life

"Behrman: 'Yes, marriage changes a man wonderfully.'
Willis: 'Why?'
Behrman: 'Before I was married a glance from Annie would intoxicate me, and now when I get home late from the lodge the look she gives actually sobers me.'"

— THE LODGE GOAT AND GOAT RIDES, 1907 [35]

Despite the turmoil brought about by political, economic and social changes of the new century, Americans still enjoyed life. Indeed, many people escaped their cares through play, and the fraternal lodge hall became a safe place to have fun. As a result of financial realities and the devaluation of self-improvement lectures and secret rituals, fraternal social life became the focal point of all other lodge activities. While Freemasons held fairs and banquets to finance their increasingly ornate temples, the Odd Fellows used similar events to pay for orphanages and homes. In rural areas, the

Although not part of
the ritualistic ceremony,
some fraternal groups
offered unsuspecting
new brothers an oppor-
tunity to ride blind-
folded on a mechanical
goat. Freemasonry and
other fraternities con-
demned this and other
types of hazing, yet for
a period of time these
spontaneous pranks
existed and the expres-
sion "riding the goat"
has persisted.

*DeMoulin Bro. & Co.,
Greenville, IL, ca. 1905.
National Heritage
Museum, 96.048.
Freemasonry – Oh,
What a Time!, W. S.
Heal, ca. 1914. National
Heritage Museum,
A96/066/0839.*

Grange held picnics and agricultural fairs; in city neighborhoods, the
Knights of Pythias and others took train excursions to parks and the country-
side. Insurance and ethnic fraternities held dances and festivals to attract
new members and foster ethnic pride. Upper-class men joined the Shrine
and other social clubs for trips to resorts and conventions.[36]

A product of the renewed desire for fun was the proliferation of un-
official "side degrees" or hazing ceremonies. The Shrine's popularity and
competition for members' free time also encouraged practical jokes. Long
a part of American fraternal life, it took on vaudevillian and scientific cruelty between 1890 and 1930. The most popular trick among some groups
was to blindfold a new member and make him ride a mechanical goat. Such
escapades were refreshingly spontaneous compared to the plodding pre-
dictability of official rituals. Despite the continual condemnation of hazing
by nearly all fraternal leaders, the practice became widespread. By the turn
of the century, regalia manufacturing companies were offering collapsible
chairs, water pistols and slapstick paddles.[37]

With all the hilarity and hijinks going on, it was not long before women's
auxiliaries joined in the fun. Wives of Shriners in Wheeling, West Virginia,
formed the Ladies of the Oriental Shrine in 1903, and Shriners' wives in
Seattle created the Daughters of the Nile in 1913. Similarly, wives of Prince
Hall Shriners began the Daughters of Isis in 1910. The Prophets of the

Grotto accepted the Daughters of Mokanna in 1919, and with the Daughters came, what must be acknowledged as the most powerful of all fraternal titles, the "Supreme Mighty Chosen One."[38]

The diversification of American fraternal orders at the turn of the 20th century reveals an inherent weakness in Freemasonry and all voluntary associations. People who chose to join them could also choose to quit. Like George Washington and Benjamin Franklin, ambitious people stay in organizations only if it satisfies both their altruistic impulse and desire for prestige. The golden age of fraternities occurred partly out of necessity of the times and partly from novelty of the rituals. As new organizations catered to specific markets, Freemasonry lost the monopoly it had held 100 years before. By 1912, there were many reasons for men to join the craft, but only its upper-class reputation and social activities seemed relevant.

Freemasonry and the World

"The Form of a Lodge Is oblong. In length from east to west, in breadth between north and south, as high as heaven and as deep as from the surface to the centre. A Lodge is said to be thus extensive to denote the universality of Freemasonry, and teaches that a Mason's Charity should be equally extensive."

— MASONIC LECTURE, 1899[39]

Masonic leaders remained largely oblivious to the societal forces building within the fraternity and reshaping the larger world. Membership continued

The Masonic Temple, (Colored),
4th Ave. and 17th St.,
Birmingham, Ala.—42

SOUVENIR FROM BIRMINGHAM, ALA.

to rise, as new lodges were chartered and bigger temples were erected. The York Rite, Scottish Rite and Shrine remained the pinnacles of American community organizations. But within the lodges, institutional and historical legacies were being tested. Should the lodge remain a quiet refuge from the world or become an active agent in the world? Was being a Freemason the highest honor or was the third degree only a means to something greater? The answers to these questions came not through studying the tenets or speculating on Masonic symbols but by reacting to the realities of the outside world. Of the forces that broke these tensions, one was domestic and the other foreign. One was fought in courtrooms and the other fought in trenches.

The relationship between white and black American fraternal orders in the 1800s reflected the nation's own segregation. With the new century came a new black resistance to racism and white attacks on black fraternities. During these battles African-American Masons answered the call of their communities. Ever since the founding of Prince Hall Freemasonry in the late 1700s, African-Americans had continued to create "separate but equal" fraternal Orders. In the 1840s, Peter Ogden began the Grand United Order of Odd Fellows, and by 1910, there were parallel white and black Knights of Pythias, Woodmen, Elks and Moose. Prince Hall Masonry grew alongside their white brethren by developing their own Eastern Star, York Rite, Scottish Rite and Shrine.[40]

The popularity of these parallel orders coupled with uniquely national black fraternities, such as the Order of St. Luke or Knights of Tabor, brought about

MASONIC TEMPLE POSTCARDS, BIRMINGHAM, ALABAMA

At the top is the Masonic temple for the Prince Hall Grand Lodge of Alabama. Below is Birmingham's Masonic temple for white Masons.

Prince Hall Masonic building, Birmingham, AL, E. C. Kropp Co., Milwaukee, WI, ca. 1925. National Heritage Museum, A96/066/461. Masonic temple, Birmingham, AL, Adolph Selige Publishing Co., St. Louis, MO, ca. 1907. National Heritage Museum, A96/066/BL7.

Building Freemasonry and American Community

the resentment and hatred of their white counterparts. Between 1905 and 1929, some white fraternal leaders orchestrated civil and criminal court attacks, especially in the South, aimed at destroying the black organizations. Fighting in local, state and federal courts — even in the U.S. Supreme Court — African-American lawyers relied on national membership resources to sustain them through long legal battles.[41] Ultimate victory came to them by way of arguments that insisted that their white counterparts had failed to take legal action during their first years of operation, thus demonstrating the common law doctrine of laches, whereby the consent of a party is implied by its inaction.[42]

The legal challenges to black fraternal orders brought a renewed determination within the African-American community to fight for all their civil rights. The 1903 publication of W.E.B. Dubois' *The Souls of Black Folks* challenged old fraternal tenets of self-reliance and Christian piety. The establishment of the National Association for the Advancement of Colored People (NAACP) in 1909 and the Urban League in 1910 further directed African-Americans toward direct legal and public confrontation of institutionalized racism. Hearing the needs outside their lodge doors, Prince Hall Freemasons and other fraternal leaders joined the fight. The tactics and strategies learned in their fraternal court cases were used to win future civil rights cases, and many NAACP lawyers, directors and activists were also proud Freemasons.[43] In 1914 John H. Murphy, Imperial Potentate of the Prince Hall Shriners, declared:

> Segregation has now been added to disenfranchisement and Jim Crow laws. . . . I cannot refrain from calling your attention to the splendid work being done by the NAACP. . . . We must give of our strength and our means, and thus encourage them in their fight for us and common humanity.[44]

Black fraternal organizations continued this mission even as their membership declined and their rituals emphasizing self-improvement were forgotten.

The second force that invaded American Masonic lodges came in April 1917, when the United States was pulled into the war against Germany and the Central Powers. Within 18 months, more than 4.8 million Americans were mobilized, and two million were sent "over there." Col. Charles E. Stanton, a member of General Pershing's staff, arrived in France and declared, "Lafayette, we are here!" Between the first American combat deaths on November 3, 1917, and Armistice Day on November 11, 1918, more than 53,513 Americans were killed.[45]

American voluntary associations did their part in the war effort. Following the lead of the Red Cross, the Young Men's Christian Association cre-

IMPERIAL POTENTATE

Between 1919 and 1931, Caesar L. Blake of Charlotte, North Carolina, served as Imperial Potentate of the Ancient Egyptian Shrine. He guided it through numerous crises and ultimately died in office.

Caesar R. Blake, Carolina Studio, Charlotte, NC, ca. 1940. National Heritage Museum, 99.044.1.

WORLD WAR I
"MASONIC TRENCH ART"

Since its earliest days, many Masons in military service have decorated their arms and equipment with Masonic symbols. This artillery shell casing was made in France in 1919 and is marked "Merriman to Caroline Harris."

1919. National Heritage Museum, 91.015.

ated clubs and canteens for soldiers. The Knights of Columbus responded with equal vigor and within 16 months of America's involvement had nearly 150 clubs for servicemen in Europe.[46] Other organizations serving overseas included the Jewish Relief Board, Salvation Army, American Library Association and Young Women's Christian Association. Even the fledgling Rotary Club received high praise for its service.[47]

Conspicuously absent from the honor roll of organizations was American Freemasonry, even as General John Pershing (a Freemason) led the American Expeditionary force and Corporal James D. Heriot (also a Freemason) earned the Medal of Honor.[48] Although local lodges and state grand lodges looked after individual brethren in the service, the fraternity's institutional structure and historical legacies prevented it from coordinating relief. Freemasonry remained divided into 49 grand lodges (48 states and the District of Columbia). The U.S. War Department preferred to deal with national organizations and simply refused to allow such a disjointed organization to work overseas.[49]

Frustrated by the government, envious of the Knights of Columbus and reacting to the pleas of military brothers, Iowa Grand Master George L. Schoonover called a Masonic convention in Cedar Rapids two weeks after the end of the war.[50] With representatives from 22 grand lodges present, the Masonic Service Association (MSA) was created. Its purpose was to provide "the Service of Mankind through education, enlightenment, financial relief and Masonic visitation, particularly in times of disaster and distress . . ."[51] Every American grand lodge was invited to join, and funding for the MSA came through voluntary grand lodge contributions.[52] The MSA was not universally accepted; several grand lodges withdrew their support, and many remained suspicious of the MSA. To alleviate fears of a "national grand lodge" that might usurp the authority of state grand lodges, MSA membership remained voluntary, and resolutions were passed to preclude the formation of such a body.[53]

Between the end of the Great War and 1920, the tensions between the traditional and modern world finally snapped. The war destroyed the old European aristocracies and with them the ideals of chivalry. Communists, nationalists, and democrats all fought to fill the void. The influenza pandemic of 1918-19 was devastating. More Europeans were killed by influenza than were killed by the war, and nearly 675,000 Americans died from the disease. President Wilson's dream of international cooperation and security dissolved as troubles erupted at home. Embittered steelworkers staged major strikes in 1919. Race riots occurred in the North, while membership in the Klan continued to rise across the nation. Women were given the right to vote, and prohibition of alcohol became constitutional law. Immi-

Officers of Overseas Lodge No. 40 F&AM
Class of May 1923.

gration was nearly cut off through fear of communists, and the "Red Scare" threatened citizens' civil rights. Even the national pastime was damaged by the 1919 Chicago "Black Sox" World Series bribery scandal.[54] Heralding the coming new age, the bands at the 1920 Republican convention "played a song called *Mr. Zip Zip Zip* instead of *John Brown's Body.* The last veterans of the Civil War shuffled offstage; their successors — the veterans of the Great War — wanted to forget their own experience in a hurry."[55]

Freemasonry also felt the impact of the unleashed forces. Between 1917 and 1920, membership increased by more than 386,000 and for the first time surpassed two million.[56] Freemasonry's future rested with men who had little respect for their fathers' history and great expectations for the future. Through their labors, the craft would be pulled into the modern world and become one of America's major charitable and social organizations. In this process, however, the fraternity would lose its preeminence and social prestige to Rotary and to organizations for women and children.

PART THREE

Adorning American Communities

1920–2000

CHAPTER 9

Plain Dealing

The Rotarian Age and Freemasonry's New Personality, 1920–1941

"[America's clubs and lodges] are a revelation, not a puzzle. Through their mysteries and ceremonies we progress literally by degrees to an understanding of the motives that lay hold upon men in group behavior. . . . We may observe the alignment of men one by one, but we must not lose sight of the fact that, taken together, they make the mass, the flesh and blood of a nation."

— CHARLES W. FERGUSON, 1937[1]

A S PRESIDENT WARREN HARDING moved into the White House in 1921, the nation was entering the Roaring Twenties. These few fast years unleashed new forces that shaped America's future. The automobile brought a new freedom to average citizens and made the world run on oil. The radio and the phonograph brought jazz and country music into every home. "Talking" motion pictures became a popular alternative to the drama and comedy of the stage. The advent of airlines, highways, supermarkets and radio networks transformed the United States into a more international, commercial and secular nation. The 1920s also had an impact on Freemasonry. The fraternity that had been the most prominent fraternal and civic group was becoming over-shadowed by more streamlined and task-oriented organizations.

Of all the many changes during the Jazz Age, perhaps three had the greatest impact on the United States and Freemasonry. First, the American economy moved decisively from heavy industry to the manufacturing of consumer goods. The growing middle-class purchased furniture and appliances to fill their new homes. Through the power of mass advertising, national brand-name products began eliminating regional companies and markets. Corporations like Coca-Cola and General Motors joined U.S. Steel and Union Pacific among Wall Street's blue chip stocks.

Second, the family structure changed as women earned the right to vote and more children attended high school and college before work and marriage. With jazz music, young Americans became enraptured with a new style of dancing, fashion and slang. Prohibition only enhanced the romance of drinking and flaunting authority. The new popular culture focused on youth, often at the expense of adults and tradition.

Third, the domination of big business — and later big government and labor — changed the way Americans earned their living and cared for their families. Centralized planning, mass production and worldwide distribution

As more men participated in Freemasonry and attended state and national conventions, they received appreciation gifts and souvenirs. Shown here are some popular examples. Those attending the Shrine Imperial convention in San Francisco in 1932 received an aluminum emblem to display on the bumper of their cars. Masonic watch fobs became popular items in the 1800s and let men advertise their membership in the Knights Templar by displaying a diamond and ruby cross and crown. A popular Masonic gift in the 1920s was a watch. This Swiss-made watch has various Masonic symbols for each hour. In the center are the words, "Love your Fellow Man, Lend him a Helping Hand." By the 1920s, Victorian whiskers were out of fashion and men were expected to be clean-shaven. The stainless steel shaving kit contains a razor and blade box with the Masonic emblem on the front.

Auto emblem, Frank C. Kubeck, San Francisco, CA., 1932. National Heritage Museum, gift of Marjorie B. Healey, 2001.069a-b. Watch fob, 1906, National Heritage Museum, gift of Mabel H. Quick, 76.44. Pocket watch, ca. 1920. National Heritage Museum, gift of Mrs. Willis R. Michael, 75.66.3a-c. Shaving kit, Gillette, ca. 1925. National Heritage Museum, gift of Richard W. Parker, 2001.072a-g.

convinced generations of Americans that any problem could be solved with the right regulations and sufficient resources. Where once Americans fiercely competed to lay claim to the most land or build the largest cities, 20th-century Americans — enticed by aggressive mass marketing — developed an obsession to acquire material goods.[2]

Freemasons struggled to keep up with the increased pace of life. In a time when marketing and personality began to mean everything, Freemasonry's once stellar "brand" suffered because of its emphasis on secrecy and an entrenched and sometimes stodgy leadership. In an age of flappers, jazz and speakeasies, younger men were less attracted to the fraternity's ancient mythology and Enlightenment ethos. The colonial legacy of state-based grand lodge sovereignty prevented any attempt to successfully focus the craft's resources in one direction. Despite the best of intentions, American society became increasingly distant from Freemasonry.

The fraternity, whose members did so much to help establish the United States in the 1700s and build it in the 1800s, found itself relegated to a peripheral role by the end of the 1900s. The thousands of local lodges, with their millions of members and the hundreds of millions of dollars devoted to charity, could not prevent the public image of Freemasonry from appearing to be that of an odd, perhaps sinister, but more likely eccentric and silly club for older men. By 2000, most Americans had little knowledge of Freemasonry, and some considered it nothing more than a quaint family tradition. The fraternity seemed to fade into the background of a rushing and ever-changing world.

City Hall, Masonic Temple and Congregational Church, Norwich, Conn.

"The tenets of your profession as a Mason are Brotherly Love, Relief and Truth."

— AMERICAN MASONIC LECTURE, 1920[3]

This part of the book shows how American Freemasons adapted to the changes wrought since the 1920s as the fraternity struggled to keep up with new voluntary associations. There are many reasons why men joined Freemasonry in the 20th century, but three became particularly important — business and professional networking (Chapter 9), family tradition and youth organizations (Chapter 10), and community service and charitable activities (Chapter 11). As a result, Freemasons reinterpreted their tenets to follow other organizations and to conform to the modern world. The tenet of "truth" was modified to mean honest business, professional dealings and improving one's personality and social networks. The youth culture and Jazz Age expanded "brotherly love" to include members of the entire family. Masonic "relief" turned toward hospitals and foundations to address community health and welfare problems.

ROTARIAN BADGE

While Freemasons and Odd Fellows wore aprons to distinguish themselves and members of ethnic orders wore brightly colored ribbons and sashes, Rotarians had adopted nametags by the 1920s.

Adcraft Mfg. Co., Chicago, ca. 1930. National Heritage Museum, 2001.058.

The Rotarian Age

"But how dwarfed the soul of those who recognize no virtue save within the membership of their own little group or sect. They still live in the atmosphere of the Middle Ages. They know nothing of the problems of this world because they are not of this world. Their heroes are of the dead past. They sequester themselves lest they become contaminated. Contributing nothing, they gain nothing; theirs only to criticize those who work."

— PAUL HARRIS, 1935[4]

After World War I, a new economy based on consumption steadily transformed American society. The establishment and growth of a middle class from the Gilded Age encouraged industry to shift from producing raw materials to manufacturing consumer goods. Economists of the 1920s considered the economic depressions of the Gilded Age as things of the past, for the stock market boom promised perpetual prosperity. As President Calvin Coolidge put it, "The business of America is business."[5]

Driving the American consumer economy was a new business persona. The old work ethics of patience and character were replaced by pep and personality. Salesmen had to be enthusiastically modern, and their products equally so. Everything tried and true was out, and everything new and improved was in. Through mass advertising, salesmanship became the means to create lifestyles and shape popular culture. Suddenly

Adorning American Communities

Americans were lulled into thinking that they could acquire success and happiness by simply buying the right automobile, radio, clothes and even soap. The ad-men joined the loan officers and movie directors as the makers of the American dream.[6]

Luncheon clubs for businessmen were perfectly positioned to meet the demands of the new economy. Paul Harris understood this when he organized the first Rotary club in 1905. His idea spread so rapidly that by 1917, there were 356 clubs. Within three years, the number of clubs more than doubled (758), and the membership increased by 17,000.[7] Similar businessmen's clubs soon followed. In 1914, Allen Brown, a Moose lodge organizer, began the Kiwanis in Detroit to provide for the exchange of business connections between members. Kiwanis was believed to have derived its name from an Indian word for "we trade" or "we share our talents." Melvin Jones, a Freemason, founded the Lions in 1917 by organizing a number of independent commercial clubs in Chicago. Inspired by Rotary and Kiwanis, the Lions chose the motto "to serve most and to serve best." Smaller clubs, such as the Optimists, Jaycees and women's clubs, such as Zonta or Soroptimists, mushroomed in big cities and small towns in the 1920s.[8] By the end of the decade the three largest and most well-known clubs — Rotary, Kiwanis and Lions — together claimed more than 400,000 members and 7,000 clubs.[9]

The success of Rotary came about through Paul Harris' perceptive and shrewd understanding for the potential for voluntary associations in America. Rotary found its niche by differing from fraternal lodges in several ways. Rather than meeting in the evenings in specially built lodge halls, the new clubs met for lunch at noon in local restaurants or hotel dining rooms. Rotarians dispensed with grandiose fraternal titles and simply called each other by first names or nicknames. Furthermore, they did not wear aprons or fraternal hats but rather the uniform of a businessman or professional — a three-piece suit adorned with a lapel pin. Rather than concentrating on ancient rituals and ceremonies, club meetings consisted of songs, jokes, and a presentation addressing important issues or events of the day. Unlike the Masonic lodge, attendance was required and those who missed a meeting paid small fines toward a charity fund.[10]

In 1910, the first Canadian Rotary club opened, and by 1912, ten clubs

SONGS of KIWANIS

"WE BUILD"

THE OFFICIAL SONG BOOK of THE INTERNATIONAL ORGANIZATION OF KIWANIS CLUBS

KIWANIANS SING

Kiwanis, like most other business clubs, usually met in large restaurants for lunch. After the meal, they listened to an informative talk, conducted a business meeting and sang songs.

Songs of Kiwanis, compiled and edited by Charles A. Gage, Chicago, 1924. National Heritage Museum.

were operating in England. Paul Harris' small-town club became Rotary International, and Kiwanis and Lions soon followed the Rotarians' lead by spreading to other parts of the world. Rotary's Chicago headquarters coordinated all its resources to address national and even international issues, as its annual convention moved from country to country. Rotary's internationalism, however, meant more than an opportunity to travel. It encouraged a greater understanding between cultures, religions and politics.[11] The appearance of Rotarians in South America, Africa and Asia in the 1920s heralded the globalization of American culture.

Lastly, Rotary did something that no fraternity had previously done and no fraternity was willing to do. It restricted its membership by class and profession. Furthermore, by holding its weekly meetings at a luncheon, it limited the number of wage-earning workers who could attend.[12] This type of class and occupational discrimination guaranteed a level of exclusivity that Freemasonry could no longer claim. So it seemed that by the mid-1920s: "The man who goes weekly to Rotary will confess he gets around to the Masons 'only two or three times a year.'"[13]

Masonic Professional Networks

". . . while influenced by this principle [of Truth], hypocrisy and deceit are unknown among us; sincerity and plain dealing are our distinguishing characteristics, and the heart and tongue join in promoting each other's welfare and rejoicing in each other's prosperity."

— WILLIAM PRESTON, 1775[14]

Rotary's growing popularity before the Great War dovetailed with Freemasonry's huge influx of new members after the war and the "golden age of fraternity" begot "a nation of joiners."[15] This new half-Mason-half-Rotarian generation, however, reinterpreted Freemasonry's purpose. No longer was the tenet of "truth" considered a personal calling to greater spirituality and moral or intellectual enlightenment. In the 1920s truth became an outward expression of fair dealing, honest negotiation and mutual profit.

From its earliest days in London, Freemasonry had always provided opportunities for its brethren to come in contact with each other in ways that were conducive to trade. It was no coincidence that the craft flourished within the European mercantile empires of the 18th century. Many local artisans and businessmen joined a lodge hoping to find a ready clientele. Local tavern owners hosted lodge meetings, and milliners sold Masonic

Adorning American Communities

Bark Lincoln, W. H. Polleys Master Laying at anchor in Smyrna July 4th, 1853.

aprons. In London, Laurence Dermott sold them wine; William Preston sold them Masonic books.

The commercial benefits of the fraternity were perhaps even greater in America — a land with more than its fair share of dreamers and speculators looking for a pot of gold and a partner to share the risk. Benjamin Franklin's membership helped him to gain access to and move among Philadelphia's elite. Just as Franklin was able to print and sell the first Masonic book in America, Paul Revere was able to sell his silver work to lodges. Throughout the 1700s and much of the 1800s, Masonic membership became an important point of introduction between strangers and merchants entering a new town or market. Acceptance into a Masonic lodge heightened a man's reputation and was strong proof of his trustworthiness. In a time when business was often sealed by a handshake and a word, a Mason's obligations to live honestly and deal fairly were respected.[16] Out on the frontier, Masonic lodges provided a sense of stability and a welcome rest for traveling men. Freemasons were expected to "meet on the level, act by the plumb and part on the square."

FLYING A MASONIC FLAG

On sailing vessels, captains often flew a Masonic flag when entering port. This was an invitation for Masons in the port to come aboard for an informal Masonic meeting, hear the latest news and possibly trade.

Bark Lincoln in Smyrna, July 4, 1853, Raphaele Corsini, Smyrna, Turkey, 1853. National Heritage Museum, 85.9.

Following the lead of other business organizations, Freemasons began social and professional groups, which were often called "Square and Compass Clubs." Meeting in restaurants or office buildings at lunchtime, these clubs allowed Freemasons to interact across professional and geographical lines.

Masons in front of Prince Hall Square Clubhouse, 115 West 131st Street, Harlem, April, 1933. Harry A. Williamson Photograph Collection, Photographs and Prints Division, Schomburg Center for Research in Black Culture, The New York Public Library, Astor, Lenox, and Tilden Foundations.

As commerce expanded after the Civil War and Freemasonry affirmed its place as the leading fraternal order, enterprising men began to exploit the fraternity's good name. Since the 1700s, Freemasons were taught that "the internal, not the external, qualifications of a man are what Masonry regards."[17] Throughout the 1800s, Masons disdained the open pursuit of crass commercial advantages within the lodge, yet some brothers used Masonic emblems on business cards, and one company even attempted to use them to sell flour.[18] Although one grand lodge officially banned emblems on cards and successfully sued the flour manufacturing company, individual initiatives could not be stopped. The small lodge supply companies of the 1850s grew into a multi-million-dollar fraternal regalia industry by 1900.[19] Joseph Cerneau and his followers sold Scottish Rite degrees to anyone able and willing to pay for them, spawning an entire breed of traveling degree-peddling hucksters. African-American entrepreneurs created dozens of clandestine Masonic grand lodges for black men that competed with Prince Hall Freemasonry. Even as white fraternal leaders attempted to stop African-American lodges, Prince Hall grand lodges were unsuccessful in curtailing spurious black groups.[20]

Before Paul Harris' first Rotary club, urban Freemasons were meeting each other in restaurants and clubs; indeed, the Shriners started in such a club. These casual groups of Masons allowed tradesmen and professionals to socialize outside the formality and ceremony of the lodge. Over time, some groups acquired the name "Square and Compass Clubs," referring directly to the Masonic working tool and indirectly to the popular phrase "a square deal." Men who lived in surrounding suburbs and were members of different lodges met weekly at a downtown or neighborhood square club meeting. In 1905, New York square clubs organized into a state body, and in 1922, the National League of Masonic Clubs was incorporated.[21]

By the late 1920s, lodge membership virtually was a prerequisite for a middle management position for some employers. Success in reciting the ritual was perceived as a sign of intelligence, poise and dedication. Serving as a Master of a lodge gave men valuable managerial experience. Employees within a corporation formed initiation degree teams that traveled to various lodges to initiate their fellow employees into the fraternity. This allowed men who worked together but lived in different suburbs to spend the evening together as co-workers and brothers. Sharing the Masonic experience developed teamwork among executives and greater loyalty to both the corporation and the craft.[22]

Seeing the success of the luncheon clubs within the Rotary, Kiwanis, Lions and similar clubs, E.C. Wolcott (1881-1975) organized a High Twelve Club in 1921 in Sioux City, Iowa. "High Twelve" is the Masonic term for noon, the time of day when the Masonic ritual indicated that the stonemasons who worked on King Solomon's Temple suspended their labors for refreshment and instruction. High Twelve adopted the motto, "To reflect upon the truth; to talk little; to hear much." Many business clubs restricted membership by profession, but Wolcott, a Congregational pastor and insurance executive, limited High Twelve membership to Freemasons. The idea spread rapidly by working through the established network of Masonic lodges. When the clubs expanded into Canada, the organization followed the lead of Rotary by changing its name to High Twelve International. Despite the Great Depression, High Twelve continued to grow, reaching more than 25 clubs by 1939 and 223 clubs by 1959.[23]

The Roaring Twenties created a new archetype for the American character — the booster. In his 1922 novel *Babbitt,* Sinclair Lewis created the icon of the congenial backslap. The protagonist, George F. Babbitt — a good Rotarian, Elk and Freemason — came to represent every small-time businessman who supported community and moral activities outwardly but inwardly remained a selfish hypocrite. "Babbittry" defined the worst of American materialism, conformity, and provincialism.[24] Despite such ridicule by Lewis and others, the growing middle class knew instinctively something that their intellectual detractors did not. Corporate enterprise, salesmanship and consumerism were indeed the means to prosperity at home and power abroad.[25] In 1935, Paul Harris unabashedly co-opted G.K. Chesterton's criticism by titling the history of his club, *This Rotarian Age.*[26]

Prosperity and Patriotism

"The beehive is an emblem of industry, and recommends the practice of that virtue to all created beings . . . Thus was man formed for social and active life, the noblest part of the work of God; and he that demeans himself as not to be endeavoring to add to the common stock of knowledge and understanding, may be deemed a drone in the hive of nature, a useless member of society, and unworthy of our protection as Masons."

— THOMAS SMITH WEBB, 1808[27]

Freemasonry's new age began as the United States declared war on Germany. With great fervor and earnestness, young men joined a Masonic lodge before, during or after their tour of duty in the armed forces. Between 1917 and 1920, Freemasonry in America grew by nearly 25 percent and continued to initiate more than 100,000 per year throughout the 1920s. This trend was also reflected in other Masonic groups. The Knights Templar and the Scottish Rite each surpassed 300,000 members, the Shrine counted more than 400,000 Nobles, and the Order of the Eastern Star, a group comprising both men and women, had 1.3 million members.[28] By 1930, Freemasonry reached a new level when its 3.3 million members equaled 12 percent of the native white adult male population.[29]

Prince Hall Freemasonry also enjoyed great growth in the 1920s. Restricted immigration, the promise of steady factory work in the North, and the boll weevil cotton plague encouraged millions of rural African Americans to leave the South. Chicago's South Side, Pittsburgh's Hill District and New York City's Harlem became proud centers of black Americans' prosperity and culture. In Northern cities,

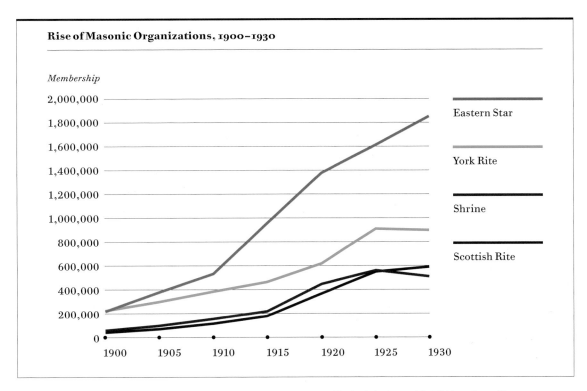

Rise of Masonic Organizations, 1900–1930

Membership

Eastern Star

York Rite

Shrine

Scottish Rite

Source: S. Brent Morris, A Radical in the East, *Iowa Research Lodge No. 2, Siegler Printing and Publishing, Ames, IA, 1994.*

Prince Hall lodges provided aid and comfort to men and their families arriving from other locations. Southern states also saw a great rise in Prince Hall Masonry. Texas, with only 2,000 members in 1903, increased to 20,000 by 1927, while the Prince Hall Grand Lodge of Alabama grew from 264 to 22,600 between 1904 and 1924.[30]

Older Masons remained ambivalent toward the youth invasion. They were elated to be strengthened by more members and the income they represented but concerned about losing something more valuable. Said one commentator:

> The impersonal feeling about their reception into the lodge will inevitably reduce to a minimum if not smother . . . that impression of brotherly love and friendship, which is the great, the real, the ineffable and incommunicable, secret of Freemasonry.[31]

Such protests went unheeded as more men knocked on the lodge room door. So great was the demand for admission that many lodges met more frequently to confer the degrees. Ultimately, the influx resulted in the formation of new lodges. Between 1920 and 1930, Massachusetts chartered 75 additional lodges, Illinois, 137, and California, 193.[32]

Grant Wood, 1939.
National Heritage
Museum, 84.16.

But as Freemasonry increased in size, it failed to fully orient and assimilate the new members. Whereas older and younger middle-class men could bond within a single Chamber of Commerce or Rotary Club in a community, many Masons felt isolated from other Masons with more than one lodge in a town. Young men in the Jazz Age often preferred to join their friend's new lodge rather than their father's or grandfather's old lodge. Furthermore, some forward-thinking professionals found the rituals tiresome, Masonic symbolism useless and the romantic ancient history of the craft laughable.[33] They wanted to have fun, spend more time with their wives and improve their communities — traits more common among Rotarians or Lions. In the 1920s, Freemasonry's starched, Eastern urban character was replaced by a jovial, Midwestern personality, and pride replaced prudence as — for better or worse — the rush of "Babbitts" into the lodge trampled the American craftsmen.

These "new men" brought with them into the lodges not only their energy, desire for fun and civic-mindedness but also the narrow-mindedness and suspicion of foreigners that characterized the country in the 1920s. Indeed, the post-war years witnessed a rejection of President Wilson's internationalism and the Versailles treaty, the highest tariffs in history, the sharp curtailment of immigration, and increased race riots in the North and lynchings in the South. The social dislocations brought about by the end of the war, the influenza pandemic and the fears among many Americans that foreigners were threatening their way of life led many native-born Protestant whites to join the Ku Klux Klan. Thus, many younger progressive Freemasons, especially in the Northeast, preferred Rotarian internationalism, while the vast majority of Midwestern, Southern and Western Masons remained staunchly conservative and isolationist. Their beliefs were so strong in the 1920s that the craft came dangerously close to losing its political neutrality and threatened its very identity as a fraternity.

The Communist revolutions in Russia and Europe at the end of World War I caused unrest at home and created a national "Red Scare" in the United States in 1919. Attacks were aimed not only at Communists but also at Socialists, trade union organizers and recent Eastern European Jewish and Catholic immigrants.[34] Behind the banner of "Americanism," organizations took on a patriotic flair as each called for greater loyalty to the United States. The Elks claimed Flag Day for their particular sponsorship, while the Veterans of Foreign Wars (1899) and the American Legion (1919) supplanted the fading Grand Army of the Republic.[35] Freemasonry quickly joined the nation's parade of patriotism. Officers of the armed forces who were Freemasons, for example, organized the National Sojourners in 1919. Grand lodges passed resolutions condemning Bolshevism and other "isms" that were, in their collective judgment, antithetical to the meaning of America.[36] Despite Freemasonry's strict ban on discussing politics in the lodge, America's Masonic leaders did not consider patriotism, or appropriate modes of display, a political issue.

Ironically perhaps, given the views of later-minded theorists, some contemporary Masonic leaders feared that Communist revolutionaries and other foreign "secret societies" might instigate attacks on Freemasonry and rekindle the anti-Masonic accusations that had nearly overwhelmed the fraternity a century before.[37] Their fears were heightened by the appearance of *The Protocols of the Elders of Zion.* This widespread forgery purported to reveal the details of an international Jewish conspiracy bent on the destruction of Christian civilization. Through its many mutations, the book claimed that the evil machinations of the Elders of Zion were controlling the Catholic Church, Freemasonry and even Communism.[38] *The Protocols* became the foundation for future paranoid conspiracy theories and of Adolf Hitler's attacks. To counter such malicious propaganda, the Masonic Service Association, grand lodges and individual brothers published books and pamphlets extolling the virtues of American patriots who were Freemasons, with special emphasis on Freemasons' role in establishing American democracy.[39]

The rebirth of the Ku Klux Klan after 1915 revealed the hatred all-too-many white Protestant Americans had for blacks, Jews and Roman Catholics. By 1925, the Klan claimed four million members.[40] Among the Klansmen were a great number of Freemasons, including Alabama Senator and later U.S. Supreme Court justice Hugo Black.[41] The Klan also took control

GROWTH OF MASONIC TEMPLES

Changes in tax laws, a booming economy and civic boosterism all launched Free-masons into a second golden age of buildings (1915–30). Across the country aging Victorian temples were replaced by modern multifunctional edifices built in city centers. Shown here are (left) St. Louis, (top) Cincinnati and (bottom) Detroit. The Detroit temple is the largest Masonic building in the world and at its dedication in 1926, an estimated 40,000 Freemasons attended — the largest gathering for any Masonic event.

Masonic temple, St. Louis, MO, Tichnor Bros., Boston, ca. 1930. National Heritage Museum, A96/066/2162. Masonic temple, Cincinnati, OH, Curt Teich & Company, Chicago, ca. 1935. National Heritage Museum, A96/066/3105. Masonic temple, Detroit, MI, United News Co. Detroit, ca. 1935. National Heritage Museum, A96/066/1902.

THE GEORGE WASHINGTON MASONIC NATIONAL MEMORIAL

MASONIC TRIBUTE TO
GEORGE WASHINGTON

Joining forces from
around the country,
Masons paid tribute to
the nation's first presi-
dent by building the
George Washington
Masonic National
Memorial in Alexandria,
Virginia. The building
is visible from airplanes
approaching Reagan
National Airport.

*Curt Teich & Co.,
Chicago, ca. 1950.
National Heritage
Museum, A96/066/
pub15.*

of some Northern state and local governments, most notably Indiana, North
Carolina, and Denver, Colorado.[42] But the organization was limited in its
national political goals, because it lacked affluence and respectability. To
acquire these qualities, Klansmen attempted to infiltrate Freemasonry.
Masonic leaders in such states as Oregon, Minnesota and Texas fought to
keep the fraternity politically neutral even as Klan membership grew within
their lodges.[43] The Klan's internal scandals and infighting as well as the
lack of evidence of black or Roman Catholic conspiracies to materialize
brought about its downfall.[44] By 1930, the organization was no longer considered a serious political power.[45] Its influence within certain Masonic
jurisdictions, particularly in some states of the old Confederacy, lingered.
Maintaining an "Americanism" ideology, Klan members did not hesitate
to bully many older ethnic lodges and prevent many good men of all races
and religions from joining.

The most forceful demonstration of Masonic prosperity and patriotism
came with the erection of the George Washington Masonic National Memorial. Beginning in 1910, members of Alexandria-Washington Lodge No.
22 in Alexandria, Virginia, established an association to create a memorial
for the memory of their first elected Master and to safely care for the Washington memorabilia in their possession. Through the association and under
the leadership of Joseph W. Eggleston, Grand Master of Virginia, and later
Louis A. Watres, a Past Grand Master of Pennsylvania, every recognized

grand lodge in the country was solicited for funds. So successful were these efforts that by 1922 ground was broken for a building on Alexandria's Shooters Hill.[46] In 1923, Watres proclaimed:

> The two and a half million Masons in the United States, prompted by a deep reverence for his memory and an undying love of country, as well as by the enduring ties of brotherhood, are erecting this monument to Washington as Mason. Were our memorial to him as enduring as the pyramids, it could not exceed the esteem in which we hold him in our hearts as one whose name has glorified our land for all time.[47]

On November 1, 1923, President Calvin Coolidge laid the cornerstone with the aid of the same trowel that President George Washington had used to lay the cornerstone of the U.S. Capitol in 1793. The trowel was then passed to every U.S. Grand Master present to symbolize the cement of brotherhood among all people. Despite the onset of the Great Depression, the $8 million construction project continued until the work was completed. On May 12, 1932, President Herbert Hoover, although not a Mason himself, dedicated the memorial before a gathering of several thousand Freemasons.[48]

Fraternalism and the Great Depression

"Is there any beautiful ritualism or human tenderness in a government bureau?"

— BINA WEST, 1936[49]

The prosperity that America enjoyed in the 1920s quickly ended after the stock market crash of October 1929. The total amount of wealth that investors lost in the crash was twice the amount of all the hard currency then in circulation. To meet their own debts, banks, brokers and individuals called the loans owed to them. This triggered a cascading effect across the country and a general collapse of America's antiquated financial structure. Many companies struggled to maintain solvency only to declare bankruptcy; workers were laid off with little prospect of finding jobs; families failed to pay their bills and mortgages, and the country's economy sank into a depression.[50]

Freemasonry, of course, was not immune and was hit with the same level of devastation suffered by so many brothers after 1930. Unemployed members could no longer afford the dues, let alone the expense of attending banquets and other social functions. As lodges lost members, the depression

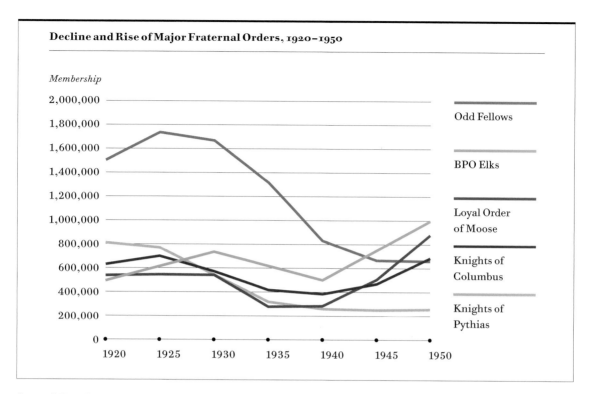

Decline and Rise of Major Fraternal Orders, 1920–1950

Membership

Odd Fellows

BPO Elks

Loyal Order of Moose

Knights of Columbus

Knights of Pythias

Source: S. Brent Morris, A Radical in the East, *Iowa Research Lodge No. 2, Siegler Printing and Publishing, Ames, IA, 1994.*

also inhibited new membership. The troubles were often compounded by the burden of mortgages and maintenance expenses for the grand edifices begun in happier days. Between 1930 and 1935, Freemasonry lost more than 600,000 members.[51]

The election of Franklin D. Roosevelt to the presidency in 1932 ushered in new ideas about the roles of government, business and labor. Even as FDR's New Deal reshaped American society, it challenged — albeit unintentionally — each of the major historical reasons for joining Freemasonry and other fraternal organizations.

The fundamental desire for self-improvement and education, which the lodge had always provided, was overshadowed by the growth of the public school system as well as colleges and universities. Further filling the niche for self-improvement were new non-ritual organizations, such as Toastmasters International. These Rotary-like organizations taught public speaking and business skills and encouraged professional networking. Founded in 1924, Toastmasters had more than 138 clubs across the country by 1938.[52] The ultimate answer to success, however, was found in a book. In 1936, Dale Carnegie's *How to Win Friends and Influence People* was published. It sold more than ten million copies within a few decades.

Thus began the modern age of the motivational speaker and the inspiration of countless books promising fame, fortune and fulfillment.

Of all the fraternal associations affected by the Great Depression, the old ritual-based fraternities were hit the hardest. The Odd Fellows, Knights of Pythias and Red Men enjoyed a brief membership increase during and immediately after World War I. With the arrival of commercial radio, jazz music and talking movies, however, the morality plays and mysterious ceremonies seemingly lost their power over the imagination. The Knights of Pythias lost 550,000 members between 1925 and 1940, while the Improved Order of Red Men lost more than 300,000.[53] The Odd Fellows declined by a staggering 62 percent from 1920 to 1940.[54] Even the post–World War II recovery could not save most of these groups, and they slowly dwindled until they were all but forgotten by later generations.

Intertwined with the ritual-based fraternities were the mutual benefit orders. Since the late 1800s, they were diverging into three different groups. The Great Depression and New Deal only solidified their future. The first and oldest group — that of workers' beneficial associations, such as the Ancient Order of United Workmen — moved away from cooperation with management and owners and toward politically active trade unions, such as the American Federation of Labor and the Congress of Industrial Organizations. These unions and others received legal authority to organize when President Roosevelt signed the Wagner Act into law in 1935. The second group — insurance-based orders organized through a fraternal lodge, such as the Tribe of Ben Hur — simply dropped their fraternal pretenses and reconfigured themselves as commercial life insurance corporations.[55]

The third group — consisting of mostly ethnic and religious fraternities, such as the Polish Falcons and the Greek Catholic Union — suffered most from the Great Depression. They were already constricted by America's "closed door" immigration policy, but the economic hardships crippled their membership and destroyed their reserve funds. FDR's implementation of Social Security and other health and welfare programs replaced much of their activities. Working together in the National Fraternal Congress of America, however, they were able to survive the 1930s and 1940s to see prosperity return in the 1950s with an influx of post-war European immigrants.[56]

Social fraternal organizations, like the Shriners, Elks and even the Moose, were weakened for a time by the Great Depression. Tens of thousands dropped their membership, and many lodges closed, as men looked for cheaper forms of entertainment. Following Pearl Harbor and America's entry into World War II, membership began to climb again as people sought a distraction from their worries and the limits of a war economy. Member-

Rotary International 1939 Assembly
THE GREENBRIER
WHITE SULPHUR SPRINGS, W. VA., U. S. A.
JUNE 12 to 16

ship in the Elks, for example, dropped from 735,000 in 1930 to 500,000 in 1940, but by 1950 it was approaching a million members.[57]

The least affected groups were those that focused on professional networking and business connections. Men with families could no longer spend the money required for dues and ritual paraphernalia when their jobs were uncertain. They could, however, rationalize retaining their membership to the business luncheon club, because it provided opportunities to help those in need and maintained business connections in the event of job loss. Furthermore, each of the clubs had little overhead cost and few, if any, were burdened with mortgages or debt. While membership in Rotary, Kiwanis and Lions did drop between 1930 and 1934, only 50 Rotary clubs were forced to close during the 1930s. By 1940, membership in these three clubs was again at an all-time high and continued to expand through World War II and well into the post-war generation. In 1955, Rotary International had more than 268,000 members in North America, Kiwanis had over 228,000, and Lions grew to more than 325,000 in the United States and Canada.[58]

The wealth, Jazz Age rhythms and booster optimism of the Roaring Twenties had indeed re-energized Freemasonry. Within a few short years, a new generation overhauled traditional lodge structures and rebuilt them according to modern designs. These new brothers no longer sought refuge from the world but were eager to live in it. Through their efforts, Freemasonry reached new heights of popularity and influence. But such success came at a cost. In a rush to "improve" the lodge and shift the emphasis, new members of the craft ignored the fraternity's spiritual and moral foundation and its Enlightenment ornamentation. Craftsmanship and toleration continued to play a major role, but the Masonic lodge lost its elite status

Plain Dealing: The Rotarian Age and Freemasonry's New Personality

In 1935, President
Franklin D. Roosevelt
attended the Masonic
initiation of two of his
three sons in New York
City's Architect Lodge
No. 517. Standing
directly behind FDR in
the center are James
and Franklin D. Jr. Also
attending the meeting
was Mayor Fiorella
LaGuardia (second row,
fifth from left), New
York Grand Master
Robert Elliott Owens
(right of FDR), mem-
bers of the New York
State Supreme Court
and other distinguished
guests.

*1935. Courtesy of the
Archives of the Supreme
Council, 33°, Southern
Jurisdiction, Washington
DC.*

in the 1920s and had to struggle to ward off mediocrity and not succumb
to bigotry.

The Great Depression curbed the pride of Americans, but it did not
destroy the era's youthful optimism and faith in corporate planning. In
his 1933 presidential inaugural address, President Roosevelt asserted his
firm belief that "the only thing we have to fear is fear itself." During FDR's
first 100 days in office, "New Dealers" passed a flood of regulatory legislation and chartered numerous federal bureaus and agencies to create a
new foundation for economic opportunity. As Americans struggled to
overcome the depression, Freemasons sought to rebuild their fraternity
through youth programs and community service projects.

CHAPTER 10

One Family

The Masonic Good Life, 1942–1965

"Reaching out with interlocking membership to all parts of the country, embracing all ages, classes, creeds, and ethnic groups, they [joiners] have constantly demonstrated the underlying unity that warrants diversity. They have served as a great cementing force for national integration."

— ARTHUR M. SCHLESINGER, 1944[1]

THE GENERATION OF AMERICANS born after 1890 shared a new attitude toward life. The pursuit of material wealth of the Gilded Age had an adverse effect. The spread of consumerism and the triumph of materialism helped undermine families and transform, if not corrupt, society. More and more citizens became alienated from the traditional political parties as politicians failed to address the nation's industrial problems. The devastation of the Great War and the failure of political leaders in Washington and diplomats in Europe to secure a stable peace further divided younger people from their elders. This younger generation did not fully reject the moral standards of their parents; rather, they wanted to learn through their own experience and in their own way. Many members of this new generation seized upon any craze or fad, welcomed any new technology and embraced any new ideology just for fun. To be sure, they also started many new organizations for social or political purposes. At the same time, older and more conservative Americans created new organizations to channel this youthful energy into what they hoped would be healthy activities.[2]

This younger generation — identified by Sinclair Lewis as "Babbitts," but most often called "joiners" — reshaped 20th-century American society. As emphasis shifted from a production-based to a consumption-based economy, young professional men joined Rotary, Kiwanis and Lions to reach larger markets. Their wives and sisters, empowered by the right to

vote and buoyed by the success of the prohibition movement, sought to address deeper problems in society, while their children or younger siblings participated in youth clubs and college fraternities. Each group in its own way provided community service through projects and crusades to improve the health and welfare of society.

This new breed of joiners had an impact on American Freemasonry. They created new organizations for their children and expanded the Masonic tenet of "brotherly love." By the 1950s, Freemasonry had shifted from a men's secret ritual organization to a more family-oriented fraternity. In the process of making their craft more friendly and community-oriented, Freemasons began to lose sight of their stated purpose to "make good men better."

Women were primarily responsible for changing the way the family participated in public affairs. They began this work before the Civil War fighting for abolition and temperance. From the Gilded Age to the Jazz Age, some fought for the right to vote with their involvement in the suffrage movement, and others moved toward intellectual and professional networking.[3] Some women organized the Women's Christian Temperance Union and other groups that fought specific ills of the country, such as child labor and illiteracy. Women's fraternal organizations, including the auxiliaries to men's orders, also prospered. In 1915 the Ladies of the Maccabees changed their name to the Women's Benefit Association. Under the leadership of Supreme Record Keeper Bina West, the association became the

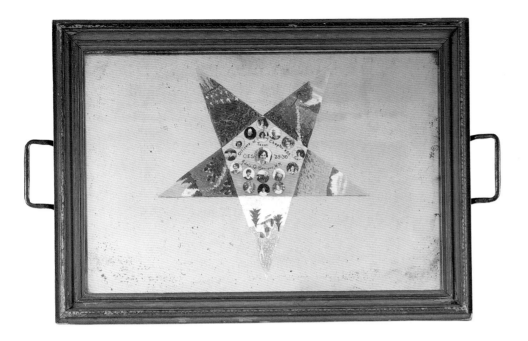

seventh largest fraternal beneficial organization in the United States and the largest women's beneficial order with more than 200,000 members.[4] Female relatives of Freemasons joined not only the Eastern Star but also the Order of Amaranth, White Shrine of Jerusalem, Social Order of the Beauceant, Heroines of Jericho and Daughters of Isis.[5] The Great Depression, the New Deal and America's entry into World War II all had an impact on women's voluntary associations as they moved away from political reform and self-improvement to focus on community service projects.

While adults undertook social and political reform in the 1910s and 1920s, a new generation came of age. Born after the turn of the century, these children graduated from high school in greater numbers and often went to college before they considered marriage or a career.[6] Stretching out the time between childhood and adulthood created a new identity as teenagers. Child labor laws in the 1920s prohibited children from working and created more leisure time. Along with the new forms of popular entertainment, the Jazz Age generation dispelled Victorian anxieties about relationships between the sexes. Young men and women began to "date" instead of "court."[7] A child's school took on a more prominent role with the growing importance of extra-curricular activities. Teenagers gained confidence by belonging to teams and clubs, but participation came at a price. Peer pressure often demanded conformity and the renunciation of individuality. Those who stepped out of line faced exclusion and were often cruelly ostracized.[8]

EASTERN STAR
MIRROR TRAY

The hand-painted tray was likely displayed at Texas Chapter No. 35, Order of the Eastern Star. It may have served as an appreciation gift to the Worthy Matron, the chapter's female leader, for her year of service. The illustrations on the star's points show different seasons of the year. In the center are small photographs of the 1930 officers.

*San Antonio, TX, 1930.
National Heritage
Museum, 2001.037.*

LAMDA CHI ALPHA

In the 1920s, college fraternities and sororities became immensely popular. Pledge pins, paddles and frat house living all became part of the American youth culture.

Fraternity Brothers, ca. 1928. Courtesy of Fort Collins Public Library, Fort Collins, CO.

Perhaps the most visible peer groups of the 1920s were college fraternities and sororities — also called "Greek-letter" fraternities because their names usually derived from the Greek initials of their motto. The first college fraternity — Phi Beta Kappa — had been organized at the College of William and Mary in Virginia in 1776. One of its founders, Thomas Smith, was a member of the Masonic lodge at Williamsburg. By 1781, Phi Beta Kappa had chapters at Princeton, Yale and Harvard.[9] After the 1780s, Greek-letter clubs, fraternities and literary societies spread to other colleges. A significant set of developments occurred between 1825 and 1827 at Union College in Schenectady, New York, where three fraternities — Kappa Alpha, Sigma Phi and Delta Phi — were organized at the same time that the anti-Masonic period was engulfing the state of New York. In 1831, Phi Beta Kappa dropped its secrecy and rituals, and it was the "Union Triad" of fraternities that became the parent of the dozens, if not hundreds, of college fraternities in America.[10]

Women's sororities were not formed until after the Civil War. The first all-women's college organization was the P.E.O. Sisterhood organized at Wesleyan College in Mount Pleasant, Iowa, in 1869. It soon accepted non-students as members and evolved into a women's fraternal Order.[11] Pi Beta Phi and Kappa Kappa Gamma, both founded at Monmouth College in Illinois, followed P.E.O., and these groups went on to become the foundation for most other sororities.[12]

Greek-letter societies grew steadily on college campuses after the Civil War and reached their greatest prominence after World War I. The societies borrowed heavily from Masonic rituals and used similar secret handshakes and words.[13] The 25 national fraternities and 10 sororities recorded in 1891 increased substantially after 1910. The number of local chapters of national fraternities more than doubled between 1912 and 1930, while the number of members per chapter tripled.[14] After 1920, the college football game, all-night "cram" sessions and co-ed frat parties became rites of passage for the American middle class.

Freemasonry officially became part of the college scene with the formation of the Acacia fraternity at the University of Michigan in 1904. An

Adorning American Communities

outgrowth of a Masonic club on campus, the fraternity was originally restricted to men who were
Freemasons. Acacia later changed its membership requirements to allow non-Masons as members. Among the fraternity's distinguished alumni
was Clifton Hillegass (University of Nebraska,
1938) creator of those abridged paths to knowledge, "Cliff Notes."[15] In 1993, Acacia recorded
40 chapters throughout the country and more
than 41,000 brothers.[16]

By the end of the 1930s, fraternal organizations had filled nearly every market niche from
cradle to grave. In every phase of life, there was
a group to absorb the individual — Cub Scouts,
Boy Scouts, Little League, YMCA, Sunday School
choirs, college fraternities, glee clubs and cheer-
leader squads. The various groups were supervised by parents, teachers, coaches and other
adults. The factory or office in the Industrial Age
had separated families. In the modern era, the
clubs or teams began to reunite father to son and
mother to daughter. Indeed, in the 1920s, adult "joiners" often met the
college fraternity or sorority students at the big game and "matched them
cheer for cheer."[17]

"My Friend, Dan Beard," by Charles Dana Gibson

DANIEL CARTER BEARD

Woodsman, illustrator,
and naturalist Daniel
Carter Beard was a pio-
neering spirit of Ameri-
can Scouting. Already
60 years old when the
Boy Scouts of America
was formed, he merged
it with his own boys'
organization, the Sons
of Daniel Boone. "Uncle
Dan," as he was called,
was a member of
Mariners' Lodge No. 67,
F&AM, New York City.

Boys' Life, *illustrated
by Joseph Cummings
Chase, February 1925.
National Heritage
Museum.*

The Masonic Family

*"By the exercise of brotherly love we are taught to regard the whole
human species as one family, the high and low, the rich and poor,
created by one Almighty Parent, and sent into the world for the aid,
support and protection of each other."*

— WILLIAM PRESTON, 1775[18]

The changes that took place within the American family in the late 1800s
began to impact Freemasonry in the 1920s. Although sons occasionally
played musical instruments in fraternal bands and daughters helped their
mothers at fraternal banquets and picnics, Freemasonry and other fraternities had no official place for children within the lodge hall. The rapid
growth of the Order of the Eastern Star as well as middle-class prosperity
disrupted the all-male stability of the Masonic lodge. As Masons increasingly

The New York Masonic Outlook

15¢

JANUARY 1927

In This Issue: S. Parkes Cadman *and* Stephen Vincent Benet

THE PROUD FATHER

A father shows his son and Masonic brother the proper way to wear his apron. Since the mid-1800s, Masons and state grand lodges published magazines. Most included local, state and national Masonic events and news along with short stories, poems and advertisements.

New York Masonic Outlook, *illustrated by Samuel Emmons Brown, January 1927. National Heritage Museum.*

looked beyond the lodge room, their sons and daughters were formally welcomed into the Masonic organizational structure. With the creation of new family organizations, the Masonic tenet of brotherly love was reinterpreted. But undergirding these innovations was a rededication to patriarchal values and conservative traditions. From the 1920s into the 1960s, young men had a new reason to become Freemasons — their family expected them to join.

The Masonic lodge was considered a pillar within the community, and membership for many became a tradition within the family. Many sons often followed their fathers into lodge so that by the 1930s some families could claim four or more generations within the same lodge. The rituals served as a rite of passage for some families, as all male relations became "brothers." For many Freemasons, there is perhaps no moment more poignant than when a father is present to witness his son become a Master Mason.

On a broader level, families with multigenerational American heritage often touted their colonial and early American ancestry. Indeed, the Society of the Cincinnati, largely created by Freemasons, was founded in 1783 for Continental Army officers and their heirs.[19] The western migrations and European immigration of the late 1800s caused many older native-born Americans to reassert their "ancient" lineage through hereditary societies. In 1889, the Sons of the American Revolution was formed. Following in quick succession were the Daughters of the American Revolution (1890), Colonial Dames (1891), Daughters of the War of 1812 (1892), and the Society of Mayflower Descendants (1897). These were joined by new orders that perpetuated the memory of those who fought in the Civil War, such as the Military Order of the Loyal Legion, the Sons of Union Veterans and the United Daughters of the Confederacy.[20]

Throughout this evolution, Freemasonry became intertwined with the hereditary societies and absorbed their conservative nature. The morality and virtues taught within the Masonic lodge took on new purposes with the patriotic fervor of World War I, the Red Scare of 1919 and the rise of the Ku Klux Klan. Fueling these impulses was the perceived threat of an increasingly secular and promiscuous society brought on by the youth cul-

Adorning American Communities

ture associated with jazz music, smoking, dancing, drinking and "heavy petting." Schools, congregations and the "Y" diversified their activities to keep children off the street and out of pool halls.[21] As parents, Masonic brothers and Eastern Star sisters turned their focus toward raising healthy and morally upright children and to proclaim Freemasonry as "the brotherhood of man under the Fatherhood of God."

Masonic Youth Organizations

"And in all the land were no women found so fair as the daughters of Job and their father gave them inheritance among their brethren."

— BOOK OF JOB, 42:15; INTERNATIONAL ORDER OF JOB'S DAUGHTERS RITUAL[22]

The conservative nature of 20th-century Masonry was reflected in the creation of three new youth organizations associated with the Masonic fraternity. All three groups sprang up in the Midwest between 1919 and 1923. The first organization taught knightly virtues to teenage boys; the other two taught feminine virtues to teenage girls.

Frank S. Land (1890-1959) was a highly charismatic man, who taught Sunday school at the age of ten and had become a successful businessman by the age of 28. As a member of Ivanhoe Lodge No. 446 in Kansas City, Missouri, Land was asked to help Louis Lower, a teenage orphan of a deceased lodge brother. The boy's sincerity inspired Land to bring together eight of Louis' friends to form a club that met at the Kansas City Masonic temple.[23] When a friend asked him what was new with the club, Frank Land replied:

> What's new is not what you might expect. I have a new title. The boys call me "Dad." They had been at a loss as to just what to call me. It seems they were reluctant to call me Frank because of our age difference and felt that Mr. Land was sort of formal. . . . "Dad" is just right. It carries respect and confidence and I am proud to be so designated.[24]

Frank Land offered a number of suggestions for the name of the club, one of which was DeMolay, in honor of Jacques DeMolay, the legendary last Grand Master of the medieval Knights Templar.[25] As the success of the club was brought to the attention of Masons in other areas, Land offered assistance in establishing chapters around the country. Masonic lodges accepted the responsibility of sponsoring the chapters, and Frank Land devoted all his time to managing the growth of the boys' organization. From nine original members in 1919, there were 1,171 active chapters with

"DAD" FRANK LAND

The beloved founder and executive secretary of DeMolay for Boys for nearly 40 years, Frank S. Land also served in various capacities for many other Masonic organizations, including Imperial Potentate of the Shrine in 1954. When he passed away in 1959, he was eulogized by many of his "boys," including Walt Disney and John Cameron Swayze.

ca. 1955. Courtesy of DeMolay International.

114,798 members by 1924. The first Canadian chapter was chartered in 1924.[26] Among the first generation of "Dad" Land's boys were Walt Disney, John Steinbeck, Walter Cronkite and U.S. Senator Henry "Scoop" Jackson.[27] The Great Depression and World War II severely curtailed the growth of DeMolay, but in the 1950s, the Order quickly recovered. When Frank Land died in 1959, there were 135,000 DeMolay boys and 2,097 chapters in 14 countries.[28]

During a 1922 address to the Eastern Star chapter in McAlester, Oklahoma, Rev. William Mark Sexson (1877-1953) noted the phenomenon of DeMolay. Rhetorically, the Freemason asked the assembled sisters why there could not be a similar organization for young girls. The Eastern Star ladies quickly accepted Brother Sexson's suggestion and began assembling their daughters, nieces and granddaughters. They then pressed Sexson, who was known for his poetic talents, to write a basic ritual. Within two months of Sexson's rhetorical question, 171 girls were assembled in the McAlester Scottish Rite temple and initiated into the Order of Rainbow for Girls. A month later, a supreme governing body was formed, and other local "assemblies" of rainbow girls were created in surrounding communities.[29] Sexson, who later served as Grand Chaplain for the Grand Lodge of Oklahoma and Worthy Grand Patron for the Order of the Eastern Star in that state, continued to serve Rainbow as its executive director. By 1955, assemblies had opened in other countries, and the official name became the International Order of Rainbow for Girls. Former members have included Supreme Court Justice Sandra Day O'Connor, U.S. Senator Olympia Snow, 1955 Miss America and actress Lee Meriwether, and comedian Lily Tomlin.[30]

Rainbow, however, did not extend everywhere, because another Masonic organization for girls had started in Nebraska. Ethel Mick (1881-1957) founded a Masonic youth organization in Omaha in 1920. Called Job's Daughters, its one-degree initiation ritual and five lectures were based on the teachings from the Book of Job. With the assistance of her husband, Dr. William Mick, and other Masons, Job's Daughters Bethel No. 1 recorded 118 girls in 1921. Growing strongest in the Northern and Western states, the organization listed 132 bethels in 1925. Within 20 years of its founding, "Jobies," as they came to be called, had 479 bethels and 33,664 members. For many years both organizations for girls maintained a requirement that membership be limited to those who had a male relative who was a Freemason. While the Rainbow organization dropped this requirement, Job's

JOB'S DAUGHTERS

An issue of *Life* magazine showed an installation ceremony of officers for Job's Daughters. Kneeling in front is Sallie Hodgins of St. Paul, Minnesota. In the background are her suite of officers and past officers.

Life, *October 8, 1956. National Heritage Museum.*

RAINBOW GIRLS'
MERIT AWARDS

After being initiated into the Order of the Rainbow, a girl earns seven colored bars for participating in different activities. When she earns all the colored bars of the Order, she receives a pot of gold charm.

ca. 1975. National Heritage Museum, gift of Laura E. Coulter Cook, 2003.003.8.

Daughters still maintains it. The Job's Daughters spread to Canada and Mexico, and in the 1950s bethels were formed in Australia and Germany. "Mother" Mick passed away in 1957, but Job's Daughters continued to grow toward a peak of 145,625 members and 1,584 bethels in 1961.[31]

The popularity of these youth groups inspired the Knights of Columbus to sponsor the Columbian Squires for boys in 1923 and the Prince Hall Masonic lodges to start the Order of Pythagoras in 1936.[32]

Like the USO, Masonic
grand lodges and the
Masonic Service Associ-
ation opened "service
centers" for men and
women serving in the
military during World
War II. The postcard
shows scenes from the
center in Chicago.

*ca. 1944. National
Heritage Museum,
A96/066/4548.*

CHINA MASONIC CLUB
DUES CARD

While serving in the
China-Burma theater
during World War II,
Brother John Q. Timbrel
joined a Masonic Square
Club. General Claire L.
Chennault, leader of
the famous American
Volunteer "Flying
Tigers" Fighter Group,
signed his dues card.
Gen. Chennault was a
member of League City
Lodge No. 1053, League
City, Texas, before join-
ing the Army in 1917.

*1944. National Heritage
Museum, gift of John Q.
Timbrel, A83/002/1.*

Freemasonry and World War II

*"At this very moment, in foxholes, on ships at sea, beneath the sea
and in the air, countless hands are being clasped in fraternal recognition
of each other in darkness as well as in the daylight. And countless
fathers, bravely wishing Godspeed to their departing sons, are saying
'Boy, when your hour of darkness and loneliness comes, find a
Freemason, and tell him you are a son of a Freemason, and there
you will find a friend.'"*

— HARRY S. TRUMAN, 1944 [33]

With Hitler's invasion of Poland in 1939, the United States slowly pulled
out of an isolationist mode. The passage of the Selective Service Act in
June 1940 introduced Americans to the first peacetime draft, but millions
of men volunteered for the armed services when Japan bombed Pearl Harbor and Germany and Italy declared war on the United States. Among the
draftees and volunteers were tens of thousands of Freemasons. The troops
were led by such noted Masons as Army Generals George Marshall, Douglas
MacArthur and Omar Bradley, Navy Admiral Ernest King, and Army Air
Corps General Henry "Hap" Arnold. [34] As Masons found fellow Masons
within the service, they informally organized "Square and Compass Clubs."
These clubs were not lodges and could not confer degrees to initiate new
members. At most, they provided a chance for brothers to relax and share
their Masonic experience with other Masons. Meeting in Quonset huts,

ship surgeries and "liberated" buildings, Masons recited familiar Masonic phrases that reminded them of home.[35]

Whereas Freemasons were left out of any effort to offer assistance during the First World War, they were now prepared to take an active role. Under executive director Carl Claudy, the Masonic Service Association (MSA) was reinvigorated and an advisory committee of several U.S. congressmen and senators was established. Through the Masonic network, the MSA began opening service centers — similar to the USO canteens — for all men and women in uniform, more especially Masons. To help promote the centers, Senator Harry Truman made radio broadcasts and Hollywood produced the film *Your Son is My Brother* in 1944. By the end of the war in 1945, the MSA had raised more than $5 million to support some 40 service centers at home and abroad.[36]

As Masons returned home following the victory in Europe and Japan in 1945, the Masonic fraternity realized the profits of its hard labor between the Great Depression and World War II. The craft was more accepted and appreciated than it had been prior to 1929. Perhaps the crowning achievement of Freemasonry's assimilation into American society was the 1948 presidential election. From across the political spectrum, all four candidates were Freemasons — Democrat and incumbent President Harry Truman of Missouri, Republican Governor Thomas Dewey of New York, Progressive Party nominee and former Vice President Henry Wallace of Iowa, and States' Rights or "Dixiecrat" Party candidate Strom Thurmond of South Carolina.[37]

Harry Truman, who won the 1948 election, is one of the greatest of all American Freemasons. A member of Belton Lodge No. 450 since 1909, Truman served as Grand Master of Missouri in 1940-41. He also received the York and Scottish Rite degrees and was an active Shriner in Kansas City. The farmer and failed haberdasher lacked a college degree, yet he won every political contest he entered. First elected as a Missouri county official in 1922, Truman was elected U.S. Senator from Missouri in 1934 and was reelected in 1940 before becoming Roosevelt's vice presidential nominee in 1944. Upon the death of FDR in 1945, Truman assumed the presidency and was elected to a full term in 1948. As president he helped form the United Nations, desegregated the U.S. armed forces, supported the founding of Israel, initiated the Marshall Plan for Europe and defended Greece, Turkey and Korea against hostile Communism. After leaving the presidency, Truman remained an active Mason for many years and on several occasions remarked, "The greatest honor that has ever come to me, and that can ever come to me in my life, is to be Grand Master of Masons in Missouri."[38]

GRAND MASTER
HARRY S. TRUMAN

An extremely active and proud Freemason, in 1940 Truman was elected Grand Master of Masons in Missouri and reelected to the U.S. Senate. Both elections were contested. The portrait of him as Grand Master was commissioned in 1949.

Original portrait by Greta Kempton, 1949. Postcard, Harry S. Truman as Grand Master, ca. 1980. National Heritage Museum, A96/066/0915.

Let the Good Times Roll

"But we, as free and accepted Masons are taught to make use of [the Trowel] for the more noble and glorious purpose of spreading the cement of Brotherly Love and affection; that cement which unites us into one sacred band, or society of friends and brothers, among whom no contention should ever exist, but that noble contention, or rather emulation, of who best can work, or best agree."

— THOMAS SMITH WEBB, 1808 [39]

In the 20 years between 1945 and 1965, both the United States and Freemasonry experienced an unprecedented era of growth and prosperity. The pessimism of the Great Depression gave way to the optimism made possible by America's military victory. The shortages and sacrifices during the war years turned into domestic wealth in the post-war decades. During the 1930s, massive public works projects provided employment for millions by building dams, bridges, and highways that improved commerce, curtained floods and provided electricity. During the war, engineers built airstrips on coral reefs, aided allies around the world and created the atomic bomb.

After VJ Day, these talents were channeled toward rebuilding America and the world. The Seabees and engineers who kept the Marines island-hopping and the Army rolling applied their talents to building massive housing subdivisions, interstate highways and international airports. Factories quickly retooled from war production to providing automobiles and durable goods, and corporations learned the power of television advertising and precision marketing. American diplomatic and military power remained preeminent in the face of growing Russian and Chinese Communist aggression.

The life of an average man typifies the monumental changes in American society during this period. Born into a working-class family in the isolationist and Jazz Age of the 1920s, he grew up during the worst of the Depression and Dust Bowl of the 1930s, only to be sent overseas to fight his way home through Tokyo or Berlin. Through the GI Bill, the returning veteran earned a college degree, bought a house or received a small-business loan. Through either a strong union or highly profitable corporation, he was able to earn a respectable wage and achieve a middle-class affluence undreamed of by his parents. By 1965, he probably owned his own house and car, while his wife cared for the home and raised children who looked forward to attending college or exploring other opportunities after graduating from high school. All this before his 45th birthday! [40]

Peace at home and power abroad, however, did not mean that life was free of social anxiety. On the contrary, those who sought the American dream were often compelled to conform to implicit, but nonetheless real, social standards. In neighborhoods and cities, adults and children were expected to exhibit proper manners, wear proper clothes, shop at the right stores, drive the right cars, and be members of the right congregations.[41]

Part of the phenomenon of the 1950s "establishment" was an expectation to belong to the right clubs and civic associations. Throughout the country, membership in all organizations grew. Freemasonry, as an established institution in the community, continued to enjoy greater respectability. Between 1945 and 1960, Masonic membership rose by more than a million members, from 2.8 to 4 million, and in 1960, there were more than 15,800 lodges throughout the 50 states. With this flowing tide of brothers, all other parts of the craft rose. In 1960, the York Rite Royal Arch Masons grew to 700,000 members, the Order of the Eastern Star had 2.5 million members, the Scottish Rite surpassed the one million mark, while the Shrine surpassed the York Rite with 750,000 nobles. Each of the Masonic youth groups — DeMolay, Rainbow and Job's Daughters — also grew substantially in the 1950s.[42]

But even as the craft struggled to absorb these huge numbers, its fundamental character mutated from within. The once elite lodges were inundated with applicants from the growing middle class. Some Masonic leaders sought to maintain exclusivity by raising annual dues and demanding higher standards for membership, while others felt that the positive statistic and growing revenues alone proved the success of the fraternity. What

Beginning in the 1930s, a Conference of Grand Masters was held annually in Washington, DC. The Grand Masters gathered on the steps of the George Washington Masonic National Memorial in 1956 for a cover photograph to accompany an article in *Life* magazine.

Life, *October 8, 1956. National Heritage Museum.*

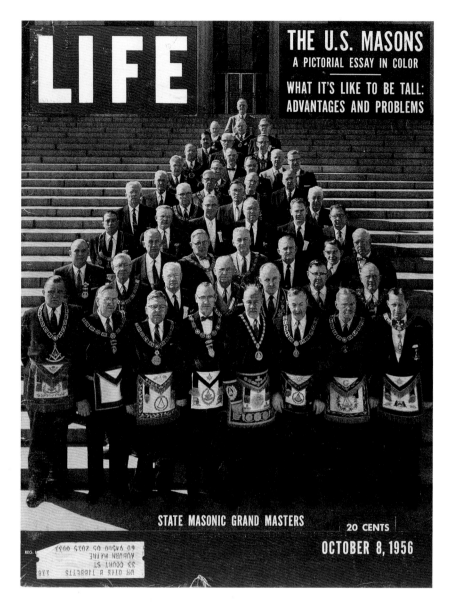

they failed to realize was that many respected community leaders were leaving the lodge room behind for suburban country clubs. Like a luxury brand whose mystique fades when more and more consumers acquire it, Freemasonry's prestige was being exchanged in the 1950s for popularity.[43] Or as New York Yankee catcher Yogi Berra once said, "No one goes to that restaurant any more — it's too crowded."[44]

The Scottish Rite

"Time was; time is; but no man may say that time shall be. For the Sublime Prince of the Royal Secret, therefore, the hour is always — NOW."

— SCOTTISH RITE, NMJ

Of the many Masonic groups that enjoyed unprecedented growth in the 1950s, none grew faster and more prominently than the Scottish Rite. From a mere 40,000 members in 1900, the Scottish Rite grew to 589,000 in 1930. Although it lost members during the Depression and the War, it rebounded with a membership of more than a half million by 1945. More impressively, the membership doubled to over a million members between 1945 and 1965. By the end of World War II, the Scottish Rite had surpassed the York Rite in membership.[45]

The rapid expansion of the Scottish Rite in the 20th century can be attributed to several factors. The 29 degrees had become stage productions with elaborate sets, costuming, makeup and state-of-the-art technology. The productions required many actors, theatrical specialists and stage-hands. Each degree was recognized for its entertainment value as it taught a moral lesson. To the generation of joiners, who felt more comfortable within a team, participation in the Scottish Rite degrees offered both the camaraderie and the accolades of an opening night. In most instances the presentations took place only twice a year, but they became a major drawing card for the members. Since there was a limited number of local Scottish

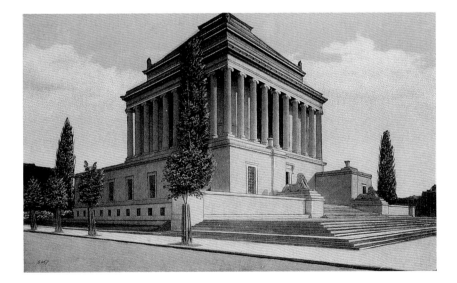

HOUSE OF THE TEMPLE

The headquarters for the Scottish Rite Southern Jurisdiction in Washington, DC, was designed by Russell Pope and based on the mausoleum at Halikarnossos (ca. 325 B.C.). The building was dedicated in 1916.

Scottish Rite House of the Temple, Washington, DC, B. S. Reynolds Co., Washington, DC, ca. 1914. National Heritage Museum, A96/066/pub33.

SCOTTISH RITE,
OAKLAND, CALIFORNIA

Membership in the Scottish Rite Valley of Oakland doubled between 1920 and 1925 to 4,313. Consequently the leadership built a new facility on the shore of Lake Merritt in 1927.

Scottish Rite temple, Oakland, CA, Pacific Novelty Company, San Francisco & Los Angeles, 1936. National Heritage Museum, A96/066/ pub36.

INDIANAPOLIS SCOTTISH
RITE CATHEDRAL

Indianapolis Scottish Rite Masons moved into a new cathedral in 1929. With highly carved stones, brass fixtures and many stained glass windows, the $2.5 million structure is considered by many to be the most beautiful Scottish Rite building in the nation.

Scottish Rite cathedral, Indianapolis, IN, Craft Greeting Card Co., Indianapolis, IN, ca. 1935. National Heritage Museum, A96/066/pub3.

10:-SCOTTISH RITE CATHEDRAL, INDIANAPOLIS, INDIANA.

Rite "valleys" in any state, many members traveled by car a considerable distance to witness the degrees. Their circle of acquaintances increased as they met Scottish Rite Masons from many lodges in the surrounding area.[46]

The Scottish Rite's rapid growth was facilitated by its centralized leadership. In the early 1800s, Scottish Rite Freemasonry was divided into two jurisdictions, which continue to exist today. Each jurisdiction is governed by a separate Supreme Council. The headquarters for the Northern Jurisdiction, consisting of 15 Northeastern and Midwestern states, is located in Lexington, Massachusetts. The Southern Jurisdiction, covering the re-

Ancient Accepted Scottish Rite

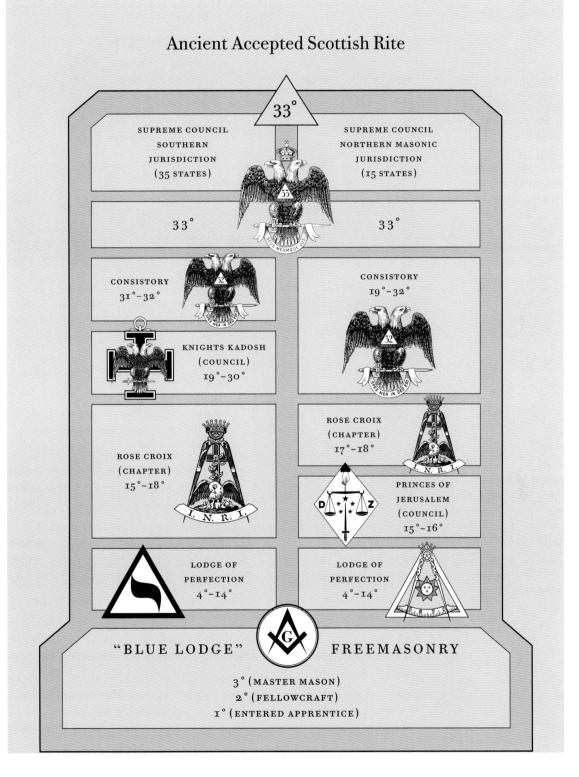

33°

| SUPREME COUNCIL SOUTHERN JURISDICTION (35 STATES) | SUPREME COUNCIL NORTHERN MASONIC JURISDICTION (15 STATES) |

33° 33°

| CONSISTORY 31°–32° | CONSISTORY 19°–32° |

KNIGHTS KADOSH (COUNCIL) 19°–30°

ROSE CROIX (CHAPTER) 17°–18°

ROSE CROIX (CHAPTER) 15°–18°

PRINCES OF JERUSALEM (COUNCIL) 15°–16°

| LODGE OF PERFECTION 4°–14° | LODGE OF PERFECTION 4°–14° |

"BLUE LODGE" FREEMASONRY

3° (MASTER MASON)
2° (FELLOWCRAFT)
1° (ENTERED APPRENTICE)

maining 35 states, is headquartered in Washington, DC. Each Supreme Council has the authority to confer the 33rd degree, which is by invitation only and is presented to a limited number of Scottish Rite Masons in recognition of their contribution to Freemasonry, their community, the nation or the world.[47]

The title of the presiding officer of a Supreme Council is a Sovereign Grand Commander. During the Scottish Rite growth periods in the first half of the 20th century, the Commanders of both jurisdictions held the position of leadership for more than 20 years. Melvin M. Johnson, an attorney and Dean of the Boston University School of Law, served the Northern Jurisdiction from 1933 to 1954. Henry A. Cowles, a Kentucky businessman and a captain during the Spanish-American War, led the Southern Jurisdiction from 1921 to 1953. Partly due to their length of Masonic service and partly due to their private achievement, both men commanded a great deal of respect from leaders in all branches of Freemasonry. While most Masonic organizations changed leaders every year, these two men maintained stable and preeminent leadership roles for more than two decades.[48]

The Space Race of the 1960s launched Americans into a new frontier. Despite the vigor and vitality of Martin Luther King Jr., Elvis Presley and

MASONIC PAVILION

At the 1964 World's Fair
at Flushing, New York,
the Grand Lodge of
New York sponsored
a Masonic pavilion that
included an exhibition
of early American
Masonic artifacts and
an 11-foot-high statue
of George Washington
as a Mason. With the
theme "Brotherhood,
the Foundation of World
Peace," the pavilion also
included dioramas and
displays highlighting
such famous Masons as
Lewis and Clark, Admi-
ral Byrd and Will Rogers.
A world map identified
the location of all 112
recognized grand lodges
in 1964.

*1964 World's Fair
Masonic Building,
Dexter Press, West
Nyack, NY, 1964.
National Heritage
Museum, A96/066/4384.*

John F. Kennedy, the greatest power in the 1960s was held by those born before World War I. The older "generation of joiners" had overcome economic depression, conquered fascism and crafted the containment policy of the Cold War. This generation also transformed Freemasonry. They turned their Victorian fathers' Masonic temples into community centers for the entire family. Husbands were in the lodge, wives in the Eastern Star and children in the youth groups, yet it was the grandparents who controlled the building associations and Masonic charity funds. Like the United States, Freemasonry was governed by wise men and managed by the best and brightest, and it hummed with the regimented efficiency of a beehive.

Yet behind this facade of harmony and prosperity were many incongruities and injustices. The nation that overcame the Great Depression still had millions living in poverty in 1965. Victory over the German and Japanese "master races" did not end the brutal racism at home. The resolve to combat Communist totalitarianism and aggression created a vast "military-industrial complex," and suspicions of those with different ideas stifled personal freedom and creativity.[49] The older generation of Freemasons turned their large membership and vast resources toward resolving each of these issues. The growing white middle-class Masons sought to alleviate the suffering of children and fight "Godless Communists," while upper-class Prince Hall Freemasons joined the civil rights movement to end racism. The high price of their community service would not become fully evident, however, until the last decades of the 20th century.

CHAPTER 11

They Are All Exhausted

Freemasons' Service for New Communities, 1966–2000

"These new mass-membership organizations are plainly of great political importance. From the point of view of social connectedness, however, they are sufficiently different from classic 'secondary associations.'... For the vast majority of their members, the only act of membership consists in writing a check for dues or perhaps occasionally reading a newsletter. Few ever attend any meetings of such organizations, and most are unlikely ever (knowingly) to encounter any other member."

— ROBERT D. PUTNAM, 1995[1]

FREEMASONS AND ALL AMERICANS witnessed stark changes during the last 35 years of the 20th century. The growth of the consumer economy of the 1920s, the expanding role of government in the 1930s, and the changing foreign policy of the 1940s reached their limits in the 1970s. Industrial cities "rusted" as corporations sent jobs overseas and Japan manufactured higher-quality products. Despite the best of intentions, the United States withdrew from Vietnam, Watergate consumed President Nixon, and government programs failed to bring victory to the war on poverty or drugs. Within the family, the divorce rate increased, more wives went into the work force and more husbands cooked, cleaned and raised children. But even as the nation reasserted its global role in the 1980s and enjoyed renewed prosperity in the 1990s, civic life declined as people spent more time alone in front of a television or computer screen.[2]

This shift had an even greater impact on Freemasonry. Membership nationwide dropped by more than 71 percent over a 40-year period as failing lodges merged or closed.[3] Many large Masonic buildings became difficult to maintain. The fraternity, like the nation, became burdened by the decisions of the past. Older Masons dutifully served their lodges and liberally

contributed to Masonic charities, but many failed to inspire their sons to join the fraternity. The craft's troubles were further compounded by anti-Masonic attacks from the political left and the religious right. On the other hand, the Grand Lodge of Washington constituted a new grand lodge in Alaska (1981), and the Grand Lodge of California constituted a new grand lodge in Hawaii (1989). More importantly, many grand lodges and Prince Hall grand lodges officially recognized each other, and the philanthropic efforts of Masonic organizations reached extraordinary heights. Even as Masonic lodges faded from many American communities, Freemasons continued to practice the virtue of charity.

MASSACHUSETTS GRAND MASTER'S APRON
ca. 1950. Courtesy of the Grand Lodge of Masons in Massachusetts.

American Service

*"I tell you, fellow Rotarians, service is the greatest thing in the world. . . .
If we can all get down to service – honest service, humble service . . .
then there will come out of the great despondency and discouragement
and distress of the world a new order."*

— PRESIDENT WARREN G. HARDING, 1923 [4]

JANE CUNNINGHAM CROLY

A *New York Tribune* journalist whose pen name was "Jennie June," Croly (1829–1901) was the first woman to write a syndicated column. She founded the Sorosis club for women in 1868 and the Women's Press Club of New York City in 1889. She also organized the General Federation of Women's Clubs.

ca. 1868. General Federation of Women's Clubs Archives.

Between 1900 and 1960, the nation's wealth and ingenuity were directed toward overcoming great engineering and technological problems, such as electrifying rural America, building interstate highways, curing polio and harnessing atomic energy. During the next 40 years, America turned more of its attention to social problems, like poverty, drugs, corruption and racism. An underlying force driving these changes was a small but powerful word: service. For most of the 19th century, "service" was associated with servitude. After the Civil War, Protestant theologians and women reinterpreted it to mean broader social charity. By the 1920s, service took on commercial connotations as customer satisfaction produced more profits.[5] "Service" became so powerful that the federal government established agencies and bureaus to serve citizens. By the 1970s, an entire business sector was identified as the "service economy." Community service in the radical 1960s generated countless grass-roots organizations. Americans shifted their volunteerism and political activism toward single-issue organizations. Rather than working within the two-party system, citizens joined special interest groups that paid professional lobbyists to work for them. As part of this process, the emphasis of fraternal organizations shifted more and more to charity.[6]

Women were the first to introduce "service" to voluntary associations. Journalist Jane Croly organized Sorosis, a New York women's club, in 1869. Like Hannah Crocker Mather in the 1700s, Croly hoped "to establish a kind of Freemasonry among women . . . [to] bridge over the barrier which custom and social etiquette place in the way of friendly intercourse."[7] In 1890, she took her idea one step further by organizing 63 women's clubs across the country into the General Federation of Women's Clubs. The group's main purpose was to encourage higher education for women and the support of cultural institutions. Quickly turning away from the arts, the clubs sought to end child labor, improve community health and support public libraries and adult literacy. The GFWC, representing more than 500,000 upper-middle-class women in 1914, endorsed women's suffrage.[8]

Following the women's example, middle-class men adopted "service" as their creed. Paul Harris' Rotary International centered its mission on

LIONS YOUTH CONGRESS
PARADE

As part of an inter-
national convention
in Dallas, TX, in 1968,
Lions International
hosted a World Youth
Congress. Young men
and women representing
Lions clubs arrived in
Dallas from all over the
free world.

*Central Studios
photography, 1968.
Author's collection.*

the service ideal. Lions, Kiwanis and others sought ways to establish community charities and improve towns and neighborhoods. Rotarians in professional occupations were expected to plan, organize and execute events, while merchants donated hardware, food or other supplies to support the projects. Other members — many times with the assistance of their families — provided the labor. Through the 1920s and 1930s, city service clubs built parks and playgrounds, beautified roads and neighborhoods, and raised money for the YMCA, Red Cross or other charities.[9]

The very concept of fraternal and voluntary associations was changed — in many ways quite radically — with the emphasis on service. Initiation rituals were overshadowed by community service projects. Mutual benefit for members was replaced by a broad outreach that extended beyond the fraternal community. Challenged by Helen Keller in 1928 to become "Knights for the Blind," Lions clubs began assisting those without sight by providing glasses and eye exams to needy people all over the world.[10] Kiwanis focused more efforts on developing youth, creating a wide range of clubs from K-Kids (under 12 years of age) up to Circle K clubs (for college students).[11] Long known for their international student exchange program in the 1980s, Rotary adopted a worldwide mission to eradicate polio.[12]

The severity of the Great Depression brought about Franklin D. Roosevelt's New Deal that promised people assistance from the government. Since many religious and fraternal charitable resources were overburdened, the federal government often took over community welfare through Social Security, the Works Progress Administration and other programs. During World War II, those who were not in uniform were expected to serve on the home front. In the 1950s and 60s, the range of government services grew exponentially. President Lyndon Johnson's Great Society created the modern social welfare state as it underwrote medical assistance, provided food stamps, funded the arts and sciences and established the Department of Housing and Urban Development.[13]

American voluntary associations went through a transformation during the 1960s and 1970s. Many sought government grants to support local projects, and others focused on national issues. The civil rights movement and the Vietnam War protest spawned new organizations. Many groups — such as the National Organization for Women (1966), Greenpeace (1971), and Moral Majority (1979) — offered a wide range of services while raising millions of dollars to lobby the government. The flood of fundraising appeals became a common occurrence. By the 1990s most Americans still belonged to at least one voluntary association. Unlike the organizations of their grandparents or parents, however, these new associations rarely had any initiation, a member code of conduct or even local chapters.[14]

During the "American Century," millions of Americans were sent all over the globe to fight tyranny or serve in the Peace Corps, and the federal government gave billions of dollars in foreign aid. United States citizens donated billions more through charity to alleviate the suffering of others. Despite the boorish reputation of Americans for crass commercialism, no other people in history have been more charitable.

Freemasonry and Community Service

"To soothe the unhappy, to sympathize with their misfortunes, to compassionate their miseries, and to restore peace to their troubled minds, is the grand aim we have in view. On this basis we establish our friendships and form our connections."

— WILLIAM PRESTON, 1775 [15]

As clubwomen and Rotarians adopted "service" as a calling, Freemasons remained aloof. Since the late 1800s, grand lodges built and maintained Masonic Homes for aged Masons and orphans of departed members, but only in times of great disaster had they extended relief beyond their jurisdiction. The Masonic Board of Relief did provide national coordination, but its primary purpose was to prevent unworthy people from exploiting

Adorning American Communities

the fraternity and receiving Masonic help. America's entry into the First World War made Freemasons aware of the need to reach out beyond the membership.

Like large federal government programs, the fraternity's transition from a private charitable organization to a public charity started at the top. Leaders of grand lodges and other Masonic groups took it upon themselves to reinterpret Freemasonry's purpose. The tenet of relief among the early stonemasons became service for all. The metaphor of craftsmen building spiritual temples within themselves expanded to building real hospitals or clinics for anyone who needed treatment. The emphasis of Freemasonry in the 20th century turned from improving the individual to improving the community.[16]

The Nobles of the Mystic Shrine led the Masonic crusade into the world of service. When it was founded in the 1870s, the Shrine was dedicated to fulfilling upper-class men's taste for the exotic in the make-believe world of the *Arabian Nights.* By 1920, the Shrine had over 300,000 members and 144 Shrines in North America.[17] With the ratification of the 18th Amendment (Prohibition) in 1919, however, Shriners' "oases" were about to go dry. Imperial Potentate (and later Mayor of Philadelphia) Freeland Kendrick of Lulu Shrine began to survey his "desert empire" looking for a project worthy of the organization's attention. He focused on a hospital for crippled children sponsored by the Scottish Rite Masons in Atlanta. Plans for a similar project were brought before the Shriners' 1920 convention in Indianapolis. The rank and file Nobles resisted the proposal because it called for an assessment of $2 per member. The turning point came when Forrest Adair of Yaarab Temple in Atlanta rose to speak. During what was later called the famous "Bubbles Speech," Adair questioned the true meaning of the Shrine. Late the night before, he said, he was awakened by a wandering Shriner playing "I'm Forever Blowing Bubbles" on his tuba. He asked rhetorically if this was indeed what all Shriners were forever doing.[18] He cited the magnificent edifices that Shriners had built for their own merriment and then challenged the members to do something greater:

> For God's sake, let us lay aside our soap and water and stop blowing bubbles and get down to brass tacks. . . . And if there is a Shriner in North America, after he sees your first crippled child treated, in its condition, and objects to having paid the two dollars, I will give a check back to him for it myself.[19]

The speech removed all opposition, and a resolution was unanimously passed to build not one but several hospitals for crippled children. Within two years, facilities in Shreveport, Louisiana, and St. Louis were admitting

MASONIC CONTRIBUTION BANK

Founded in 1866, the Masonic Orphans Home & Infirmary in Louisville, Kentucky, is the oldest Masonic Home in America. A second facility, was opened in Shelbyville, Kentucky, in 1901. Freemasons collected coins in boxes for an Operation Craftsmen Fund to support widows in the 1960s.

ca. 1960. National Heritage Museum, 2001.053.

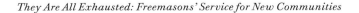

patients, and sites in ten other cities had been selected. The number of hospitals increased to 22 in the decades ahead, and each child received free treatment.[20]

Even as the Imperial Shrine was answering its call to work, the Masonic Service Association (MSA) was broadening its activities. A number of grand lodges combined their efforts in 1918 to create the MSA as a way of coordinating resources to help Masons in the armed forces. Melvin M. Johnson, a Past Grand Master of Massachusetts, urged delegates at the MSA's second convention in 1920 to rethink the very purpose of Masonic lodges: "If this Association can persuade the Masters of lodges in this country that the function of Masonry is not the mere conferring of degrees, we have got our money's worth, not for $25,000 but for $250,000."[21]

Grand Masters also authorized MSA to coordinate charity in times of major disasters. The first such occasion was the 1923 Japanese earthquake, after which the MSA delivered $1,577 to help those in need. In the 1920s and 1930s, MSA sent Masonic money to Chile, Canada, Austria and the Philippines. During the great Mississippi flood of 1927, more than $600,000 was raised to help some 700,000 displaced persons from Illinois to Louisiana.[22]

Following the pattern of the good works of the Shrine and the MSA, Freemasons started other charitable programs or partnered with existing foundations. In 1934, the Northern Jurisdiction of the Scottish Rite established a fund for researching the causes of dementia praecox, which later became known as schizophrenia. In the Southern Jurisdiction, Scottish

Partial List of Masonic Disaster Relief, 1923–2000

LOCATION	YEAR	AMOUNT
Japanese earthquake	1923	$ 1,577
Florida hurricane	1926	114,237
Austrian relief	1938	5,202
Chilean earthquake	1939	7,387
Philippine relief	1945	46,798
Manitoba relief	1950	19,210
Holland relief	1953	29,985
Tamaulipas (Mexico) relief	1955	18,024
Italy flood	1967	20,009
Peru relief	1970	19,221
Guatemala relief	1976	66,130
Mississippi flood	1979	80,561
Chilean flood	1985	32,500
South Carolina hurricane	1989	243,325
California earthquake	1989	62,000
Hawaii hurricane	1992	76,900
Midwestern flood	1993	460,925
Oklahoma City bombing	1995	89,962
Washington flood	1996	32,487
Nevada flood	1997	48,850
Central American hurricane	1999	171,600
New Mexico wild fires	2000	60,325

Source: Masonic Service Association, Silver Spring, MD.

"We have assumed a place of leadership unequalled by any other organization. We have moved out of the seclusion of our halls . . . into the community to serve the country, the race, the community and God."

— PRESIDENT OF INTERNATIONAL CONFERENCE OF PRINCE HALL GRAND MASTERS, 1952 [23]

Rite Masons in Georgia and Texas opened hospitals, financed a dormitory building for women at the University of Texas, and donated money and equipment to the Gallaudet School for the Deaf in St. Louis. [24]

RESEARCH LAB,
UTICA, NEW YORK

In its first 35 years,
the Masonic Medical
Research Laboratory at
Utica was mainly dedi-
cated to basic scientific
research in cardiology.
Located on the grounds
of the New York Masonic
Home, the laboratory
opened in 1958. The
Grand Royal Arch Chap-
ter donated $150,000
for the construction of
a wing attached to the
main research facility
in 1974. A second floor
was added to the wing
in 1988.

2002. Printed with
permission of Masonic
Medical Research
Laboratory, Utica, NY.

The Second World War had spurred further Masonic commitment to good works. By 1980, nearly every branch of the fraternity had aligned itself with a charitable outreach program. In 1955, the Knights Templar started the Eye Foundation to help children born with visual disabilities. The General Grand Chapter of Royal Arch Masons began funding Central Auditory Processing Disorders in 1974. Other Masonic charities included Dentistry for Handicapped Children (Grotto) and support of the Muscular Dystrophy Association (Tall Cedars of Lebanon). The Eastern Star and the Amaranth made direct donations to the American Cancer Society, the Heart Fund and the American Diabetes Association.[25]

Many grand lodges began their own charities. In 1958, for example, the Grand Lodge of New York opened a medical research laboratory in Utica. Among its research projects today are abnormal heart rhythm and sudden infant death syndrome. In 1966, the Grand Lodge of Kansas established a foundation that later provided financial support for cancer research at the University of Kansas Medical Center.[26] The way in which charities were selected for support by the fraternity was usually based on the personal decision of a Grand Master or the leader of another Masonic group.

Challenged in the courts to defend their right to organize in the early 1900s, Prince Hall grand lodges supported the creation of the NAACP in 1909 and encouraged African-Americans to stand up for their civil rights. Beginning in the 1920s, northern Prince Hall grand lodges officially supported federal anti-lynching legislation.[27] In the South, Prince Hall grand lodges partnered with churches and NAACP chapters to gain greater voting rights. Prince Hall magazines "unofficially" endorsed brothers running for political office. Although some Prince Hall leaders worried about the fraternity becoming overly political, persistent racism in America made civil rights an issue of universal concern among the brothers.[28] In 1951, the International Conference of Prince Hall Grand Masters created the Prince Hall Masons Legal Research Fund under the control of the NAACP.[29] In 1958, Thurgood Marshall, chief legal counsel for the NAACP and a Freemason, stated, "Whenever and wherever I needed money and did not know any place to get it, Prince Hall Masons never let me down."[30] Between 1951 and 1962, Prince Hall Masons spent $250,000 in support of civil rights, and in 1961-62 they spent $750,000.[31]

206   *Adorning American Communities*

The Structure of Freemasonry

By 1965, American Freemasonry had become more like a national conglomerate than a group of independent state organizations. It was as complicated as any modern bureaucracy with the dozens of affiliated organizations, numerous charitable foundations and millions of members. State grand lodges no longer simply supervised the ritual work of local lodges or maintained Homes for older Masons. They began to allocate millions of dollars for charity. Instead of focusing on a single initiative, however, individual lodges and grand lodges chose their own philanthropic causes. Although post-war Freemasonry achieved unity through the ideal of community service, Masonic programs usually failed to have great impact. Becoming the Master of a lodge was no longer the highest honor in the craft, but the first rung on many Masonic "corporate ladders." Local Masonic leaders sought positions at the district or grand lodge level. Similar ladders existed within the York Rite, Scottish Rite, Shrine, and other Masonic clubs. It became common for Masons to simultaneously find themselves on various rungs on several ladders. Many active Masons lost their effectiveness by spreading their energy among so many positions.

THE STRUCTURE OF
FREEMASONRY

Life, *October 8, 1956.*
National Heritage
Museum.

Decline of American Freemasonry

"The hour-glass is an emblem of human life; behold! how swiftly the sands run, and how rapidly our lives are drawing to a close. We cannot, without astonishment, behold the little particles which are contained in this machine, how they pass away almost imperceptibly, and yet, to our surprise, in a short space of an hour, they are all exhausted. Thus wastes man."

— THOMAS SMITH WEBB, 1808 [32]

SHRINER GERALD FORD

A Freemason since 1949 and a member of many branches of the craft, President Ford joined Saladin Shrine at Grand Rapids, Michigan, in 1959. He received the 33rd degree from the Scottish Rite in 1962. Ford is the most recent Freemason to serve as president of the United States.

ca. 1976. Shriners International.

In 1965, Freemasons continued to bask in the afterglow of their fraternity's long history of success and social prestige. Freemasons were prominent among many professions. There were entertainers such as Red Skelton, preachers such as Rev. Norman Vincent Peale, athletes such as Bart Starr, judges such as Chief Justice Earl Warren and politicians like Barry Goldwater. They were so much a part of the establishment that FBI Director J. Edgar Hoover congratulated his brother Shriners in leading the fight against communism. [33]

The fraternity was still humming like a big Detroit-built engine. MSA's *Short Talk Bulletins* and Masonic libraries continued to bring history and knowledge to the brethren. The York Rite and Scottish Rite provided dramatic ritual and pageantry that appealed to the growing membership base. Grand lodges continued to expand their Masonic Homes into modern retirement communities. Local lodge banquets were supplemented by state and national gatherings, while Shriners continued to thrill children with parades and circuses and to celebrate exuberantly at conventions. Being a good Mason was a sign of respect within corporations and between small businessmen and salesmen. DeMolay, Rainbow and Job's Daughters welcomed children of the post-war baby boom. Masonic community service projects were contributing to the relief of some of America's social and public health problems. Keeping the fraternity's extended structure firing on all cylinders, however, required a great amount of energy and coordination.

Unfortunately, leaders in the craft, like leaders in the nation at large, failed to appreciate fully the fundamental transformation that America was experiencing in the mid-1960s. A younger generation was not accepting the social lines drawn by earlier generations. During the 1960s, forces were unleashed that threatened 50 years of sacrifice and ingenuity. Those demanding civil rights and a withdrawal from Vietnam led a multi-generational rebellion against societal convention and conformity. As teenage drug use and pregnancy rose, so did adult crime, divorce and alcoholism. American core values of morality, religion and justice were eroded by the limits of military power and political, union and corporate corruption. By 1980, the economic prosperity of the post-war period had turned into inflation, recession and the loss of millions of manufacturing jobs. Attendance at traditional religious services declined, as new spiritual and philosophical movements phased in and out.[34]

Three major social earthquakes severely tested the fraternity and undermined Freemasonry's place within American society. First, the expansion of leisure time, the ease of travel and the growth of disposable personal income allowed more Americans in the 1970s to watch television, shop and eat out. Masonic leaders spent money on bigger banquets, parades and more opulent affairs to entice more men to join, but the events could scarcely hope to compete with the spectacles readily available in color in living rooms or at shopping malls across America. While this approach attracted Masons who wanted to socialize, it did nothing to strengthen the fraternity or to "make good men better." Only the Scottish Rite and the Shrine, whose new members were already Masons, continued to show growth. In 1965 the Scottish Rite crossed the one million mark and Shrine membership of 800,000 Nobles remained steady until 1980.[35]

Second, "counter-culture" freedom ran contrary to the views of the fraternity's middle-class hierarchy. Unable or unwilling to accept the changes, Freemasons resisted the trends of the modern world and the 1960s "youth movement." Parental pressure to join youth organizations faced peer pressure that warned, "Don't trust anyone over 30." DeMolay, in particular, suffered as a direct result. There were young men who joined their father's and grandfather's lodge but rarely attended meetings. By the 1980s, a growing Masonic generation gap existed.[36] Conspicuously absent from the lodge was the vast middle-class suburban generation that equated Freemasonry to the cartoon depiction of the "Loyal Order of Water Buffaloes" in *The Flintstones*.

The seismographic shift in American morality in the 1960s and 1970s disturbed older Freemasons. Proudly proclaiming their patriotism and their stalwart faith in God, they reaffirmed their unshakable belief that Masonic morality was America's morality. Masonic publications ignored Watergate, the failures in Vietnam and other harsh realities. Instead they contained inspiring articles on such famous Masons as Paul Revere and Clark Gable. Grand Lodges continued to provide financial support in the

OKLAHOMA INDIAN MASONIC DEGREE TEAM

Freemasons from different lodges often form special degree teams to perform the ritual in unique and entertaining ways. Founded in 1948, the Oklahoma Indian Masonic degree team, composed of Native Americans from several tribes, has been invited to perform the third degree in more than 40 states.

Curt Teich & Co., Chicago, ca. 1955. National Heritage Museum, A96/066/4333.

In celebration of America's bicentennial, the Scottish Rite Masons in the Northern Jurisdiction created the Museum of Our National Heritage and dedicated it to "America, her history, her patriots and builders, her ideals and to faith in her future." Since its opening in 1975, the museum has presented more than 200 exhibitions and has welcomed more than one million visitors. The name was changed to National Heritage Museum in 2001. An extensive collection of fraternal material is a vital part of the museum and the accompanying Van Gorden-Williams Library.

Hutchins Photography, Inc., Belmont, MA, 1975. National Heritage Museum.

1980s and 1990s to restore national monuments — Fort McHenry, the Valley Forge Memorial Arch, the Statue of Liberty and the Peace Garden in North Dakota.[37]

Failing to adjust to post-modern, post-industrial America, Freemasonry became alienated from society. With the passing of each member of the "joiner" generations and the closing of each lodge, the fraternity slipped slowly from America's consciousness. Americans increasingly found Freemasonry less attractive with each new television channel, sporting event or tourist attraction, and greater demands from work, commuting and family. The old Masonic temples in many urban centers became dark and dreary places as lodges moved to the suburbs for better parking and easier access. Harsher realities hit Prince Hall Masons. Inner-city black neighborhoods were cleared to make way for urban renewal and highways. Middle-class blacks that could afford to move relocated to integrated suburbs, while many working-class blacks were laid off as industries disappeared.[38] Historians of the civil rights movement ignored the earlier contributions made by Prince Hall Masons.[39]

The Quality of Mercy

"[Freemasonry] stands for fraternity and philanthropy, truth and justice, reverence for God; and enlightenment in all spheres, civil, religious, and intellectual."

— CONSTITUTIONS OF THE GRAND LODGE OF MASSACHUSETTS, 1989[40]

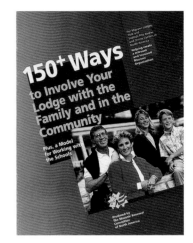

Masonic leaders did not seem to be overly concerned about the drop in membership numbers and the fading image in the community until the 1980s. They pacified themselves with the knowledge that other civic and fraternal organizations were also losing members and that Freemasonry had survived temporary membership losses in the past. But with the realization that membership had declined by more than 20 percent between 1965 and 1980, leaders within the fraternity began to act.[41] In the next 20 years, the leadership used every resource available to make it easier, quicker and cheaper to join while continually offering more social activities and charitable programs. The community outreach effort was designed to make the public aware of the good works of the fraternity and induce men to seek membership.

Overcoming longstanding unwritten codes of Masonic conduct, Grand Masters finally turned to direct advertising and mass marketing to reenergize the brethren. In 1988, a group of Masonic leaders created a Masonic Renewal Task Force to identify the problems facing the fraternity and to provide solutions. A firm was hired to conduct a survey among men who were not Masons to determine their attitude toward Freemasonry. Only 30 percent of those surveyed were familiar with the fraternity, and another 11 percent were not even aware of its existence. After reviewing the results of the survey, the task force prepared brochures, videotapes and guidebooks to assist lodges in promoting the fraternity. This marketing approach was met with mixed emotions. Many grand lodges rejected the idea of soliciting for members and preferred the usual custom of having the prospective member seek out a Mason. In some instances, however, the inquisitive prospect had difficulty finding the location of a Masonic lodge, let alone the whereabouts of a Mason.[42]

In the struggle to maintain credibility and improve membership statistics, some Grand Masters explored different approaches to attract new members. In 1992, the Grand Lodge of the District of Columbia arrived at a unique solution — degree festivals. These one-day events allowed men who were "too busy" to attend regular lodge meetings to receive all three degrees in a mass initiation. Other grand lodges picked up on the idea, and within a few years the Scottish Rite and Shrine joined in the festivals.

LODGE ASSISTANCE

The Masonic Renewal Committee of North America has published a number of brochures and other material to help Masons attract more members, increase lodge meeting attendance and participate in their communities. The committee was created in 1990 as a joint project among U.S. and Canadian Masonic grand lodges, the Scottish Rite and the Shrine.

150+ Ways for Lodges in Community Service, 1996. National Heritage Museum.

They Are All Exhausted: Freemasons' Service for New Communities

In several states, a man could go "all the way in one day" — from the first degree through the 32nd and into the Shrine.[43] What had typically taken as much as eight or more months and $500 in the 1920s now took as little as eight hours and $300 in the 1990s. The desire for more men even compelled the Shrine to drop its original membership requirement. Since 1877, a brother had to become either a 32nd degree Mason in the Scottish Rite or a Knight Templar in the York Rite before he could become a Shriner. The prerequisites were dropped in 2000 so that any Master Mason was welcome to join the Shrine.[44]

To raise public awareness and entice men to join, Masonic leaders sought new ways to involve the fraternity in charitable endeavors and community service. No longer focused on members and their families, Masonic charity was now more broadly directed toward anyone who needed assistance. In the 1970s, the Shrine expanded its hospital program by building centers for children with severe burns and later for those with spinal cord injuries. The Southern Jurisdiction of the Scottish Rite had been assisting children with learning disabilities since 1953, and the Northern Jurisdiction introduced a program in 1994 to provide learning centers for one-on-one

SHRINERS HOSPITAL POSTER

Since the opening of the first hospital in 1922, Shriners have spent $6.5 billion to help more than 700,000 children. Today they support 18 orthopedic hospitals, three burns centers and one spinal cord injury rehabilitation center. In every case, treatment is provided without charge to the parents of the children.

Shriners . . . Building a Better Tomorrow for Kids, 1990. National Heritage Museum, gift of the Shrine, A2004/001/1.

Adorning American Communities

tutoring of children with dyslexia. Many grand lodges and other affiliated Masonic groups have provided scholarships and supported hundreds of charities.[45] In 1989, Ralph Head, editor of the *California Freemason,* identified this new Masonic worldliness as "Applied Freemasonry." Just as speculative Freemasonry had evolved out of operative stonemasonry, Head could see Applied Freemasonry moving brothers from simply contemplating morality to putting it into action. Or more specifically, "For Masonry to live on in the future, it must demonstrate its usefulness to mankind."[46] Even though the combined Masonic philanthropies were contributing over $2 million per day — 70 percent of which went to the general public — the fraternity's 1995 membership figures had dropped below the 1920 level.[47]

Nevertheless, those charitable efforts did not change the public's general perception of Freemasonry. Compounding its other troubles was a resurgence of anti-Masonry. In some ways more severe than those of the 1830s, these attacks came from many directions on the political spectrum. In 1987, Judge David B. Sentelle's appointment to the U.S. Court of Appeals for the District of Columbia was delayed because he was a Freemason. Believing the craft to be discriminatory, several members of the Senate judiciary committee questioned whether a Mason on the bench might carry a bigoted attitude. Only after a lengthy debate was Judge Sentelle confirmed, and Freemasonry exonerated, by an 87-0 Senate vote.[48]

Attacks also came from the religious right. In 1990, evangelical pastors revived old accusations that Freemasonry was a satanic cult. So loud were the accusations that the Southern Baptist Convention commissioned a thorough study of the craft. After a great deal of controversy and recrimination, the delegates to the 1993 national convention ultimately decided that Masonic membership was a matter of an individual's own conscience and responsibility.[49] The severity of these attacks led to the establishment of the Masonic Information Center to provide information to the media and to correct erroneous or misleading statements made about the fraternity. John Robinson, an articulate spokesman for Freemasonry, was the

ANTI-MASONIC COMICS

Religious attacks against Freemasonry were renewed in the 1980s. One of the most widely circulated was "The Curse of Baphomet," a comic book that attempts to create the impression that the fraternity is evil.

Jack T. Chick, The Curse of Baphomet, *One Accord Ministries, Dubuque, IA, 1990. National Heritage Museum.*

driving force behind its creation.[50] The Center became a part of the Masonic Service Association.

Journalists and writers had long sniped at Freemasonry, but along with the popularity of the Internet in the 1990s came an eruption of anti-Masonic accusations and paranoid fantasies. Websites produced views that attempted to link Freemasonry to every conceivable conspiracy, cabal and unexplained phenomenon in history — from the Pyramids of Giza to John F. Kennedy's assassination.[51] Other books and websites have attempted to link Freemasonry to the Holy Grail, the medieval Knights Templar and hidden symbols within the street plan of Washington, DC.[52] And if these attacks and falsehoods were not enough, the Wiccan/Pagan movement plagiarized Masonic rituals and claimed them to be of ancient origin.[53]

Undermining each of Freemasonry's problems was a deeper issue, one that Masonic leaders were inherently unable to recognize. Freemasonry was losing the one commodity that every craft must hold dear: quality. The post-war prosperity and social equality of the 1960s and 1970s opened the door for membership in formerly exclusive clubs. In the rush to compete with the growing number of civic organizations and to be more inclusive, Freemasons altered their standards in a vain attempt to make quantity as valuable as quality. At the same time, many professional and inquisitive men sought other interests. The honor and status once earned by being accepted as a Mason and being recognized as "a good man and true" was blurred with the emphasis on philanthropy. The Shrine, for instance, was no longer the "playground" for affluent Masons but preferred to proclaim itself "the world's greatest philanthropy."

Amidst the membership loss and confusion of the 1990s, Freemasons in most states were at least able to resolve an old irregularity. Since Prince Hall received a lodge charter from England in 1787, predominantly white and predominantly black lodges had coexisted independently. Despite occasional examples of white and black men recognizing each other as Masons and brief attempts by grand lodges to recognize each other, larger forces thwarted attempts of official recognition.[54] Finally, after much discussion the Grand Lodge of Connecticut and the Prince Hall Grand Lodge of Connecticut formally recognized each other in 1989.

> It is mutually agreed . . . on this 14th day of October 1989, that we dwell together in peace and harmony, and each do hereafter fraternally recognize the other as legitimate proponents of Brotherly Love, Relief and Truth within the state of Connecticut . . .[55]

Their action brought immediate denunciation from some grand lodges, but other states soon followed Connecticut's lead. Two other barriers were

JOINT MASONIC BANQUET

In 1994, mainstream and Prince Hall Freemasons held a joint social event for the first time in Pennsylvania history. Among the 1,500 Freemasons and guests attending the banquet was Pittsburgh Mayor Thomas J. Murphy. The photograph shows the two Grand Masters of Freemasons in Pennsylvania: George H. Hohenshildt (front row, 2nd from left) and Roland K. Lee (front row, 4th from left).

Photograph by Robert Binnie, 1994. Courtesy of Herbert C. Wolstoncroft Jr.

overcome. Both of the Northern Jurisdictions of the Scottish Rite recognized each other in 1995, and more importantly, the United Grand Lodge of England formally recognized the Prince Hall Grand Lodge of Massachusetts on December 14, 1994. By 2001, a total of 32 grand lodges had joint recognition agreements and more were being debated.[56] It is unlikely, however, that the two grand lodges within each state will ever merge, because there is little reason to do so and both enjoy their autonomy. Each grand lodge has its own traditions and history and each serves its own communities. While integration might appear the logical end to 200 years of separation, Freemasons understand that brotherly love only occurs when human beings, regardless of Masonic affiliation, willingly recognize each other as such and not through grand lodge decrees.

The debate over the state of Freemasonry goes on. No doubt, it is one that will never end. Is its 40-year membership decline a sign of obsolescence or is the fraternity returning to a more normal membership level after the great influx of the post-war years?[57] If indeed the lodge is an anachronism, then — to borrow a turn of phrase from the ritual — Masons may at least look forward to the prospect of enjoying the happy reflection of a well-spent life. Like Father Abraham, they may look about and see their progeny as countless as the stars in heaven. If, on the other hand, Freemasonry has a productive future within the American community, then the men who join its lodges will most likely continue to work as their brothers did in the past — trusting in God and patiently practicing the tenets of brotherly love, relief and truth.

"May the blessing of Heaven be with us and all regular Masons; to beautify and cement us with every moral and social virtue. Amen."

— WILLIAM PRESTON, 1772[58]

"The lapse of time, the ruthless hand of ignorance, and the devastations of war, have laid waste and destroyed many valuable monuments of antiquity. Even the Temple of King Solomon, so spacious and magnificent, and constructed by so many celebrated artists, was yet laid in ruins, and escaped not the unsparing ravages of barbarous force. Freemasonry, notwithstanding, has been able to survive. The attentive ear receives the sound from the instructive tongue, and its sacred mysteries are safely lodged in the repository of faithful breasts. The tools and implements of architecture, symbols the most expressive! imprint on the memory wise and serious truths, and transmit unimpaired, through a succession of ages, the excellent tenets of this institution."

— WILLIAM PRESTON, *Illustrations of Masonry*, 1772

THE LIGHT OF MASONRY

The Light of Masonry, W.C. Doyle, 1984. National Heritage Museum, gift of Alexander A. Bird, 2000.026.10.

Name_____

E.A._____ F.C._____ M.M._____

_____ Lodge No._____ At_____

The Light of Masonry

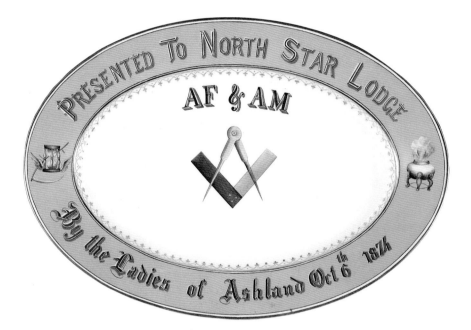

MASONIC PLATTER, 1874

Decorated by Jones, McDuffee & Stratton, Massachusetts, 1874.
National Heritage Museum, gift of North Star Lodge, AF&AM, Ashland, MA, 2000.021.

Notes

Notes to the Introduction

1. William Hillman, *Mr. President* (New York: Farrar, Straus & Young, 1952) 81.

2. Allen E. Roberts. *Brother Truman* (Highland Springs, VA: Anchor Communications, 1985) 143–49, and Dwight L. Smith, *Goodly Heritage* (Indianapolis: Grand Lodge of Masons in Indiana, 1968) 401–2. Smith attended the Beech Grove Lodge meeting with President Truman. Truman jokingly asked that his Masonic knowledge be tested before he was allowed in. Furthermore, he insisted he be introduced as a Past Grand Master of Missouri and not as President of the United States.

3. *Preston's Illustrations of Masonry,* CD-ROM, Andrew Prescott, ed. (Sheffield, UK: Academy Electronics Publications, 2001) 1775 ed., 72.

4. Masonic lectures vary from lodge to lodge and are not uniform even today. This quote derives from a speech made by Thomas Dunckerley, Provincial Grand Master of Freemasons in Hampshire, in 1769. It was printed in Wellins Calcott, *A Candid Disquisition of the Principle and Practices of the Most Ancient and Honorable Society of Free and Accepted Masons* (London: James Dixwell, 1769; facsimile reprint, Bloomington, IL: Masonic Book Club, 1989) 138–39. Later Masonic writers, particularly William Preston, edited this passage for their own purposes, and it is now quoted as it is used today in most American Masonic lodges.

5. *Preston's Illustrations of Masonry,* 1796 ed., 49.

6. *Preston's Illustrations of Masonry,* 1772 ed., 14.

7. Freemasonry's origins remain the single biggest issue in Masonic historiography. Among the best scholarly sources are: John Hamill, *The Craft: A History of English Freemasonry* (Wellingborough, England: Crucible, 1986), and David Stevenson, *The First Free-masons: Scotland's Early Lodges and Their Members* (Edinburgh: Grand Lodge of Scotland, 2nd ed., 2001).

8. See *2004 List of Lodges Masonic,* (Bloomington, IL: Pantagraph Printing, 2004), and Kent Henderson and Tony Pope, *Freemasonry Universal: A New Guide to the Masonic World,* 2 vols. (Victoria, Australia: Global Masonic Publications, 1998–2000).

9. For example, see John Robison, *Proof of a Conspiracy against All Religions and Governments of Europe, carried on in the Secret Meetings of Free Masons, Illuminati, and Reading Societies* (London: William Creech, T. Cadell Jr., W. Davies, 1797); Leo Taxil, *La Femme et l'Enfant dans la Franc Maconnerie Universelle* (Paris: A.C. De La Rive, 1894), and Pat Robertson, *The New World Order* (Dallas: Word Publishing, 1992).

10. Alan Carles Kors, *The Encyclopedia of the Enlightenment* (New York: Oxford University Press, 2003) vol. 1, 418–19.

11. *Preston's Illustrations of Masonry,* 1772 ed., 13.

12. For a basic explanation of Freemasonry's rituals, see Carl H. Claudy, *Introduction to Freemasonry,* 3 vols. (Washington, DC: Temple Publishers, 1931), and Allen E. Roberts, *The Craft and Its Symbols* (Richmond, VA: Macoy, 1974). For an example of a deeper interpretation, see W. Kirk MacNulty, *The Way of the Craftsman: A Search for the Spiritual Essence of Craft Freemasonry* (London: Central Regalia, 2002).

13. James Anderson, *The Constitutions of the Free-Masons* (1723, facsimile edition, Abingdon, UK: Burgess & Son, 1976) 61.

14. Wallace McLeod, ed., *The Old Gothic Constitutions,* facsimile reprint of four early printed texts of the Masonic old charges (Bloomington, IL: Masonic Book Club, 1985).

15. Anderson, *Constitutions*, 50–53.

16. Where this quote originated is unclear, but eminent jurist and Freemason Roscoe Pound, in his book *Masonic Addresses and Writings of Roscoe Pound* (New York: Macoy, 1953, 20–21), argued that English Freemasons in the early 1700s held to this mission. By the 1970s, the phrase was universally accepted in American Freemasonry and appears in large type in Roberts, *The Craft and Its Symbols*, 8.

17. Anderson, *Constitutions*, 56, 60–61; *Coil's Masonic Encyclopedia* (Richmond, VA: Macoy, rev. ed., 1996) 373; *Constitutions and Regulations of the Most Worshipful Grand Lodge of Ancient Free and Accepted Masons of the Commonwealth of Massachusetts*, (Boston, 1989) Sec. 416–20. In Ohio, for example, 142 men were expelled from Freemasonry in 1870; 20 men were expelled in 1920, and four were expelled in 1970. See *Proceedings of the Grand Lodge of Ohio*, 1870, 128; 1920, 353; 1970, 38.

18. *Preston's Illustrations of Masonry*, 1772 ed., 12.

19. *Preston's Illustrations of Masonry*, 1775 ed., 59. The "gentlemen" would be the lodge stewards.

20. Claudy, *Introduction to Freemasonry*, vol. 1, 8. The phrase originates at least as far back as William Preston in 1772, who wrote: "The whole is one regular system of morality, conceived in a strain of interesting allegory, which unfolds its beauties to the candid and industrious inquirer." *Preston's Illustrations of Masonry*, 1772 ed., 60.

21. *Proceedings of the Celebration of the Right Worshipful Grand Lodge of Pennsylvania . . . at Its Celebration of the Bi-Centenary of the Birth of . . . Grand Master Benjamin Franklin* (Philadelphia, 1906) 59–60.

22. According to Alexander Piatigorsky, *Freemasonry: The Study of a Phenomenon* (London: Harvill, 1999) 342: "There are more than 64,000 titles of books, articles and other publications devoted to Masonry and written by, or (though far less often) specifically about Freemasons." See also Kent Walgren, *Freemasonry, Anti-Masonry and Illuminism in the United States, 1734–1850: A Bibliography*, 2 vols. (Worcester, MA: American Antiquarian Society, 2003). Walgren's bibliography cites over 2,700 Masonic publications before the Civil War. An Internet search (*www.google.com*) for the word "Freemasonry" on May 10, 2004, returned 190,000 hits. A search within www.amazon.com on the same day listed 3,127 books under "Freemasonry."

23. Arthur M. Schlesinger, "Biography of a Nation of Joiners," *American Historical Review*, October 1944, 1–25; Eric Hobsbawn, *Primitive Rebels: Studies in Archaic Forms of Social Movement in the 19th and 20th Centuries* (New York: Frederick A. Praeger, 1963) 152–54. In most cases, however, the fraternity is simply ignored by scholars. See Piatigorsky, *Freemasonry: A Study of a Phenomenon*, 342.

24. See Mark C. Carnes, *Secret Ritual and Manhood in Victorian America* (New Haven, CT: Yale University Press, 1989); Mary Ann Clawson, *Constructing Brotherhood: Class, Gender and Fraternalism* (Princeton, NJ: Princeton University Press, 1989), and William Muraskin, *Middle-Class Blacks in White Society: Prince Hall Freemasonry in America* (Berkeley: University of California Press, 1975).

25. Lynn Dumenil, *Freemasonry and American Culture, 1880–1930* (Princeton, NJ: Princeton University Press, 1984); Steven C. Bullock, *Revolutionary Brotherhood: Freemasonry and the Transformation of the American Social Order, 1730–1840* (Chapel Hill: University of North Carolina, 1996), and Jasper Ridley, *The Freemasons: A History of the World's Most Powerful Secret Society* (New York: Arcade Publishing, 2001).

26. *Coil's Masonic Encyclopedia*, 55. Between 1738 and 1902, the Roman Catholic Church issued several bulls and encyclicals concerning the craft, including Pope Leo XIII's strong condemnation of Freemasonry in his 1884 encyclical, *Humanum Genus*. American Protestant denominations that have issued proclamations against the fraternity include the Lutheran Church, Missouri Synod. In the 1990s, leaders of the Southern Baptist Convention and other conservative evangelical denominations rigorously denounced Freemasonry. See James J. Holly, *The Southern Baptist Convention and Freemasonry*, vol. 2, including complete text of vol. 1 (Taylor, SC: Faith Printing Company, 1993).

27. The Volume of the Sacred Law would be the Bible in the case of a Christian, the Torah in the case of a Jew, the Koran in the case of a Muslim, and so forth.

28. Anderson, *Constitutions*, 48.

29. See Richard Hofstadter, *The Paranoid Style in American Politics and Other Essays* (New York: Knopf, 1965).

30. Anderson, *Constitutions*, 50.

31. See Alvin J. Schmidt, *Fraternal Organizations* (Westport, CT: Greenwood Press, 1980) 23–25, 52, 100–5, 176–78, and William R. Denslow, *10,000 Famous Freemasons* (Trenton: Missouri Lodge of Research, 1958) vol. 2, 317.

Notes to Chapter 1

1. Early Masonic rituals and lectures varied widely from lodge to lodge and are not fully uniform even today.

This quote is written as questions and answers in Samuel Pritchard's *Masonry Dissect'd* (London: printed for J. Wilford, 1730) 13. Later Masonic writers modified and edited this passage for their own purposes, but it is essentially the same that is used throughout most American Masonic lodges.

2. For the diversity of Masonic lodges around the globe, see Kent Henderson and Tony Pope, *Freemasonry Universal: A New Guide to the Masonic World*, 2 vol. (Victoria, Australia: Global Masonic Publications, 1998), and R. William Weisberger, Wallace McLeod and S. Brent Morris, eds., *Freemasonry on Both Sides of the Atlantic* (Boulder, CO: East European Monographs, 2002).

3. *Preston's Illustrations of Masonry*, CD-ROM, Andrew Prescott, ed. (Sheffield, UK: Academy Electronics Publications, 2001) 1772 ed., 12.

4. James Anderson, *The Constitutions of the Free-Masons* (1723, Facsimile ed., Abingdon, UK: Burgess & Son, 1976) 50.

5. While most early Freemasons were Anglican Protestants, Anthony, 6th Duke of Montagu, Grand Master in 1732, was a Roman Catholic; the third Grand Master, John Desaguliers, was a Huguenot minister and James Anderson, author of the 1723 *Constitutions*, was a Presbyterian minister. The first recorded Jewish Freemason was Edward Rose in 1732. See William R. Denslow, *10,000 Famous Freemasons*, 4 vols. (Trenton: Missouri Lodge of Research, 1957-60), and Jacob Katz, *Jews and Freemasonry in Europe, 1723-1939*, translated from Hebrew by Leonard Oschry (Cambridge, MA: Harvard University Press, 1970) 16.

6. The origin of this definition is unclear. The eminent clergyman and Freemason Joseph Fort Newton (1876-1950) may have first coined it in *The Builders: The Story and Study of Freemasonry* (New York: George Doran, 1914) 126.

7. Anderson, *Constitutions*, 49.

8. David Stevenson, *The First Freemasons: Scotland's Early Lodges and Their Members* (Edinburgh: Grand Lodge of Scotland, 2001) 2.

9. The charges of several stonemason guilds, ranging from the 1300s to the 1700s, still exist. "All have a common form: (a) an opening prayer; (b) a legendary history of the mason craft tracing it from biblical origins to its establishment in England; (c) a code of regulations for Masters, Fellows and Apprentices covering both craft practices and morals; (d) arrangements for large-scale 'territorial' assemblies at which attendance was obligatory; (e) procedures for the trial and punishments of offenders; (f) admission procedures 'for new men that were never charged before'

including an oath of fidelity." John Hamill, *The Craft: A History of English Freemasonry* (Wellingborough, UK: Crucible, 1986) 29-30. See also *The Regis Poem* (Bloomington, IL: Masonic Book Club, 1970 reprint).

10. Stevenson, *The First Freemasons*, 34-35.

11. Anderson, *Constitutions*, 50-51, and Hamill, *The Craft*, 41-42. For an explanation of the term "Free and Accepted," see *Coil's Masonic Encyclopedia* (Richmond, VA: Macoy, rev. ed., 1996) 4-5, 272-73. The terms "Ancient," "Free," and "Accepted" have multiple definitions. "Ancient" usually refers to the Ancient Grand Lodge of England founded in 1756. Its use demonstrates that a grand lodge traces its lineage back to this grand lodge. "Ancient" also refers to being old, or originating in remote times, and is used by such organizations as Boston's Ancient and Honorable Artillery Company. "Free" usually refers to a free-born man, or someone who is not a serf or in bondage. It also refers to having the skill to work in freestone, to design carve and sculpt and not simply to build. "Accepted" refers not only to the non-stonemasons who were accepted into stonemasons' lodges but also to the fact that the fraternity was accepted, that is, legal and fully sanctioned by the Crown and the Church.

12. Anderson, *Constitutions*, 20-21.

13. For an overview of the English Enlightenment, see Frederick C. Beiser, *The Sovereignty of Reason: the Defense of Rationality in the Early English Enlightenment* (Princeton, NJ: Princeton University Press, 1996); J.R. Clarke, "The Royal Society and Early Grand Lodge Freemasonry," *Ars Quatuor Coronatorum: Transactions of the Quatuor Coronati Lodge No. 2076*, hereafter cited as *AQC*, vol. 80, 1967, 110-20, and Alan Charles Kors, *The Encyclopedia of the Enlightenment* (New York: Oxford University Press, 2003) vol. 1, 417-18.

14. Steven C. Bullock, *Revolutionary Brotherhood, Freemasonry and the Transformation of the American Social Order, 1730-1840* (Chapel Hill: University of North Carolina Press, 1996) 14. For further reading, see Saint Thomas Aquinas, *Summa Theologica* (1485), and Sir Francis Bacon, *New Atlantis* (1626).

15. Anderson, *Constitutions*, 13.

16. Bullock, *Revolutionary Brotherhood*, 22-23. Popular books of the Solomon's Temple era included Samuel Lee, *Orbis Miraculum, or the Temple of Solomon: pourtrayed by Scripture-Light...* (1659), John Bunyan, *Solomon's Temple Spiritualiz'd; or Gospel-Light Fetcht out of the Temple at Jerusalem...* (1688), and Sir Isaac Newton, *The Chronologies of the Ancient Kingdoms* (1728).

17. *Encyclopaedia Britannica*, "Temple Architecture"

(Chicago: William Benton Publishers, 1966) vol. 21, 927. See also Rev. Harry Kelso Eversull, *The Temples in Jerusalem* (Cincinnati, OH: Masonic Memorial Chapel Association, 1946).

18. Stevenson, *The First Freemasons*, 102.

19. Samuel Pritchard, *Masonry Dissect'd: Being an Universal and Genuine Description of All Its Branches, from the Original to the Present Time, as It is Delivered in the Constituted Regular Lodges . . .* (London: printed for J. Wilford, 1730) 25-29, (Bloomington, IL: Masonic Book Club, 1977 reprint with analysis and commentary by Harry Carr).

20. Stevenson, *The First Freemasons*, 7-8. See also Frances A. Yates, *The Art of Memory* (Chicago: University of Chicago Press, 1974) 303-5.

21. Anderson, *Constitutions*, 50.

22. For an overview, see Porter, *London: A Social History* (Cambridge, MA: Harvard University Press, 1995), "Chapter Six: Commercial City: 1650-1800."

23. Hamill, *The Craft*, 41-42.

24. Harry W. Rylands, "The Masonic Apron," *AQC,* vol. 5, 1892, and Hamill, *The Craft*, 73-76.

25. David Stevens, "James Anderson: Man & Mason," *Heredom: Transaction of the Scottish Rite Research Society* (Washington, DC: Scottish Rite Research Society, 2002) vol. 10, 93-138.

26. A.C.F. Jackson, *English Masonic Exposures, 1760-1769* (London: Lewis Masonic, 1986).

27. Hamill, *The Craft*, 50-51. The rival grand lodges were the Ancient Grand Lodge or "Antients" (1750s) in London, the Grand Lodge at York (1720s, 1760-1790s), the Grand Lodge South of the River Trent (1780s) and another short-lived grand lodge in London that broke away from the "Antients" in 1770.

28. Lawrence Dermott, *Ahiman Rezon* (Bloomington, IL: Masonic Book Club, 1972 reprint), and C.N. Batham, "The Grand Lodge of England according to the Old Institutions," Prestonian Lecture for 1981; reprinted with discussion in *AQC*, vol. 94 (1981). The Ancients were also known as the "Antients."

29. Hamill, *The Craft*, 50-51.

30. Hamill, *The Craft*, 87-98. For a full listing, see John Lane, *Masonic Records 1717-1894, Lists of all the Lodges at Home and Abroad* (London: United Grand Lodge of England, 1895).

31. Hamill, *The Craft*, 100; *Coil's Masonic Encyclopedia*, 575-77. Ancient Hebrew architects did not have the knowledge to build a true arch. Although Laurence Dermott claimed to have been "exalted" into the Royal Arch degree in 1746, the oldest minute books that record the conferral of the degree are from the Fredericksburg, Virginia, lodge in 1753. For an overview of the Royal Arch, see Bernard E. Jones, *Freemason's Book of the Royal Arch* (London: George G. Harrap & Co., 1965).

32. Hamill, *The Craft*, 53-55.

33. William Preston as quoted in Colin Dyer, *William Preston and His Work* (Shepperton, UK: Lewis Masonic, 1987) 236.

34. Dyer, *William Preston and His Work*, 7.

35. Denslow, *10,000 Famous Freemasons*, vol. 3, 365-66, and Dyer, *William Preston and His Work*, 4-9. When Preston died in 1818, he willed his estate to support the Masonic Charity Fund and the Masonic Home for Female Children, and to establish a fund for the presentation of Masonic lectures. The United Grand Lodge of England still maintains this fund.

36. *Preston's Illustrations of Masonry*, 1772 ed., xiii-xvii.

37. *The Masonic Addresses and Writings of Roscoe Pound* (New York: Macoy, 1953) 20-21. See also Alexander Piatigorsky, *Freemasonry: A Study of a Phenomenon* (London: Harvill Press, 1999) 151.

38. C.N. Batham, "Chevalier Ramsay; a New Appreciation," *AQC*, vol. 81, 1968, Appendix 1, 299, 301.

39. Hamill, *The Craft*, 87-88.

40. Margaret C. Jacob, *Living the Enlightenment: Freemasonry and Politics in Eighteenth-Century Europe* (New York: Oxford University Press, 1991) 4-5.

41. Jacob, *Living the Enlightenment*, 23. For an overview of the Roman Catholic Church's official understanding of Freemasonry and a transcription of *In eminenti*, see Alec Mellor, "The Roman Catholic Church and the Craft," *AQC*, vol. 89, 1972, 60-69.

42. Jacob, *Living the Enlightenment*, 4, 225.

43. Denslow, *10,000 Famous Freemasons*, vol. 4, 8, and *Coil's Masonic Encyclopedia*, 499-504.

44. For a full treatment of the "oration," see Lisa Kahler, "Andrew Michael Ramsay and his Masonic Oration," *Heredom*, vol. 1, 1991, 19-47, and Cyril N. Batham, "Ramsay's Oration: The Epernay and Grand Lodge Versions," *Heredom*, vol. 1, 1991, 49-59.

45. Jacob, *Living the Enlightenment*, 207-9; Mary Ann Clawson, *Constructing Brotherhood: Class, Gender and Fraternalism* (Princeton, NJ: Princeton University Press, 1989) 79-80.

46. For a sampling of how different people adapted Freemasonry to their societies, see R. William Weisberger, et al., eds., *Freemasonry on Both Sides of the Atlantic* (Boulder, CO: East European Monograph, 2002).

47. George A. Newbury and Louis L. Williams, *A History of the Supreme Council of the Ancient Accepted Scottish Rite of Freemasonry for the Northern Masonic Jurisdiction of the USA* (Lexington, MA: Supreme Council, 1987) 31-33, and William L. Fox, *Lodge of the Double-*

Headed Eagle: Two Centuries of Scottish Rite Free-masonry in America's Southern Jurisdiction (Fayetteville: University of Arkansas Press, 1997) 13–14.

48. Denslow, *10,000 Famous Freemasons*, vol. 2, 76–77; Newbury and Williams, *History of the Supreme Council*, 50, and Jacob, *Living the Enlightenment*, 156. Frederick was a logical choice for this position because of his well-known Masonic membership and deep friendship with the philosopher Voltaire and because he was considered an "enlightened despot." See Alan Carles Kors, *Encyclopedia of the Enlightenment* (New York: Oxford University Press, 2003) vol. 1, 417–18.

Notes to Chapter 2

1. David Stevenson, *The First Freemasons: Scotland's Early Lodges and Their Members*, 2nd ed. (Edinburgh: Grand Lodge of Scotland, 2001) 143; Alphonse Cerza, "New Jersey," in Lewis C. Cook, ed., *Colonial Freemasonry* (Fulton: Missouri Lodge of Research Transactions, 1974) vol. 30, 106, and William R. Denslow, *10,000 Famous Freemasons* (Trenton: Missouri Lodge of Research, 1950) vol. 4, 144.

2. Conrad Hahn, "Freemasonry Comes to Our Shores," in Cook, ed., *Colonial Freemasonry*, 5, and Denslow, *10,000 Famous Freemasons*, vol. 1, 77. See also Melvin M. Johnson, *The Beginnings of Freemasonry in America* (New York: George H. Doran Co., 1924).

3. *Pennsylvania Gazette* (Philadelphia) December 3–8, 1730, in Wayne A. Huss, *The Master Builders: A History of the Grand Lodge of Free and Accepted Masons in Pennsylvania* (Philadelphia: Grand Lodge of Masons in Pennsylvania, 1986) vol. 1, 17.

4. Thomas S. Roy, *Stalwart Builders: The Grand Lodge of Masons in Massachusetts* (Boston: Grand Lodge of Masons in Massachusetts, 1971) 2–3. The current Massachusetts Grand Lodge refers to this date as the beginning of the St. John's Provincial Grand Lodge, for which Henry Price was the first Grand Master.

5. Huss, *Master Builders*, vol. 1, 17, and Walter M. Callaway Jr., "Georgia," in Cook, ed., *Colonial Freemasonry*, 59.

6. In 1737, two Philadelphia non-Masons, Dr. Evan Jones and John Remington, cruelly tricked Daniel Rees into believing he was going to be initiated into Freemasonry. During a hazing, Rees caught on fire and soon thereafter died of his burns. *Pennsylvania Gazette*, Feb. 14, 1737, 8, in Steven C. Bullock, *Revolutionary Brotherhood: Freemasonry and the Transformation of the American Social Order, 1739–1840* (Chapel

Hill: University of North Carolina Press, 1996) 50–51.

7. Letter from Benjamin Franklin to his parents, H.W. Brands, *The First American: The Life and Times of Benjamin Franklin* (New York: Anchor Books, 2002) 153.

8. Bullock, *Revolutionary Brotherhood*, 4.

9. Huss, *Master Builders*, vol. 1, 26–27. See also Julius Friedrich Sachse, *Benjamin Franklin as a Free Mason* (Philadelphia: New Era Printing Company, 1906) 93. Franklin reprinted Anderson's *Constitutions of the Free-Masons* in 1734.

10. Bullock, *Revolutionary Brotherhood*, 51.

11. Denslow, *10,000 Famous Freemasons*, vol. 2, 72–73. When Franklin was in London in 1760, he was received at the Modern Grand Lodge as a "Provincial Grand Master of Philadelphia." Sachse, *Franklin as a Free Mason*, 105. "There is not a word of mention about his Masonic life to be found in his autobiography, or any of his other letters that have come down to us; [except to his mother and father and Henry Price] almost every other subject is touched upon in his voluminous correspondence except such as relates to the craft."

12. Allen E. Roberts, *G. Washington; Master Mason* (Richmond, VA: Macoy, 1976) 87. See also William Moseley Brown, *George Washington Freemason* (Richmond, VA.: Garrett & Massie, 1952) 19–27.

13. Richard Brookhiser, *Founding Father: Rediscovering George Washington* (New York: Free Press, 1996) 144–51.

14. David Hackett Fischer, *Albion's Seed: Four British Folkways in America* (New York: Oxford University Press, 1989) 410–11.

15. David Hackett Fischer, *Paul Revere's Ride* (New York: Oxford University Press, 1994) 301–2, 306.

16. Edith J. Steblecki, *Paul Revere and Freemasonry* (Boston: Paul Revere Memorial Association, 1985) 55–56. Late in life, Revere participated in every facet of Freemasonry available, including the "higher degrees" of the Royal Arch and possibly the Masonic Knights Templar. See Denslow, *10,000 Famous Freemasons*, vol. 4, 26–27.

17. Bullock, *Revolutionary Brotherhood*, 96–97.

18. Charles H. Wesley, *Prince Hall: Life and Legacy* (Washington, DC: United Supreme Council, Southern Jurisdiction, Prince Hall Affiliation, 1977) 6, 7; David Gray, *Inside Prince Hall* (Lancaster, VA: Anchor Communications, 2004) 42–50. See also Joseph A. Walkes Jr., *Black Square and Compass: 200 Years of Prince Hall Freemasonry* (1979) 16; William Bentley, *The Diary of William Bentley, Pastor of the East Church, Salem, Massachusetts* (Gloucester, MA: P. Smith, 1962) vol. 3, 321.

19. Gray, *Inside Prince Hall,* 17. The other men initiated with Prince Hall were: Cyrus Jonbus, Bueston Singer, Prince Rees, John Carter, Peter Freeman, Benjamin Tiber, Cuff Bufform, Thomas Sanderson, Prince Taylor, Cato Spears, Boston Smith, Peter Best, Forten Howard and Richard Tilley.

20. Bullock, *Revolutionary Brotherhood,* 159-62; Gray, *Inside Prince Hall,* 22. When the St. John's Grand Lodge and the St. Andrew's Grand Lodge merged to form the Grand Lodge of Massachusetts in 1792, Prince Hall's African Lodge No. 459 did not participate but remained under the authority of the "Modern" Grand Lodge of England.

21. Loretta J. Williams, *Black Freemasonry and Middle-Class Realities* (Columbia: University of Missouri Press, 1980) 42.

22. Gray, *Inside Prince Hall,* 25.

23. Lorenzo J. Greene, *The Negro in Colonial New England, 1620-1776* (New York: Atheneum, 1968) 81-83.

24. Harry E. Davis, *A History of Freemasonry Among Negroes in America* (Philadelphia: United Supreme Council, Ancient and Accepted Scottish Rite, Northern Jurisdiction, USA, Prince Hall Affiliation, 1946) 23-24, and Bullock, *Revolutionary Brotherhood,* 159.

25. *Preston's Illustrations of Masonry,* CD-ROM, Andrew Prescott, ed. (Sheffield, UK: Academy Electronics Publications, 2001) 1775 ed., 116.

26. Bullock, *Revolutionary Brotherhood,* 112-14.

27. The nine Masons who signed the Declaration of Independence were William Ellery, Benjamin Franklin, John Hancock, Joseph Hewes, William Hooper, Robert Treat Paine, Richard Stockton, George Walton, and William Whipple. Ronald Heaton, *Masonic Membership of the Founding Fathers* (Silver Spring, MD: Masonic Service Association, 1965) xvi.

28. Cook, *Colonial Freemasonry,* 215.

29. James R. Case, "American Union Lodge," in Cook, ed., *Colonial Freemasonry,* 194-205. In 1790, Major Jonathan Heart reconstituted the lodge in Marietta, Ohio, the first in that territory.

30. Heaton, *Masonic Membership of the Founding Fathers,* Lafayette, 37-39; DeKalb, 84-85; Von Steuben, 62-63.

31. Heaton, *Masonic Membership of the Founding Fathers,* 2-3.

32. James R. Case, "American Union Lodge," in Cook, ed., *Colonial Freemasonry,* 196. For example, records of Lodge No. 17 in Queen Anne's County, Maryland, for May 29, 1777, state, "Ordered that a sum of money not exceeding 24 pounds be sent to Brother Samuel T. Wright, a distressed prisoner [of war] at New York." Edward T. Schultz, *History of Freemasonry in Maryland* (Baltimore, MD: J.H. Medair & Co., 1884) vol. 1, 65.

33. Heaton, *Masonic Membership of the Founding Fathers,* xvi. Freemasonry also helped naval officers. For instance, John Paul Jones visited Benjamin Franklin in Loge des Neufs Soeurs in Paris during the war. See Evan Thomas, *John Paul Jones: Sailor, Hero, Father of the American Navy* (New York: Simon & Schuster, 2003) 216-17, and Denslow, *10,000 Famous Masons,* vol. 2, 315.

34. Harlow Giles Unger, *Lafayette* (Hoboken, NJ: John Wiley, 2002) 98-99; Steblecki, *Paul Revere and Freemasonry,* 33, and Walkes, *Black Square and Compass,* 15-16.

35. Almost immediately after the Boston Tea Party on Dec. 16, 1773, many people speculated that it was a "Masonic event." Alphonse Cerza states: "There is no doubt that some of the men who planned the Party and took part in its execution were Masons. But, they undoubtedly also belonged to other groups which were active in the protesting of the actions of the British. It is very doubtful that the entire Party can be classified as a Masonic project." Cerza, "The Boston Tea Party," in Cook, ed., *Colonial Freemasonry,* 209-11.

36. The most important book to perpetuate these accusations is John Robison, *Proof of a Conspiracy against All Religions and Governments of Europe, Carried on in the Secret Meetings of Free Masons, Illuminati, and Reading Societies* (London: William Creech, T. Cadell Jr., W. Davies, 1797).

37. Thomas Smith Webb, *The Freemason's Monitor; or, Illustrations of Masonry* (New York: Southwick & Crocker, 1802) 40.

38. Heaton, *Masonic Membership of the Founding Fathers,* xvi. Signers of the Articles of Confederation who were known Masons: Thomas Adams, Daniel Carroll, John Dickinson, William Ellery, John Hancock, Cornelius Harnett, Henry Laurens, Daniel Roberdeau and Jonathan Bayard Smith. Signers of the U.S. Constitution who were known Masons: Gunning Bedford Jr., John Blair, David Brearley, Jacob Broom, Daniel Carroll, Jonathan Dayton, John Dickinson, Benjamin Franklin, Nicolas Gilman, Rufus King, James McHenry, William Paterson and George Washington.

39. The "George Washington Bible" is still owned by St. John's Lodge No. 1. It has been used in four other presidential inaugurations: Warren G. Harding, 1921; Dwight D. Eisenhower, 1953; Jimmy Carter, 1977; and George H.W. Bush, 1989. Of the four, only Harding was a Mason. *Masonic Hall* (New York: Grand Lodge of Masons in New York, 1984) 26.

40. Denslow, *10,000 Famous Freemasons,* vol. 3, 244; vol. 1, 102, 275.

41. Barbara Franco, *Masonic Symbols in American Deco-*

rative Arts (Lexington, MA: Museum of Our National Heritage, 1976) 17.

42. Len Travers, "In the Greatest Solemn Dignity: The Capitol Cornerstone and Ceremony in the Early Republic," in Donald R. Kennon, ed., *A Republic for the Ages* (Charlottesville: University of Virginia Press, 1999) 155–56. A description of a cornerstone ceremony is found in *Preston's Illustrations of Masonry*, 1775 ed., 128–321. See also Warren F. Mellny, "Cornerstone Customs," *The Philalethes*, June 1956, 47–50.

43. Bullock, *Revolutionary Brotherhood*, 5.

44. Alphonse Cerza & Walter M. Callaway Jr., "Virginia," in Cook, ed., *Colonial Freemasonry*, 186–87, and Brown, *George Washington Freemason*, 122–23, 126–39.

45. Prince Hall, "A Charge Delivered to the African Lodge, June 24, 1797, at Menotomy (Massachusetts)," quoted in Joanna Brooks and John Saillant, eds., *Face Zion Forward: First Writers of the Black Atlantic, 1785– 1798* (Boston, Northeastern University Press, 2002) 208.

46. Minor Myers Jr., *Liberty without Anarchy: A History of the Society of the Cincinnati* (Charlottesville: University Press of Virginia, 1983) 26.

47. For differing opinions on the legitimacy of Prince Hall Freemasonry, see Gray, *Inside Prince Hall*, and Henry W. Coil and John M. Sherman, ed., *A Documentary Account of Prince Hall and Other Black Fraternal Orders* (Fulton: Missouri Lodge of Research, 1982).

Notes to Chapter 3

1. Julius F. Sachse, *Washington's Masonic Correspondence* (Philadelphia: Grand Lodge of Pennsylvania, 1915) 109.

2. William R. Denslow, *10,000 Famous Freemasons*, 4 vols. (Trenton: Missouri Lodge of Research, 1957–60).

3. For an overview of the history of this period, see Daniel J. Boorstin, *The Americans: The National Experience* (New York: Random House, 1967).

4. Alan Gowans. "Freemasonry and the Neoclassical Style in America," *Antiques* (Feb. 1960) 172. See also Barbara Franco, *Masonic Symbols in American Decorative Arts* (Lexington, MA: Museum of Our National Heritage, 1976); Barbara Franco, *Bespangled, Painted and Embroidered: Decorated Masonic Aprons in America, 1790–1850* (Lexington, MA: Museum of Our National Heritage, 1980), and John D. Hamilton, *The Material Culture of the American Freemasons* (Lexington, MA: Museum of Our National Heritage, 1994).

5. *Preston's Illustrations of Masonry*, CD-ROM, Andrew Prescott, ed. (Sheffield, UK: Academy Electronics Publications 2001) 1775 ed., 118.

6. William Preston Vaughn, *The Anti-Masonic Party in the United States, 1826–1843* (Lexington: University Press of Kentucky, 1983) 11, and Steven C. Bullock, *Revolutionary Brotherhood: Freemasonry and the Transformation of the American Social Order, 1739– 1840* (Chapel Hill: University of North Carolina Press, 1996) 188, 371.

7. William Muraskin, *Middle-Class Blacks in a White Society: Prince Hall Freemasonry in America* (Berkeley: University of California Press, 1975) 188.

8. Thomas Smith Webb, *The Freemason's Monitor; or, Illustrations of Masonry* (New York: Southwick & Crocker, 1797) iv.

9. *Coil's Masonic Encyclopedia,* rev. ed. (Richmond, VA: Macoy, 1996) 349, 534, 579. The first chartered Royal Arch chapter was Hiram No. 1, Newton, CT, in 1791; the first recorded Royal and Select council was Columbian Council No. 1, New York, in 1807, and the first Knights Templar commandery was Pennsylvania Encampment No. 1, Philadelphia, in 1794.

10. *Coil's Masonic Encyclopedia,* 101. The First Prince Hall Royal Arch chapter was Union Chapter, Philadelphia, in 1826; the first Prince Hall Knights Templar commandery was St. George Encampment, Philadelphia, in 1820; the first Prince Hall council was not chartered until 1916 in Cleveland. It should also be noted that when Philadelphia Black Masons wrote to Prince Hall in 1797, looking for a warrant to meet, some of the brethren had already received the Royal Arch degrees. See William H. Upton, "Prince Hall's Letter Book," *Ars Quatuor Coronatorum, Transactions of Quatuor Coronati Lodge,* 1900, vol. 13, 61–62.

11. Herbert T. Leyland, *Thomas Smith Webb: Freemason, Musician, Entrepreneur* (Dayton, OH: Otterbein Press, 1965) 15–16, 61, 81, 294–95.

12. *Coil's Masonic Encyclopedia,* 567; Bullock, *Revolutionary Brotherhood,* 244. For Webb's impact on the formation of the York Rite, see Herbert C. Leyland, *Thomas Smith Webb* (Dayton, OH: Otterbein Press, 1965) 442–45. The name "York Rite" derives from the legend of 10th-century King Athelstan of England holding a national assembly of stonemasons in York. Furthermore, the first known reference to the Royal Arch and Knights Templar degrees "were described in the 'York' Lodge records as the 4th and 5th degrees, respectively," in the second half of the 1700s. See *Coil's Masonic Encyclopedia,* 560.

13. Denslow, *10,000 Famous Freemasons,* vol. 1, 269, 324. A volunteer in the Connecticut militia, Doolittle created a series of drawings of the battles at Lexington and Concord in 1775.

14. For a discussion on the development of American Masonic rituals, see *Coil's Masonic Encyclopedia*, 566–68, and Franco, *Masonic Symbols in American Decorative Arts*, 29.

15. *Coil's Masonic Encyclopedia*, 458. "Ordo ab Chaos" (Order out of Chaos) is a motto of the Scottish Rite in the United States.

16. William L. Fox, *Lodge of the Double-Headed Eagle: Two Centuries of Scottish Rite Freemasonry in America's Southern Jurisdiction* (Fayetteville: University of Arkansas Press, 1997) 25–29; George A. Newbury and Louis L. Williams, *History of the Supreme Council of the Ancient Accepted Scottish Rite of Freemasonry for the Northern Masonic Jurisdiction of the USA* (Lexington, MA: Supreme Council, AASR, NMJ, USA, 1987) 62–69. Of the eleven organizers, six were merchants, three were doctors (one of whom became an Episcopal minister) one was a rabbi and one was a French nobleman. Two were Roman Catholics, four were Jews and the rest of various Protestant denominations.

17. Newbury and Williams, *History of the Supreme Council*, 83–85.

18. Newbury and Williams, *History of the Supreme Council*, 96–98.

19. Henry W. Coil, *Freemasonry through Six Centuries* (Fulton, MO: Ovid Bell Press, 1967) vol. 2, 377–80.

20. Thomas Smith Webb, *The Freemason's Monitor; or, Illustrations of Masonry* (Boston, Joshua Cushing Printer, 1808) 48. William Preston originally began this passage as "Monarchs, in all ages, . . ." (*Preston's Illustrations of Masonry*, 1775 ed., 63). Webb's first edition of 1797 continued this opening but by 1808 he had changed it to "The greatest and best men in all ages . . ."

21. *Coil's Masonic Encyclopedia*, 277–78.

22. *Reprint of the Minutes of the Grand Lodge of Free and Accepted Masons of Pennsylvania*, vol. 4, 1817–1822 (Philadelphia: Grand Lodge of Masons in Pennsylvania, 1898) 472–79.

23. Harlow G. Unger, *Lafayette* (New York: John Wiley, 2002) 352. While in Pittsburgh, Lafayette stayed at the Masonic hall. See *History of Lodge No. 45, 1785–1910* (Pittsburgh, PA: Lodge No. 45, 1912) 115. Of the thousands of Americans who saw Lafayette, three stand out: the future abolitionist and Prince Hall Grand Master of Massachusetts, Lewis Hayden, in Kentucky; lawyer, author and Scottish Rite Grand Commander Albert Pike, in Boston, and future poet Walt Whitman, in Brooklyn.

24. Thomas S. Roy, *Stalwart Builders: Grand Lodge of Masons in Massachusetts* (Boston: Grand Lodge of Masons in Massachusetts, 1971) 116–17, and *One*

Hundred and Fifty Years of King Solomon's Lodge, 1783–1933 (Somerville, MA, 1933) 29–31.

25. George Washington, "Farewell Address" (September 1796), *The Writings of George Washington from the Original Manuscripts, 1745–1799*, John C. Fitzpatrick, ed. (Washington, DC: U.S. Government Printing Office, 1936) vol. 35, 233.

26. John Quincy Adams, *Letters addressed to William L. Stone, Esq., of New York, and to Benjamin Cowell, Esq., of Rhode-Island, upon the subject of Masonry & Anti-masonry, to which is added, A Portrait of Masonry by John C. Spencer* (Providence, RI: Edward & J. W. Cory, 1833) Letter 2, 13.

27. Denslow, *10,000 Famous Freemasons*, vol. 3, 230–31. William Preston Vaughn, *The Anti-Masonic Party in the United States, 1826–1843* (Lexington: University Press of Kentucky, 1983) 2–3. Morgan's Masonic membership is still in doubt, although he may have received the first degree and possibly the Royal Arch degree. His membership records may have been destroyed after his disappearance.

28. Bullock, *Revolutionary Brotherhood*, 277–79.

29. *Coil's Masonic Encyclopedia*, 428–30. Various 1820s and 1830s reports say he lived as a hermit in northern Canada, was hanged as a pirate, became an Arizona Indian Chief, was seen in Turkey living under the name "Mustapha" or had become a political operative in New York state under the name "Wannamaker."

30. Dorothy Ann Lipson, *Freemasonry in Federalist Connecticut 1789–1839* (Princeton, NJ: Princeton University Press), 268. Four men were tried in January 1827 on a charge of "conspiracy to kidnap" (classified as a misdemeanor). One man received a two-year sentence, two men three months, and the last man a one-month sentence. Other trials dragged on for five years with no one being tried for murder. Vaughn, *Anti-Masonic Party*, 7

31. Lipson, *Freemasonry in Federalist Connecticut*, 83. A central book for all conspiracy accusations against Freemasonry is John Robison, *Proof of a Conspiracy against All Religions and Governments of Europe, Carried on in the Secret Meetings of Free Masons, Illuminati, and Reading Societies* (London: William Creech, T. Cadell Jr., and W. Davies, 1797).

32. Lipson, *Freemasonry in Federalist Connecticut*, 8, 106, 113–116; Vaughn, *Anti-Masonic Party*, 14–17, 22–23.

33. Lipson, *Freemasonry in Federalist Connecticut*, 333; Bullock, *Revolutionary Brotherhood*, 295–96.

34. Vaughn, *Anti-Masonic Party*, 7.

35. William Wadsworth, "Address," *Anti-Masonic Convention Proceedings* (LeRoy, NY: March 1828) 11–12.

36. Kathleen Smith Kutolowski, "Freemasonry Revis-

ited: Another Look at the Grass-Roots Bases of Anti-Masonic Anxieties," in R. William Weisberger, et al., eds., *Freemasonry on Both Sides of the Atlantic*, (Boulder, CO: East European Monographs, 2002) 592. "Fully three-fifths of the [Genesee] county's office-holders (including 14 of 17 State Assemblymen and Senators) belonged to a lodge."

37. Bullock, *Revolutionary Brotherhood*, 188–89.

38. Vaughn, *Anti-Masonic Party*, 55–69.

39. Bullock, *Revolutionary Brotherhood*, 282, 292–93. "William Lloyd Garrison (a delegate to the 1832 Massachusetts Anti-Masonic Convention) founded the first national journal of immediate abolitionism in 1831."

40. Vaughn, *Anti-Masonic Party*, 187, and Allen E. Roberts, *Freemasonry in American History* (Richmond, VA: Macoy, 1985) 234–37.

41. Lipson, *Freemasonry in Federalist Connecticut*, 326–29; Wayne A Huss. *The Master Builders: A History of the Grand Lodge of Free and Accepted Masons in Pennsylvania*, vol. 1 (Philadelphia: Grand Lodge of Pennsylvania, 1986) 127, and Bullock, *Revolutionary Brotherhood*, 289–90.

42. The Scottish Rite Supreme Council for the Northern Masonic Jurisdiction did not meet between 1826 and 1840. Records were left in the hands of John J.J. Gourgas. Through his dedication, Gourgas is revered as the "Conservator of the Rite." The NMJ's highest award is named for him. See Newbury and Williams, *History of the Supreme Council*, 85, 223–226.

43. Thomas Smith Webb, *The Freemason's Monitor; or, Illustrations of Masonry* (Boston, Joshua Cushing, Printer, 1808) 80.

44. David Gray, *Inside Prince Hall* (Lancaster, VA: Anchor Communications, 2004) 30–31; Boston *Advertiser*, June 18, 1827. For a facsimile of the notice, see Henry W. Coil and John M. Sherman, eds., *A Documentary Account of Prince Hall and Other Black Fraternal Orders* (Fulton: Missouri Lodge of Research, 1982) 146.

45. Charles H. Wesley, *History of the Prince Hall Grand Lodge of the State of Ohio, 1849–1960: An Epoch in American Fraternalism* (Wilberforce, OH: Central State College Press, 1961) 24, 36, 51–56.

46. For an overview of anti-Masonic writings and their influences, see David Brion Davis, "Some Themes of Counter-Subversion: An Analysis of Anti-Masonic, Anti-Catholic, and Anti-Mormon Literature," *Mississippi Valley Historical Review* (now known as *Journal of American History*) vol. 47, 1960–61, 205–24, and Richard Hofstadter, *The Paranoid Style in American Politics* (New York: Knopf, 1965). For a summary of recent attacks on the fraternity, see Arturo deHoyos

and S. Brent Morris, *Is It True What They Say about Freemasonry?* (New York: M. Evans and Company, Inc., 2004).

47. The relationship between Freemasonry and the Church of Jesus Christ of Latter-Day Saints is complex. It is well known that many founders of the LDS Church were members of the Masonic lodge in Nauvoo, Illinois, including Joseph Smith, his brother Hyrum and Brigham Young. Denslow, *10,000 Famous Freemasons*, vol. 4, 153, 157–59, 357. See Richard Abanes, *One Nation Under Gods: A History of the Mormon Church* (New York: Four Walls, Eight Windows, 2001) and E. Cecil McGavin, *Mormonism and Masonry* (Salt Lake City, UT: Bookcraft Publishers, 1976).

Notes to Chapter 4

1. Alexis de Tocqueville, *Democracy in America*, 1831 (New York: Vintage Books, 1945 reprint) vol. 2, 118.

2. Tocqueville, *Democracy in America*, 118.

3. Lynn Dumenil, *Freemasonry in American Culture, 1880–1930* (Princeton, NJ: Princeton University Press, 1984) 225.

4. Charles W. Moore, *The Pocket Trestleboard* (Boston: Charles W. Moore, 1861) 24.

5. Edward E. Grusd, *B'nai B'rith: The Story of a Covenant* (New York: Appleton-Century, 1966) 13–15.

6. For a better understanding of the involvement of individual Freemasons in the founding of many American fraternal societies and Freemasonry's impact on American fraternal history in general, see Albert C. Stevens, ed., *The Cyclopaedia of Fraternities* (New York: E.B. Treat & Co., 2nd ed., 1907) vii. See also Alvin J. Schmidt, *Fraternal Organizations* (Westport, CT: Greenwood Press, 1980) 119–22.

7. *Preston's Illustrations of Masonry*, CD-ROM, Andrew Prescott, ed. (Sheffield, UK: Academy Electronics Publications, 2001) 1788 ed., 53.

8. Arthur M. Schlesinger, "Biography of a Nation of Joiners," *The American Historical Review*, vol. 50, no. 1 (October 1944) 6, 10.

9. Schlesinger, "Biography of a Nation of Joiners," 10.

10. Schlesinger, "Biography of a Nation of Joiners," 16.

11. See William D. Moore with John D. Hamilton, "Washington as the Master of His Lodge: History and Symbolism of a Masonic Icon," in *George Washington American Symbol*, Barbara J. Mitnick, ed. (New York: Hudson Hill Press, 1999) 78. See also Rob Morris, *The Poetry of Freemasonry* (Chicago: Knight and Leonard, Printers, 1884), and *National Masonic Convention Held at Baltimore, Maryland, May 8–17, 1843: A*

Centennial Celebration, 1943 (Baltimore: Grand Lodge of Maryland, 1943).

12. In 1835, the Grand Lodge of Connecticut waived all membership fees for clergy. See Dorothy Ann Lipson, *Freemasonry in Federalist Connecticut, 1789–1839* (Princeton, NJ: Princeton University Press, 1977) 128. By 1891 in New York state, Freemasonry attracted 26 percent of Universalist clerics, 22 percent of Episcopalian clerics and 18 percent of Methodist clerics. Mark C. Carnes, *Secret Ritual and Manhood in Victorian America* (New Haven, CT: Yale University Press, 1989) 61. Barbara Franco, *Bespangled, Painted & Embroidered: Decorated Masonic Aprons in America, 1790–1850* (Lexington, MA: Museum of Our National Heritage, 1980), 36–38.

13. Thomas Smith Webb, *The Freemason's Monitor; or, Illustrations of Masonry* (Providence, RI: Cushing & Webb, 1805) 41.

14. *Coil's Masonic Encyclopedia*, rev. ed. (Richmond, VA: Macoy, 1996) 139–40, 378. See also Michael S. Kaulback, *Masonic Libraries: A Listing of Masonic Libraries in the United States, Canada and England* (Silver Spring, MD: Masonic Service Association, 1998).

15. William R. Denslow, *10,000 Famous Freemasons* (Trenton: Missouri Lodge of Research, 1959) vol. 3, 313. See also Joseph Morcombe, *The Life and Labors of Theodore Sutton Parvin* (Clinton, IA: Allen Printing Co., 1906).

16. See Kent Henderson and Tony Pope, *Freemasonry Universal: A New Guide to the Masonic World* (Victoria, Australia: Global Masonic Publications, 1998) vol. 1, 94, 134, 162, 176.

17. Charles Wesley, *The History of the Prince Hall Grand Lodge of Free and Accepted Masons of the State of Ohio, 1849–1960* (Wilberforce, OH: Central State College Press, 1961) 29–31. William A. Muraskin, *Middle-Class Blacks in a White Society: Prince Hall Freemasonry in America* (Berkeley: University of California Press, 1975) 36–37. Between 1849 and 1869, Ohio helped form lodges in Kentucky, Indiana, Louisiana, Tennessee, Alabama and Missouri.

18. Joseph A. Walkes Jr., *Black Square and Compass: 200 Years of Prince Hall Freemasonry* (1979) 118–21.

19. Martin Delaney, *The Origin and Objects of Ancient Freemasonry: Its Introduction into the United States and Legitimacy Among Colored Men* (Pittsburgh, 1853) 40.

20. Dumenil, *Freemasonry in American Culture*, 7.

21. *Ritual of the Order of the Eastern Star* (Chicago: General Grand Chapter of the Order of the Eastern Star, 1890) 40.

22. Lipson, *Freemasonry in Federalist Connecticut*, 329–30.

23. Steven C. Bullock, *Revolutionary Brotherhood: Freemasonry and the Transformation of the American Social Order, 1730–1840* (Chapel Hill: University of North Carolina Press, 1996) 160–62.

24. Karen Blair, *The Clubwoman as Feminist: True Womanhood Redefined, 1868–1914* (New York: Holmes and Meier, 1980), 13, 20; Robyn Muncy, *Creating A Female Dominion in American Reform, 1890–1935* (New York: Oxford University Press, 1991) 4.

25. Theodore A. Ross, *Odd Fellowship: Its History and Manual* (New York: M.W. Hazen Co., 1888) 485–86. In 1851, Odd Fellow & Mason Schuyler Colfax created the Daughters of Rebekah. Colfax was vice president of the United States (1869–73) under President Grant (Denslow, *10,000 Famous Freemasons*, vol. 1, 237). In 1872, the Daughters of Rebekah had 158 lodges with 5,435 sisters, and by 1897, the numbers rose to 4,808 lodges with 178,148 sisters. (Ross, *Odd Fellowship*, 673).

26. *Coil's Masonic Encyclopedia*, 435. See also Morris, *The Poetry of Freemasonry*.

27. Mary Ann Clawson, *Constructing Brotherhood: Class, Gender and Fraternalism* (Princeton, NJ: Princeton University Press, 1989) 188.

28. James Anderson, *The Constitutions of the Free-Masons* (1723, Facsimile ed., Abingdon, UK: Burgess & Son, 1976) 49–50. See also R.A. Gilbert, "'The Monstrous Regiment': Women and Freemasonry in the Nineteenth Century," *Ars Quatuor Coronatorum: Transactions of the Quatuor Coronati Lodge No. 2076*, vol. 115 (2002), 153–78.

29. Lipson, *Freemasonry in Federalist Connecticut*, 192–95, and Mark C. Carnes, *Secret Ritual and Manhood in Victorian America*, 84–85.

30. Schmidt, *Fraternal Organizations*, 97–100. See also Robert Macoy, ed., *Manual of the Order of the Eastern Star* (Chicago: J.C.W. Bailey, 1868). While Ruth, Esther and Martha are identified in the Bible, "Adah" is the name Morris gave to Jephthah's daughter in the Book of Judges and "Electra" was created to identify "the elder unto the elect lady" in 2 John. In 1866, Rob Morris left the United States for the Palestine and turned the Order over to Masonic publisher and regalia dealer Robert Macoy. Willis D. Engle, *The History of the Order of the Eastern Star* (Indianapolis: Willis D. Engle, 1901).

31. Albert C. Stevens, ed., *Cyclopaedia of Fraternities*, 2nd ed. (New York: E.B. Treat & Co., 1907) 98.

32. Dumenil, *Freemasonry in American Culture*, 25.

33. Thomas Smith Webb, *The Freemason's Monitor*, 1802 ed., 44.

34. Denslow, *10,000 Famous Freemasons*, McClellan, vol.

3, 165; Chamberlain, vol. 1, 28; Armistead, vol. 1, 28; Pickett, vol. 3, 338; Toombs, vol. 4, 247; Stanton, vol. 4, 180; Johnson, vol. 2, 298.

35. Allen E. Roberts, *House Undivided: The Story of Freemasonry and the Civil War* (New York: Macoy, 1961) 106; Walkes, *Black Square and Compass*, 43-44.

36. Roberts, *House Undivided*, 106.

37. Anderson, *Constitutions*, 48.

38. *Proceedings of the Grand Lodge of Free and Accepted Masons of the State of Missouri* (St. Louis: M. Niedner, 1861) 12.

39. Dumenil, *Freemasonry in American Culture*, 101-2; Roberts, *House Undivided*, 111, 122.

40. Denslow, *10,000 Famous Freemasons*, vol. 3, 176-77. See also William H. Armstrong, *Major McKinley: William McKinley & the Civil War* (Kent, OH: Kent State University Press, 2000).

41. Theda Skocpol, Ziad Munson, Andrew Karch and Bayliss Camp, "Patriot Partnerships: Why Great Wars Nourished American Civic Voluntarism," *Shaped by War and Trade*, Ira Katznelson and Martin Shefter, eds. (Princeton, NJ: Princeton University Press, 2002) 134-80.

42. Denslow, *10,000 Famous Freemasons*, vol. 3, 99-100; Stevens, *Cyclopaedia of Fraternities*, 366-67.

43. Stevens, *Cyclopaedia of Fraternities*, 369.

44. Stuart C. Maconnell, *Glorious Contentment: The Grand Army of the Republic, 1865-1910* (Chapter Hill: University of North Carolina Press, 1992) 138-40. See also Mary Rulkotter Dearing, *Veterans in Politics: The Story of the Grand Army of the Republic* (Baton Rouge: Louisiana State University Press, 1952).

45. Wyn Craig Wade, *The Fiery Cross: The Ku Klux Klan in America* (New York: Simon & Schuster, 1987) 34-35; Stevens, *Cyclopaedia of Fraternities*, 416-17.

46. Wade, *The Fiery Cross*, 59. Forrest only received the Entered Apprentice degree in Masonry.

47. See Wade, *The Fiery Cross*, chapter 3: "Congress, the Klan and the End of Reconstruction, 1870-77," 80-111; Schmidt, *Fraternal Organizations*, 196-97.

48. David G. Hackett, "The Prince Hall Masons and the African American Church: The Labors of Grand Master and Bishop James Walker Hood, 1831-1918," *Church History* (December 2000, vol. 69, no. 4) 776. See also Sandy Dwayne Martin, *For God and Race: The Religious and Political Leadership of A.M.E.Z. Bishop James Walker Hood* (Columbia: University of South Carolina Press, 1999).

49. Hackett, "Prince Hall Mason and the African American Church," 772.

50. See Henderson and Pope, *Freemasonry Universal*.

51. Muraskin, *Middle-Class Blacks in a White Society*, 53; *Commonwealth of Massachusetts, Journal of the House of Representatives, 1872* and *1873*. See also Lewis Hayden, "Caste among Masons," address before Prince Hall Grand Lodge of Free and Accepted Masons of Massachusetts at the festival of St. John the Evangelist, December 27, 1865 (Boston: Edward S. Coombs, 1866), and *Proceedings of the Prince Hall Grand Lodge . . . Located at Boston . . . for the Year 1873* (1874).

Notes to Chapter 5

1. W.S. Harwood, "Secret Societies in America," *North American Review* (1897) vol. 164 no. 485, 621.

2. For an overview of this period, see Thomas J. Schlereth, *Victorian America: Transformations in Everyday Life, 1876-1915* (New York: Harper Collins, 1991) 260-69. See also Robert T. Handy, *A Christian America: Protestant Hopes and Historical Realities* (New York: Oxford University Press, 1992) and Paul S. Boyer, *Urban Masses and Moral Order in America, 1820-1920* (Cambridge, MA: Harvard University Press, 1978).

3. Thomas Smith Webb, *The Freemason's Monitor; or, Illustrations of Masonry* (Boston, Joshua Cushing Printer, 1808) 53. The reference "to that undiscovered country . . ." is from William Shakespeare's *Hamlet*, Act 3, Scene 1.

4. Alvin J. Schmidt, *Fraternal Organizations* (Westport, CT: Greenwood Press, 1980) 367-73, and Albert C. Stevens, ed., *The Cyclopaedia of Fraternities*, 2nd ed. (New York: E.B. Treat & Co., 1907) iii.

5. Harwood, "Secret Societies in America," 63.

6. Mary Ann Clawson, *Constructing Brotherhood: Class, Gender, and Fraternalism* (Princeton, NJ: Princeton University Press, 1989) 111-12.

7. Stevens, *Cyclopaedia of Fraternities*, iii.

8. Stevens, *Cyclopaedia of Fraternities*, xv. See also Lynn Dumenil, *Freemasonry in American Culture, 1880-1930* (Princeton, NJ: Princeton University Press, 1984) xi, and David T. Beito, *From Mutual Aid to the Welfare State: Fraternal Societies and Social Services, 1890-1967* (Chapel Hill: University of North Carolina Press, 2000) 296.

9. Dumenil, *Freemasonry and American Culture*, 111.

10. *Preston's Illustrations of Masonry*, CD-ROM, Andrew Prescott, ed. (Sheffield, UK: Academy Electronics Publications, 2001) 1772 ed., 14.

11. Dumenil, *Freemasonry in American Culture*, 225.

12. William R. Denslow, *10,000 Famous Freemasons* (Fulton: Missouri Lodge of Research, 1957-59) vol. 1, 148,

231–32; vol. 2, 124–25; vol. 3, 371. Laura Ingalls Wilder was a member of Mansfield (Missouri) Chapter No. 75.

13. Gerald M. Bordman, ed., *Oxford Companion to American Theater* (New York: Oxford University Press, 1984) 659, 684. See also Lawrence W. Levine, *Highbrow/Lowbrow: The Emergence of Cultural Hierarchy in America* (Cambridge, MA: Harvard University Press, 1990).

14. Dumenil, *Freemasonry in American Culture,* 82. In 1895, for example, Masonic lodges in Illinois initiated 3,229 men and rejected 600, *Proceedings of the Grand Lodge of Free and Accepted Masons of Illinois* (Bloomington, IL: Pantagraph Printing, 1895) 60.

15. Dumenil, *Freemasonry in American Culture,* 22, 86.

16. For a basic understanding of Masonic rituals, see Carl Claudy, *Introduction to Freemasonry,* 3 vols. (Washington, DC: Temple Publishers, 1931), and Allen E. Roberts, *The Craft and Its Symbols* (Richmond, VA: Macoy, 1974). For a deeper interpretation of Freemasonry's degrees, see W. Kirk MacNulty, *Freemasonry: A Journey through Ritual and Symbol* (New York: Thames and Hudson, 1991).

17. Denslow, *10,000 Famous Freemasons;* William Shakespeare (1554–1616) is often claimed to have been a Freemason, vol. 4, 125; Edward Gibbon (1737–94) was a Freemason, vol. 2, 107–8; John Bunyan (1628–88) is also claimed to have been a Freemason, and his book *Solomon's Temple Spiritualized* has many Masonic parallels, vol. 1, 153–54.

18. W.G. Sibley, *The Story of Freemasonry* (Gallipolis, OH: The Lion's Paw Club, 1904) 51.

19. Stevens, *Cyclopaedia of Fraternities,* 75, and *Coil's Masonic Encyclopedia* (Richmond, VA: Macoy, rev. ed., 1996) 101. See also Arturo deHoyos, "On the Origins of the Prince Hall Scottish Rite Rituals," *Heredom: Transactions of the Scottish Rite Research Society* (Washington, DC: Scottish Rite Research Society, 1995), 51–67.

20. Stevens, *Cyclopaedia of Fraternities,* 42, 75.

21. *Coil's Masonic Encyclopedia,* 349. See Robert L. D. Cooper, "The Knights Templar in Scotland: The Creation of a Myth," *Ars Quatuor Coronatorum: Transactions of the Quatuor Coronati Lodge,* vol. 115, September 2002. See also Father Richard Augustine Hay (1661–1736), comp. *The Genealogie of the Saintclaires of Rosslyn,* Robert L.D. Cooper, ed., John Wade, translator (Edinburgh: Grand Lodge of Scotland, 2002).

22. *Proceedings of the Grand Encampment of the Knights Templar of the United States of America, 27th Triennial Conclave* (St. Louis: Woodward & Tierman Printing Co., 1898) 98.

23. For a basic history of the Masonic Knights Templar, see Francis J. Skully, *History of the Grand Encampment of Knights Templar of the United States of America; the 850th Anniversary of Templary; the Story of Knighthood from the Days of the Ancient Templars to the 44th Conclave of the Modern Templars in 1949* (Greenfield, IN: William Mitchell Printing Co., 1952).

24. For a basic insight into the popularity of Masonic Knights Templar, see William D. Moore, "Structures of Masculinity: Masonic Temples, Material Culture, and Ritual Gender Archetypes in New York, 1870–1930" (Ph.D. dissertation, Boston University, 1999, printed by UMI Dissertation Services, Ann Arbor MI) 108–69.

25. George A. Newbury and Louis L. Williams, *History of the Supreme Council of the Ancient Accepted Scottish Rite of Freemasonry for the Northern Masonic Jurisdiction of the United States of America* (Lexington, MA: Supreme Council, 33°, Northern Masonic Jurisdiction, 1987) 178–80.

26. *Proceedings of the Supreme Council, Ancient Accepted Scottish Rite, Northern Masonic Jurisdiction, USA* (Boston: James Kempster, 1909) 196–98.

27. *Official Ritual of the Modern Woodmen of America,* 2nd rev. (Modern Woodmen of America, 1904) 27.

28. As quoted in Schmidt, *Fraternal Organizations,* 184.

29. For information about the play, see James R. Carnahan, *Pythian Knighthood: Its History and Literature* (Cincinnati, OH: Pettibone Brothers, 1909) 272. In addition to being a Mason, Rathbone was also a member of the Sons of Malta and the Improved Order of Red Men.

30. Stevens, *Cyclopaedia of Fraternities,* 264, and Harwood, *Secret Societies in America,* 620.

31. Stevens, *Cyclopaedia of Fraternities,* 266. See also Theda Skocpol and Jennifer Oser, "Organization Despite Adversity: The Origins and Development of African American Fraternal Associations," *Social Science History,* Fall 2004.

32. Stevens, *Cyclopaedia of Fraternities,* 157.

33. Este E. Buffum, *Modern Woodmen of America: A History,* vol. 1 (Rock Island, IL: Modern Woodmen Press, 1927) 1.

34. Stevens, *Cyclopaedia of Fraternities,* 158.

35. Schmidt, *Fraternal Organizations,* 218–20.

36. The relationship between the Roman Catholic Church and Freemasonry is perhaps one of the most complex subjects within the fraternity, second only to the origins of Freemasonry. In 1884, Pope Leo XIII issued the encyclical Humanum Genus that strongly condemned Freemasonry and all other "secret societies" as an attempt to undermine Church authority.

Sister M. Claudia Carlen, *A Guide to the Encyclicals of the Roman Pontiffs from Leo XIII to the Present Day* (New York, 1939) 44–46, and Christopher J. Kauffman, *Faith and Fraternalism: The History of the Knights of Columbus, 1882–1982* (New York: Harper & Row, 1982) 39, 84–85. See also *Coil's Masonic Encyclopedia*, 54–56; H.L. Haywood, *Freemasonry and Roman Catholicism* (Chicago: Masonic History Co., 1943), and Forrest D. Haggard, *The Clergy and the Craft* (Trenton: Missouri Lodge of Research, 1970).

37. Kauffman, *Faith and Fraternalism*, 71, and Schmidt, *Fraternal Organizations*, 176–78.

38. Kauffman, *Faith and Fraternalism*, 71, 133.

39. Clawson, *Constructing Brotherhood*, 227–31.

40. Carnes, *Secret Ritual and Manhood in Victorian America*, 98–99.

41. Thomas Smith Webb, *The Freemason's Monitor; or, Illustrations of Masonry* (Boston, Joshua Cushing Printer, 1808) 53.

42. Carnes, *Secret Ritual and Manhood in Victorian America*, 121–22.

43. Ann Douglass, *The Feminization of American Culture* (New York: Alfred A. Knopf, 1977) 87.

44. For a complete discussion of the separation between fathers and sons, see Carnes, *Secret Ritual and Manhood in Victorian America*.

Notes to Chapter 6

1. James Bryce, *The American Commonwealth* (New York: MacMillan, 1888) vol. 2, 239.

2. For an overview of this period, see Thomas J. Schlereth, *Victorian America: Transformations in Everyday Life, 1876–1915* (New York: Harper Collins, 1991) 33–34.

3. Hugh Brogan, *The Penguin History of the United States of America* (London: Penguin Books, 1986) 409–10, 419–20. See also John K. Mahon, *History of the Militia and the National Guard* (New York: MacMillan, 1983).

4. *Preston's Illustrations of Masonry*, CD-ROM, Andrew Prescott, ed. (Sheffield, UK: Academy Electronics Publications, Ltd., 2001) 1775 ed., 72.

5. James Anderson, *The Constitutions of the Free-Masons* (London: Grand Lodge of England, 2nd ed., 1738) (Bloomington, IL: Masonic Book Club, reprint 1978) 160–61.

6. John Hamill, *The Craft: A History of English Freemasonry.* (Wellingborough, UK: Crucible, 1986) 127–29. The English Modern Grand Lodge founded an orphanage for girls in 1789 and Prince Hall's Boston lodge made four contributions to the home. The Ancient Grand Lodge started a home for boys in 1798.

7. Melvin M. Johnson, *The Beginnings of Freemasonry in America* (New York: George H. Doran Co., 1924) 106. St. John's Lodge was known as "The First Lodge" until 1783 when it merged with "The Second Lodge."

8. Wayne A. Huss, *The Master Builders: A History of the Grand Lodge of Free and Accepted Masons of Pennsylvania*, vol. 1, 1731–1873 (Philadelphia: Grand Lodge of Pennsylvania, 1986) 62–63.

9. George Moulton, "An Orphan Succored," in John H. Brownell, ed., *Gems from the Quarry and Sparks from the Gavel* (Detroit: John H. Brownell, 1893) vol. 2, 340.

10. *Coil's Masonic Encyclopedia* (Richmond, VA: Macoy, rev. ed., 1996) 404–6. It is appropriate that Kentucky started the first Masonic home, as its state anthem is Stephen Foster's "My Old Kentucky Home." After the Chicago Fire, the Grand Lodge of Illinois received over $90,000 (*Grand Lodge of Illinois 1872 Proceeding*, 9); after the Johnstown Flood, the Grand Lodge of Pennsylvania received $44,761 (*Grand Lodge of Pennsylvania, 1891 Proceedings*, 140), and after the Galveston Hurricane, the Grand Lodge of Texas received about $75,000 (*Grand Lodge of Texas, 1900 Proceedings*, 14).

11. Lynn Dumenil, *Freemasonry and American Culture 1880–1930* (Princeton, NJ: Princeton University Press) 103–4.

12. *Coil's Masonic Encyclopedia*, "Landmarks," 358–70. There remains a persistent confusion within Masonic jurisprudence over landmarks. Important Masons such as Rob Morris, Albert Pike, Albert Mackey and Roscoe Pound all attempted to clarify the craft's "landmarks." For a good summation, see S. Brent Morris, "Landmarks and Liabilities," *A Radical in the East* (Ames: Iowa Research Lodge No. 2, 1994) 93–103.

13. William D. Moore with John D. Hamilton, "Washington as the Master of His Lodge: History and Symbolism of a Masonic Icon," in *George Washington American Symbol*, Barbara J. Mitnick, ed. (New York: Hudson Hill Press, 1999) 71–89.

14. Dumenil, *Freemasonry and American Culture*, 104.

15. Mark C. Carnes, *Secret Ritual and Manhood in Victorian America* (New Haven, CT: Yale University Press, 1989) 4.

16. Thomas Smith Webb, *The Freemason's Monitor; or, Illustrations of Masonry* (Boston: Joshua Cushing Printer, 1808) 80.

17. Mary Ann Clawson, *Constructing Brotherhood: Class, Gender, and Fraternalism* (Princeton, NJ, Princeton University Press, 1989) 216–18. William J. Simmons,

founder of the KKK in 1915, a paid manager of the Woodmen of the World and active Freemason, when asked what his profession was, explained, "I am a fraternalist." David Chalmers, *Hooded Americanism: First Century of the Ku Klux Klan* (Chicago: Quadrangle Books, 1968) 29.

18. Theodore A. Ross, *Odd Fellowship, Its History and Manual* (New York: M.W. Hazen Co., 1891) 655.

19. Theodore A. Ross, *Odd Fellowship*, 632, 655.

20. Albert C. Stevens, *Cyclopaedia of Freemasonry*, 2nd ed. (New York: E.B. Treat & Co., 1907) 128–29.

21. Stevens, *Cyclopaedia of Freemasonry*, 128–29. The Odd Fellows opened their first Home for widows and orphans in Meadville, PA, in 1872. In a curious coincidence, this author graduated from Allegheny College in Meadville in 1986, and his fraternity house was across the street from the Old Fellows' Home.

22. Keith L. Yates, *The Fogarty Years: A History of the AOUW* (Seattle: Evergreen Printing Co., 1972) 58–59.

23. Stevens, *Cyclopaedia of Fraternities*, 381.

24. Stephens, *Cyclopaedia of Fraternities*, 392, and William Denslow, *10,000 Famous Freemasons* (Trenton: Missouri Lodge of Research, 1959) vol. 3, 361, vol. 4, 187. For reference to Powderley's dislike of Knights of Labor ritual, see General Assembly of the Knights of Labor, *Proceedings* (1887) 156, as cited in Norman J. Ware, *The Labor Movement in the United States, 1860–1895* (Gloucester, MA: Peter Smith, 1959) 95.

25. Stevens, *Cyclopaedia of Fraternities*, 394. See also Jason Kaufman, "Rise and Fall of a Nation of Joiners: The Knights of Labor Revisited," *Journal of Interdisciplinary History*, 31:4 (Spring 2001) 563, and Kim Voss, *The Making of American Exceptionalism: The Knights of Labor and Class Formation in the Nineteenth Century* (Ithaca, NY: Cornell University Press, 1993).

26. Alvin J. Schmidt, *Fraternal Organizations* (Westport, CT: Greenwood Press, 1966) 252–56.

27. National Grange, *Manual of Subordinate Granges*, 10th ed. (Philadelphia: George S. Ferguson, 1910) 38–39.

28. Thomas A. Woods, *Knights of the Plow: Oliver H. Kelley and the Origins of the Grange in Republican Ideology* (Ames: Iowa State University Press, 1991) 150, 163, 207. The Grange supported the 1876 landmark Supreme Court ruling in *Munn v. Illinois* to remove grain silo storage fees. To enforce the ruling, several western states passed legislation called the "Granger Laws." See also Stevens, *Cyclopaedia of Fraternities*, 395–97.

29. Schmidt, *Fraternal Organizations*, 365–78.

30. David Gerard Iliff Jr., *The Lost Tribe of Ben Hur* (Indianapolis: Fall Creek Review, 1994), 3–4.

31. See Theda Skocpol and Jennifer Oser, "Organization Despite Diversity: The Origins and Development of African American Fraternal Associations," *Social Science History*, Fall 2004.

32. Schmidt, *Fraternal Organizations*, 368–80.

33. R.H. Gerard, *Court Degree Ritual of the Tribe of Ben Hur, Containing the Court Degree* (Crawfordsville, IN: R.H. Gerard, n.d.) 37.

34. David T. Bieto, *From Mutual Aid to the Welfare State: Fraternal Societies and Social Services, 1890–1967* (Chapel Hill: University of North Carolina Press, 2000) 4–45, 132–36.

35. Bieto, *From Mutual Aid to the Welfare State*, 14, 24. Two of the largest insurance corporations of the 20th century, Prudential Insurance and Metropolitan Life, were founded on the fraternal system.

36. Carnes, *Secret Ritual and Manhood in Victorian America*, 1–3.

37. John Hamilton, *Material Culture of American Freemasons* (Lexington, MA: Museum of Our National Heritage, 1994) 282–87 and William D. Moore, "Masonic Lodge Rooms and Their Furnishings," *Heredom: Transactions of the Scottish Rite Research Society* (Washington, DC: Scottish Rite Research Society, 1993) 99–136.

38. Clawson, *Constructing Brotherhood*, 233.

39. Clawson, *Constructing Brotherhood*, 237–38. The founder of the Odd Fellows' Patriarchs Militant, John C. Underwood, served as lieutenant governor of Kentucky between 1875 and 1879. The Knights of Pythias Uniform Rank was organized and headed by James R. Carnahan. He served as the Adjutant General of the Indiana National Guard between 1881 and 1885.

40. Beito, *From Mutual Aid to the Welfare State*, 39–40.

Notes to Chapter 7

1. Walter B. Hill, "The Great American Safety-valve," *Century Magazine*, July 1892, 383–84.

2. Theodore A. Ross, *Odd Fellowship, Its History and Manual* (New York: M.W. Hazen Co., 1899) 2.

3. For an overview of this period, see Thomas J. Schlereth, *Victorian America: Transformations in Everyday Life, 1876–1915* (New York: Harper Collins, 1991).

4. S. Brent Morris, "Boom to Bust in the Twentieth Century: Freemasonry and American Fraternities," *A Radical in the East* (Ames: Iowa Research Lodge No. 2, 1994) 30. In 1900, the 49 grand lodges included 46 states plus the territories of Arizona and New Mexico and the District of Columbia.

5. In 1900, the top five grand lodges in America with

the most lodges were New York, 745; Illinois, 723; Texas, 634; Missouri, 556, and Ohio, 501. *Proceedings of the Grand Lodge of Masons in Illinois* (1900) 237.

6. See *A Portrait Gallery with Biographical Sketches of Prominent Freemasons throughout the United States,* 5 vols. (New York: John C. Yorston & Co., 1892), and William R. Denslow, *10,000 Famous Freemasons,* 4 vols. (Trenton: Missouri Lodge of Research, 1957-60).

7. Denslow, *10,000 Famous Freemasons,* vol. 4, 41-42, The Ringling brothers were members of Baraboo Lodge No. 34, Baraboo, WI. At one meeting in 1891, each of the brothers served as the top six lodge officers and initiated their father into the lodge; vol. 4, 201, Gen. Tom Thumb, "Charles S. Stratton"; vol. 3, 322, Admiral Peary was a member of Elisha Kent Kane Lodge No. 45 in New York City, named for the first American artic explorer. For information on Buffalo soldiers, see Joseph A. Walkes Jr., *Black Square and Compass* (1979) 71-80.

8. *Preston's Illustrations of Masonry,* CD-ROM, Andrew Prescott, ed. (Sheffield, UK: Academy Electronics Publications, 2001) 1775 ed., 72.

9. In many jurisdictions, the Junior Warden (the third ranking officer in a lodge) and his assistants, the Senior and Junior Stewards, are responsible for preparing the tables for dining, overseeing the food and drink and insuring no brother overindulges.

10. *Coil's Masonic Encyclopedia,* 2nd ed. (Richmond, VA: Macoy, 1996) 385. See also "History of Table Lodges," *Proceedings of the Texas Lodge of Research* (Waco, 1977-78) 178, and Harry Carr, "Masonic Toasts," *Ars Quatuor Coronatorum: Transactions of the Quatuor Coronati Lodge No. 2076* (1969) 332-38.

11. Lynn Dumenil, *Freemasonry in American Culture, 1880-1930* (Princeton, NJ: Princeton University Press, 1989) 8.

12. Allen E. Roberts, *Freemasonry in American History* (Richmond, VA: Macoy, 1985) 305, 318.

13. The Knights Templar parade at the Triennial Conclave in Boston in 1895 was probably the largest gathering of Freemasons in the world in the 19th century. How many thousands of non-Knight Templar Masons viewed the parade is unknown, but it was estimated that "the number of men in line to have been about 26,000. The procession marched to the music of 137 bands and occupied more than five hours in its passage." See *Report of the Triennial Committee of the Grand Commandery of Knights Templar of Massachusetts and Rhode Island* (Central Falls, RI: E.L. Freemans & Son, 1895) 102-3.

14. Tony Fels, "Religious Assimilation in a Fraternal Organization: Jews and Freemasonry in Gilded Age San Francisco," in R. William Weisberger, Wallace McLeod and S. Brent Morris, eds., *Freemasonry on Both Sides of the Atlantic* (Boulder, CO: East European Monographs, 2002) 627. Fels' essay provides an initial understanding of religious and class divisions among Masonic lodges.

15. A.C.F. Jackson, *English Masonic Exposures, 1760-1769* (London: Lewis Masonic, 1986) Transcript of "Three Distinct Knocks, 1760," 84.

16. Fred Van Deventer, *Parade to Glory: The Story of the Shriners and Their Hospitals for Crippled Children* (New York: William Morrow and Co., 1959) 35, 42-43.

17. Van Deventer, *Parade to Glory,* 1-6.

18. See *The Mystic Shrine Illustrated: The Full Illustrated Ritual of the Nobles of the Mystic Shrine,* rev. ed. (Chicago: Ezra A. Cook, 1893).

19. Van Deventer, *Parade to Glory,* 23-24. The confusion and misinformation of Arabic and Moslem culture is made apparent by the title of Rabban, which is Jewish and not Moslem. AAONMS rearranged spells "A MASON."

20. Van Deventer, *Parade to Glory,* 25-26.

21. George L. Root, *History of the Shrine, the Ancient Arabic Order Nobles of the Mystic Shrine of North America* (Peoria, IL: B. Frank Brown Co., 1903) 20-21.

22. Van Deventer, *Parade to Glory,* 277.

23. Van Deventer, *Parade to Glory,* 29-30.

24. Charles W. Ferguson, *Fifty Million Brothers, A Panorama of American Lodges and Clubs* (New York: Farrar & Rinehart, 1937) 235.

25. Van Deventer, *Parade to Glory,* 277.

26. Van Deventer, *Parade to Glory,* 92, 277-79.

27. As quoted in Van Deventer, *Parade to Glory,* 274.

28. Morris, *A Radical in the East,* 42-43. In the United States in 1900, there were 55,915 Shriners and 223,391 York Rite (Royal Arch) Masons. In 1920, the Scottish Rite had 367,151 members and the Knights Templar had 313,667 members.

29. Thomas Smith Webb, *The Freemason's Monitor: or Illustrations of Masonry* (Boston, Joshua Cushing, Printer, 1808) 33.

30. Van Deventer, *Parade to Glory,* 71-72, 278. At the 1886 Knights Templar national conclave in Cleveland, the Arabic Shriners "tempted" the Christian Knights into a local hall with a "well of Zem Zem" and "camel's milk" (a bar and a beer). Between 1887 and 1888, 16 new Shrine temples were chartered.

31. Van Deventer, *Parade to Glory,* 57-58.

32. Van Deventer, *Parade to Glory,* 123-24.

33. Alvin J. Schmidt, *Fraternal Organizations* (Westport, CT: Greenwood Press, 1980) 151. See also Otto Hildebrandt, *A Peep into the Mystic Realm* (Fort Worth,

TX: Department of Printing, Masonic Home & School, 1946).

34. *Proceedings of the Supreme Council, Mystic Order of the Veiled Prophets of the Enchanted Realm* (Hamilton, NY: Republican Press, 1908) 43.

35. Schmidt, *Fraternal Organizations,* 329.

36. *Proceedings of the Supreme Forest, Tall Cedars of Lebanon* (Trenton, NJ: Harrison Press, 1925) 30.

37. Schmidt, *Fraternal Organizations,* 169.

38. Schmidt, *Fraternal Organizations,* 104. The earliest official version of the toast dates to 1906, but the earliest lodges always had some form of toast at 11 p.m. To symbolize the toast, the Elks' emblem includes a clock set at the eleventh hour.

39. Schmidt, *Fraternal Organizations,* 303–5.

40. Schmidt, *Fraternal Organizations,* 179–80.

41. Schmidt, *Fraternal Organizations,* 27. The Order took its name from the fortress in Spain where the Moors surrendered to Ferdinand and Isabella in 1492. Wearing fezzes and Arabic costumes like Shriners, the Order was never officially recognized by the Knights of Columbus.

42. Schmidt, *Fraternal Organizations,* 47–48.

43. Schmidt, *Fraternal Organizations,* 367–74.

44. Theda Skocpol and Jennifer Oser, "Organization Despite Diversity: The Origins and Development of African American Fraternal Associations," Harvard University, *Social Science History,* Fall 2004.

45. Charles E. Ellis, *An Authentic History of the Benevolent and Protective Order of Elks* (Chicago, 1910) 20–31.

46. Charles E. Redaker, *Early History of the Benevolent and Protective Order of Elks of the Dominion of Canada and Newfoundland* (Windsor, Ontario, 1937) 92.

47. Schmidt, *Fraternal Organizations,* 102.

48. Schmidt, *Fraternal Organizations,* 102, 104.

49. Arthur Preuss, comp., *A Dictionary of Secret and Other Societies* (St. Louis, MO: B. Herder Book Co., 1924; reprinted by Detroit: Gale Research Co., 1966) 60.

50. *Masonic Standard,* New York, April 4, 1908, 10.

51. William D. Moore, "Structures of Masculinity: Masonic Temples, Material Culture, and Ritual Gender Archetypes in New York, 1870-1930," Ph.D. dissertation, Boston University, 1999 (published by UMI Dissertation Services, Ann Arbor, MI) 302-4. In 1866, the state of New York changed the laws so that fraternal lodges could own property and form separate temple associations.

52. William D. Moore, "Funding the Temples of Masculinity," *Heredom: Transactions of the Scottish Rite Research Society* (Washington, DC, 1996) 35-49.

53. Schlereth, *Victorian America,* 173.

54. "A City under One Roof," *Scientific American,* February 10, 1894. It was the tallest building in the world between 1892 and 1896. Despite the fanfare of its opening, it was ultimately a financial failure and was torn down in 1939.

55. Schlereth, *Victorian America,* 173.

56. Burg, *Chicago's White City* (Lexington: University Press of Kentucky, 1979) 89.

57. Joseph A. Walkes, Jr., *History of the Shrine: Ancient Egyptian Arabic Order Nobles of the Mystic Shrine, Inc.* (Detroit: Ancent Egyptian Arabic Order Nobles of the Mystic Shrine of North and South America and Its Jurisdiction, Inc., P.H.A., 1993) 49, 57.

Notes to Chapter 8

1. Theodore Roosevelt, "Freemasonry and Citizenship," *The Trestle Board,* Feb. 1905, 509.

2. For an overview of this period, see John M. Cooper, *Pivotal Decades: The United States, 1900–1920* (New York: W.W. Norton, 1999).

3. Lynn Dumenil, *Freemasonry in American Culture, 1880–1930* (Princeton, NJ: Princeton University Press, 1984) 28–29.

4. Dumenil, *Freemasonry in American Culture,* 26–27, 230–31.

5. Thomas Smith Webb, *The Freemason's Monitor; or, Illustrations of Masonry* (Boston: Joshua Cushing, Printer, 1808) 67–68. This quotation demonstrates Webb's application of Preston. In his 1775 edition of *Illustrations of Masonry* [CD-ROM, Andrew Prescott, ed. (Sheffield, UK: Academy Electronics Publications, 2001) 94–95], Preston wrote the first half: "Geometry treats of the powers and properties of magnitudes in general, where length, length and breadth, or length, breadth, and thickness are considered."

6. For an overview of the Progressive Era, see John Whiteclay Chambers, *The Tyranny of Change: America in the Progressive Era, 1900–1917* (New York: Palgrave Macmillan, 2nd ed., 1992).

7. Paul P. Harris, *My Road to Rotary: The Story of a Boy, a Vermont Community, and Rotary* (Chicago: A. Kroch and Son, 1948) 230.

8. Charles W. Ferguson, *Fifty Million Brothers: A Panorama of American Lodges and Clubs* (New York: Farrar & Rinehart, 1937) 95.

9. Harris, *My Road to Rotary,* 307. Between 1915 and 1919, the number of clubs increased from 200 to 500 and membership surpassed 43,000.

10. Albert Pike, *Morals and Dogma of the Ancient and Accepted Scottish Rite of Freemasonry* (Charleston,

SC: Supreme Council, 33°, Southern Jurisdiction, 1871) 851.

11. Alvin Schmidt, *Fraternal Organizations* (Westport, CT: Greenwood Press, 1980) 372-75.

12. Wyn Craig Wade, *The Fiery Cross: The Ku Klux Klan in America* (New York: Simon & Shuster, 1987) 138-39, 157.

13. In 1880, the Scottish Rite Southern Jurisdiction had 1,150 members. William L. Fox, *Lodge of the Double-Headed Eagle* (Fayetteville: University of Arkansas Press, 1997) 91. The Scottish Rite Northern Jurisdiction had approximately 7,400 members. George A. Newbury and Louis L. Williams, *History of the Supreme Council, 33°, for the Northern Masonic Jurisdiction, USA* (Lexington, MA: Supreme Council, AASR, NMJ, 1987) 181. For York Rite membership, see *Proceedings of the General Grand Chapter, Royal Arch Masons, Triennial Conclave, 1883* (Buffalo, NY: Young, Lockwood & Co., 1883) 143; Dumenil, *Freemasonry in American Culture*, 225.

14. Samuel H. Baynard Jr., *History of the Supreme Council, 33°, Northern Masonic Jurisdiction of the USA* (Boston: Supreme Council, 33°, NMJ, 1938) vol. 1, 285-87, vol. 2, 3-19. Van Rensselaer was a member of the famous Albany, New York, family.

15. *Coil's Masonic Encyclopedia* (Richmond, VA: Macoy, rev. ed., 1996) 472-75. For a complete biography, see Walter Lee Brown, *A Life of Albert Pike* (Fayetteville: University of Arkansas Press, 1997).

16. Fox, *Lodge of the Double-Headed Eagle*, 52. Albert Mackey is one of the most important American Freemasons of the 19th century. See *Coil's Masonic Encyclopedia*, 394-96.

17. See Rex R. Hutchens, *A Bridge to Light* (Washington, DC: Supreme Council, 33°, SJ, USA, 1988).

18. See Pike, *Morals and Dogma,* and Rex R. Hutchens, *Pillars of Wisdom: Writings of Albert Pike* (Washington, DC: Supreme Council, 33°, Southern Jurisdiction, 1995).

19. Charles S. Lobringer, *The Supreme Council, 33°, Ancient and Accepted Scottish Rite, Southern Jurisdiction, U.S.A.* (Louisville, KY: Standard Print, 1931) 358, 361.

20. Jack P. de Vise, *A Magnificent Heritage: 150 Years of the Scottish Rite Freemasonry in the Valley of Cincinnati* (Cincinnati, OH, 2003) 63. See also C. Lance Brockman, "Creating Scenic Illusion for the Theater and the Fraternity" in *Theater of the Fraternity: Staging the Ritual Space of the Scottish Rite of Freemasonry, 1896-1929* (Minneapolis: Frederick R. Weisman Art Museum, University of Minnesota, 1996) 99.

21. Brockman, *Theater of the Fraternity*, 99-102.

22. Brockman, "Catalyst for Change: Intersection of the Theater and the Scottish Rite," *Heredom: Transactions of the Scottish Rite Research Society* (Washington, DC, 1994) 125-26, 131.

23. James D. Carter Jr., *History of the Supreme Council, 33°, Southern Jurisdiction, U.S.A., 1891-1921* (Washington, DC: Supreme Council, 33°, SJ, USA, 1971) 167.

24. In 1900, the Southern Jurisdiction had 10,560 members. Lobringier, *Supreme Council*, 735. In 1920, the Southern Jurisdiction had 192,231 members. See *Transactions of the Supreme Council, 33°, Southern Jurisdiction, 1920-21*, 238. Newbury and Williams, *History of the Supreme Council, 33°, NMJ, USA*, 239-40.

25. Loyal Order of Moose, *Initiatory Ceremony* (1908) 10.

26. There were occasions when individual Masons organized insurance agencies for their brothers, such as the Masonic Life Association. Arthur Pruess, comp., *A Dictionary of Secret and Other Societies* (St. Louis, MO: B. Herder Book Co., 1924; Detroit: Gale Research Co., 1966 reprint) 266. However, these companies were not officially sanctioned by grand lodges. Many grand lodges even went so far as to require men applying for membership to acknowledge that Freemasonry does not promise any form of insurance or benefits to its members.

27. Schmidt, *Fraternal Organizations*, 53, and Alan Axelrod, *The International Encyclopedia of Secret Societies and Fraternal Orders* (New York: Facts on File, Inc., 1997) 230.

28. *2000 Statistics of Fraternal Benefit Societies* (Naperville, IL: National Fraternal Congress of America, 2001). Among the membership of the National Fraternal Congress of America were Union Saint Jean Baptiste, the Greek Catholic Union, Polish Women's Alliance of America and the Lutheran Brotherhood.

29. David T. Beito, *From Mutual Aid to the Welfare State* (Chapel Hill: University of North Carolina Press, 2000) 116, 128-29.

30. William R. Denslow, *10,000 Famous Freemasons* (Trenton: Missouri Lodge of Research, 1957) vol. 1, 290-91, and James J. Davis, *The Iron Puddler: My Life in the Rolling Mills and What Became of It* (New York: Grosset & Dunlap, 1922) 345.

31. Robert L. Uzzel, "Puddler Jim Davis: Labor Leader, Mason and Moosepuddler," *The Philalethes*, June 2001, 63. See also Joe M. Chapple, *Our Jim: A Biography* (Boston: Chapple Publishing Co., 1928).

32. Davis, *The Iron Puddler*, 257, 262, and Beito, *From Mutual Aid to the Welfare State*, 65.

33. Schmidt, *Fraternal Organizations*, 221.

34. Denslow, *10,000 Famous Freemasons*, vol. 1, 290-91, and Charles W. Ferguson, *Fifty Million Brothers*, 290.

35. James Pettibone, ed., *The Lodge Goat, Goat Rides, Butts, and Goat Hair: Gathered from the Lodge Room of Every Fraternal Order* (Cincinnati, OH: James Pettibone, 1907) 412.

36. Thomas J. Schlereth, *Victorian America: Transformations in Everyday Life, 1876–1915* (New York: Harper Collins, 1991) 212–13.

37. John D. Hamilton, "The Lodge Goat," *The Northern Light*, vol. 29, no. 1, Feb. 1998, 12–13. When and where the practice of forcing new members to be blindfolded and ride a goat is unknown, but the goat was used in some Odd Fellows lodges in the 1850s. See also John D. Hamilton, *Material Culture of the American Freemasons* (Lexington, MA: Museum of Our National Heritage, 1994) 86–89 and "Appendix I: Dealers of Fraternal Regalia and Paraphernalia." The most famous manufacturers of these hazing devices were De-Moulin Brothers Company of Greenville, IL, and Pettibone Brothers of Cincinnati.

38. Schmidt, *Fraternal Organizations*, 85–87. The Knights of Pythias' Shrine-like group, the "Dokeys," also had a women's auxiliary called the Nomads of Avrudaka. Schmidt, 180.

39. As quoted in George E. Simons, *Standard Masonic Monitor* (New York: Macoy, 1899) 31.

40. Theda Skocpol and Jennifer Oser, "Organization Despite Adversity: The Origins and Development of African American Fraternal Association," *Social Science History*, Fall 2004. In 1916, the Grand United Order of Odd Fellows' female auxiliary, the Household of Ruth, had 197,000 members and 5,000 lodges. See Beito, *From Mutual Aide to Welfare State*, 50. See also Arturo de Hoyas, "On the Origins of the Prince Hall Scottish Rite Rituals," *Heredom*, vol. 5, 1996, 51–67.

41. Ariane Liazos and Marshall Ganz, "Duty to the Race: African-American Fraternal Orders in Defense of Right to Organize," *Social Science History*, Fall 2004.

42. Liazos and Ganz, "Duty to the Race."

43. Liazos and Ganz, "Duty to the Race." Lawyers who were Masons include: T. Gillis Nutter, E. Burton Ceruti, Warner T. McGuinn and D.W. Perkins.

44. Joseph A. Walkes Jr., *History of the Shrine: Ancient Egyptian Arabic Order Nobles of the Mystic Shrine, Inc.* (Detroit: Ancient Egyptian Order Nobles of the Mystic Shrine of North and South America and Its Jurisdictions, P.H.A., 1993) 78.

45. To understand these numbers better, compare them to the United States involvement in Vietnam. In 13 years (1960–73), 47,393 Americans were killed in battle. During World War One, 53,513 were killed in 12 months.

46. Christopher Kauffman, *Faith and Fraternalism: The History of the Knights of Columbus, 1882–1982* (New York: Harper & Row, 1982) 216.

47. Allen E. Roberts, *Freemasonry's Servant: The Masonic Service Association of the United States, the First Fifty Years* (Washington, DC: Masonic Service Association, 1969), 7, and Harris, *My Road to Rotary*, 254.

48. Denslow, *10,000 Famous Freemasons*, vol. 3, 331, and S. Kenneth Baril, comp., *Medal of Honor: The Letter G in Valor* (Cheshire, CT: Weidner Publishers, 1994) 60.

49. Roberts, *Freemasonry's Servant*, 1.

50. Roberts, *Freemasonry's Servant*, 7–8, 19–20.

51. Roberts, *Freemasonry's Servant*, 20.

52. Roberts, *Freemasonry's Servant*, 21.

53. Roberts, *Freemasonry's Servant*, 31–32, 36.

54. For an overview of this period, see William E. Leuchtenburg and Daniel J. Boorstin, *The Perils of Prosperity, 1914–1932* (Chicago: University of Chicago Press, 2nd ed., 1993).

55. Hugh Brogan, *The Penguin History of the United States of America* (London: Penguin Books, 1986) 506.

56. In 1916, the total Masonic membership in the United States was 1,656,324. *1915 Proceedings of the Grand Lodge of New York, F&AM* (New York: J.J. Little & Ives Co., 1916) 104. In 1920, the total membership was 2,043,133. *1920 Proceedings of the Grand Lodge of New York, F&AM* (New York: J.J. Little & Ives Co., 1921) 72.

Notes to Chapter 9

1. Charles W. Ferguson, *Fifty Million Brothers: A Panorama of American Lodges and Clubs* (New York: Farrar & Rinehart, 1937) 15.

2. For an overview of the 1920s and consumerism, the youth movement and big business, see Warren I. Susman, *Culture as History* (New York: Pantheon Books, 1984) Chapter 8; Paula S. Fass, *The Damned and the Beautiful: American Youth in the 1920s* (New York: Oxford University Press, 1977) Chapter 1, and Glenn Porter, *The Rise of Big Business, 1860–1920* (New York: Harlan Davidson, 1992).

3. *King Solomon and His Followers: A Valuable Aid to the Memory* (New York: Allen Publishing Co., 1920) 44.

4. Paul Harris, *This Rotarian Age* (Chicago: Rotary International, 1935) 59–60.

5. Hugh Brogan, *Penguin History of the United States* (London: Penguin Books, 1986) 508–10, 522.

6. Susman, *Culture as History*, xxiv, 111, 127–28.

7. Jeffrey A. Charles, *Service Clubs in American Society: Rotary, Kiwanis and Lions* (Urbana: University of Illinois Press, 1993) 44–45.

8. Ferguson, *Fifty Million Brothers*, 94–107. For a history of the Lions Club, see Robert J. Casey and W.A.S. Douglas, *World's Biggest Doers* (Chicago: Wilcox and Follett, 1959). For Kiwanis, L.A. Hapgood, *The Men Who Wear the K* (Indianapolis, IN: Kiwanis International, 1981).

9. Charles, *Service Clubs in American Society*, 45.

10. Clifford Putney, "Service over Secrecy: How Lodge-style Fraternalism Yielded Popularity to Men's Service Clubs," *Journal of Popular Culture*, Summer 1993, 186.

11. Charles, *Service Clubs in American Society*, 124, 131. The German novelist Thomas Mann was a member of the Dresden Rotary Club. In 1930, he encouraged Rotarians to find a middle path between the extreme right- and left-wing politicians.

12. Charles, *Service Clubs in American Society*, 38–39, 52–53. Rotary also established a membership classification system that restricted each profession to one member per club. This encouraged a wider circle of business networking and reduced competition among Rotarians for new clients and customers. Such classifications, however, were often overlooked, as more men demanded to join and greater varieties of occupations developed. For instance, insurance agents became subdivided into life insurance, auto insurance, homeowners insurance, etc.

13. Robert S. and Helen M. Lynd, *Middletown; A Study in American Culture* (New York: Harcourt, Brace & World, 1956) 306.

14. *Preston's Illustrations of Masonry*, CD-ROM, Andrew Prescott, ed. (Sheffield, UK: Academy Electronics Publications, 2001) 1775 ed., 72–73.

15. Arthur M. Schlesinger, "Biography of American Joiners," *American Historical Review*, Oct. 1944, 1–25. The term "joiners" dates back to the late 1800s and was often written in slang as "jiners."

16. Steven C. Bullock, *Revolutionary Brotherhood* (Chapel Hill: University of Northern Carolina Press, 1996) 198–202; Lynn Dumenil, *Freemasonry and American Culture, 1880–1930* (Princeton, NJ: Princeton University Press, 1984) 22, 30.

17. Wellins Calcott, *A Candid Disquisition of the Principle and Practices of the Most Ancient and Honorable Society of Free and Accepted Masons* (London: James Dixwell, 1769) 138–39.

18. Dumenil, *Freemasonry and American Culture*, 22; *Coil's Masonic Encyclopedia* (Richmond, VA: Macoy, rev. ed., 1996) 631. See also Alphonse Cerza, *The Courts and Freemasonry: Case Histories That Have or Could Affect Freemasonry* (Highland Springs, VA: Anchor Communications, 1986).

19. John Hamilton, *Material Culture of American Freemasons* (Lexington, MA: Museum of Our National Heritage, 1994) 282–87.

20. David Gray, *Inside Prince Hall* (Lancaster, VA: Anchor Communications, 2004), 193, 200–10. Gray lists more than 200 irregular grand lodges in the United States.

21. *Coil's Masonic Encyclopedia*, 138. See also Bruno Bertuccioli, *The Level Club: A New York Story of the Twenties: Splendor, Decadence, and Resurgence of a Monument to Human Ambition* (Owings Mills, MD: Watermark Press, 1991).

22. Dumenil, *Freemasonry and American Culture*, 209–11.

23. Louis P. Black, *History of High Twelve International, 1920–1960* (St. Louis, MO: High Twelve International, 1989) 21, 41, 54. See also Alvin Schmidt, *Fraternal Organizations* (Westport, CT: Greenwood Press, 1980) 159–60.

24. H.L. Mencken, *Minority Report* (New York: Alfred J. Knopf, 1956) 178–79. See also Bruce Bliven, "The Babbitt in His Warren," *Scribner's Magazine*, Dec. 1928, 899–901, and Sinclair Lewis, *Babbitt* (New York: Harcourt, Brace, 1922).

25. Susman, *Culture as History*, 109–12.

26. Harris, *This Rotarian Age*, 1–2. Chesterton's speech, "This Rotarian Age," quoted in C.P. Hewitt, *Towards My Neighbour: The Social Influence of the Rotary Movement in Great Britain and Ireland* (London: Longman, Green and Co., 1950) 148.

27. Thomas Smith Webb, *The Freemason's Monitor; or, Illustrations of Masonry* (Boston, Joshua Cushing Printer, 1808) 78–79.

28. S. Brent Morris, "Boom to Bust in the Twentieth Century: Freemasonry and American Fraternities," *A Radical in the East* (Ames: Iowa Research Lodge No. 2, 1994) 30–34.

29. Dumenil, *Freemasonry and American Culture*, 225.

30. William A. Muraskin, *Middle-Class Blacks in White Society: Prince Hall Freemasonry in America* (Berkeley: University of California Press, 1975) 29, 184.

31. *Tyler-Keystone*, 34, Aug. 1920, 115–16, as quoted in Dumenil, *Freemasonry and American Culture*, 271.

32. *List of Regular Lodges, A.F.& A.M., 1920* (Bloomington, IL: Pantagraph Printing, 1920) MA, 86; IL, 55; CA, 14. *List of Regular Lodges Masonic, 1930* (Bloomington, IL: Pantagraph Printing, 1929) MA, 96; IL, 64; CA, 14.

33. Dumenil, *Freemasonry and American Culture*, 156–

63, and Mark C. Carnes, *Secret Ritual and Manhood in Victorian America* (New Haven, CT: Yale University Press, 1989) 155–56.

34. Brogan, *Penguin History of the United States,* 503, 512.

35. The remaining 16 members of the Grand Army of the Republic closed the last post at the 1949 Grand Encampment in Indianapolis. Mary R. Dearing, *Veterans in Politics: The Story of the Grand Army of the Republic* (Baton Rouge: Louisiana State University Press, 1952) 497–98.

36. *Keystone-Tyler,* 32, Aug. 1919, reprinted from *Illinois Freemason; The Builder, Journal for the American Student,* Jan. 1920, 8, as quoted in Dumenil, *Freemasonry and American Culture,* 135. The Masonic Service Association affirmed these sentiments by stating as its mission: "Teach every member of the Fraternity what is required of a loyal citizen," and "Help outgeneral the strategy and propaganda of those enemies of America, who are working now from within." *Builder,* 2.

37. Dumenil, *Freemasonry and American Culture,* 120–22; William L. Fox, *Lodge of the Double-Headed Eagle: Two Centuries of Scottish Rite Freemasonry in America's Southern Jurisdiction* (Fayetteville: University of Arkansas Press, 1997) 240–41.

38. Norman Cohn, *Warrant for Genocide: The Myth of the Jewish World Conspiracy and the Protocols of the Elders of Zion* (London: Penguin Books, 1970) 49–54, 72–73.

39. Dumenil, *Freemasonry and American Culture,* 131–34.

40. Wyn Craig Wade, *The Fiery Cross: The Ku Klux Klan in America* (New York: Simon & Schuster, 1987) 183.

41. Wade, *The Fiery Cross,* 197; Fox, *Lodge of the Double-Headed Eagle,* 207–8, and William R. Denslow, *10,000 Famous Masons* (Trenton: Missouri Lodge of Research, 1959) vol. 1, 99.

42. Mark David Chalmers, *Hooded Americanism: The History of the Ku Klux Klan* (Durham, NC: Duke University Press, 1987) 92–93, 127, 170, and Richard K. Tucker, *The Dragon and the Cross: The Rise and Fall of the Ku Klux Klan in Middle America* (Hamden, CT: Archon Books, 1991) 101, 126, 155.

43. Chalmers, *Hooded America,* 24, 149, and Lynn Dumenil, *Freemasonry and American Culture,* 122–23.

44. Chalmers, *Hooded America,* 292–93, 296.

45. Brogan, *Penguin History of the United States of America,* 519.

46. William Adrian Brown, *History of the George Washington Masonic National Memorial, 1920–1974* (William Adrian Brown, 1980) 4–10.

47. *Minutes of the 13th Annual Convention of the George Washington Masonic National Memorial Association, 1923* (Alexandria, VA, 1923) 9.

48. Brown, *History of the George Washington Masonic National Memorial,* 25, 56–57.

49. Bina West, president of the Women's Benefit Association, as quoted in David T. Beito, *From Mutual Aid to the Welfare State: Fraternal Societies and Social Services, 1890–1967* (Chapel Hill: University of North Carolina Press, 2000) 230, Endnote 20, 288.

50. Brogan, *Penguin History of the United States of America,* 527.

51. S. Brent Morris, *Radical in the East,* 30.

52. Ralph Smedley, *The Story of Toastmasters* (Rancho Santa Margarita, CA: Toastmasters International, 1993) 74.

53. Carnes, *Secret Ritual,* 151–52.

54. Morris, *Radical in the East,* 14–15.

55. The AOUW National Grand Lodge died in 1929. State grand lodge congresses existed until 1952. Various state grand lodges merged or were bought out thereafter until the last AOUW organization in Washington state passed away in the 1980s. See Keith L. Yates, *The Fogarty Years: A History of the AOUW* (Seattle: Evergreen Printing Co., 1972). The Tribe of Ben Hur became the National Assurance Company in 1940. See David Illiff, *The Lost Tribe of Ben Hur* (Indianapolis, IN: Fall Creek Review, 1944) 31. Bina West's Ladies of the Maccabees became the Women's Benefit Association in 1926 and then the North American Benefit Association in 1966. See Keith L. Yates, *An Enduring Heritage: The First One Hundred Years of the North American Benefit Association* (Port Huron, MI: North American Benefit Association, 1992) 232, 361.

56. In 2000, the National Fraternal Congress of America represented 94 organizations with over seven million members and more than $278 billion in fraternal life insurance policies in force. *2000 Statistics of Fraternal Benefit Societies* (Naperville, IL: National Fraternal Congress of America, 2001).

57. Morris, *A Radical in the East,* 33.

58. Charles, *Service Clubs in American Society,* 107–8, 148.

Notes to Chapter 10

1. Arthur M. Schlesinger, "Biography of a Nation of Joiners," *American Historical Review* (vol. 50, no. 1, October 1944) 25.

2. Paula Fass, *The Damned and the Beautiful: American Youth in the 1920s* (New York: Oxford University Press, 1977) 19–20.

3. Karen J. Blair, *The Clubwoman as Feminist: True Womanhood Redefined, 1868–1914* (New York: Holmes & Meier Publishers, 1980) 1–5.

4. Keith L. Yates, *An Enduring Heritage: The First One Hundred Years of the North American Benefit Association* (Port Huron, MI: North American Benefit Association, 1992) 123.

5. *Coil's Masonic Encyclopedia,* rev. ed. (Richmond, VA: Macoy, 1996) 7–14.

6. Fass, *The Damned and the Beautiful,* 124. Between 1900 and 1930, high school enrollment increased 654 percent. Colleges and universities experienced a three-fold increase.

7. Fass, *The Damned and the Beautiful,* 75, and Mark C. Carnes, *Secret Ritual and Manhood in Victorian America* (New Haven, CT: Yale University Press, 1989) 153–55.

8. Fass, *The Damned and the Beautiful,* 163.

9. Richard Nelson Current, *Phi Beta Kappa in American Life: The First 200 Years* (New York: Oxford University Press, 1990) 10. Phi Beta Kappa, for example, stands for Philosophia Biouy Kubernetes, or "Love of wisdom, the guide of life."

10. Jack L. Anson and Robert Marchesani, eds., *Baird's Manual of American College Fraternities,* (Indianapolis: Baird's Manual Foundation, Inc., 20th ed., 1991) I-11.

11. Stella Clapp, *Out of the Heart: A Century of P.E.O., 1869–1969* (Des Moines, IA: P.E.O. Sisterhood, 1968) 73–74.

12. Anson and Marchesani, *Baird's Manual of American College Fraternities,* I-12.

13. Albert C. Stevens, ed., *Cyclopaedia of Fraternities* (New York: E.B. Treat & Co., 2nd ed., 1907) xix.

14. Fass, *The Damned and the Beautiful,* 143.

15. Donald W. Solanas Jr. and Donald W. Lawson, *Pythagoras: The Membership Manual of the Acacia Fraternity* (Indianapolis, IN: Acacia Fraternity, 1994) 95.

16. Anson and Marchesani, *Baird's Manual of American College Fraternities,* III-2.

17. Fass, *The Damned and the Beautiful,* 365.

18. *Preston's Illustrations of Masonry,* CD-ROM, Andrew Prescott, ed. (Sheffield, UK: Academy Electronics Publications, 2001) 1775 ed., 71–72.

19. Minor Myers Jr., *Liberty without Anarchy: A History of the Society of the Cincinnati* (Charlottesville: University of Virginia Press, 1983) 26.

20. Charles W. Ferguson, *Fifty Million Brothers: A Panorama of American Lodges and Clubs* (New York: Farrah & Rinehart, 1937) chapters 14 and 18. See also Wallace Evan Davies, *Patriotism on Parade: The Story of Veterans and Hereditary Organizations in America,* 1783–1900 (Cambridge, MA: Harvard University Press, 1955).

21. Fass, *The Damned and the Beautiful,* 140–41, 190–91. See also Clifford Putney, *Muscular Christianity: Manhood and Sports in Protestant America, 1880–1920* (Cambridge, MA: Harvard University Press, 2001).

22. *Official History of the International Order of Job's Daughters* (Omaha, NE: Supreme Guardian Council, IOJD, 1966) 2.

23. Herbert E. Duncan, *Hi Dad! A Biography of Frank S. Land* (Fulton, MO: Ovid Bell Press, 1970) 23–25.

24. Duncan, *Hi Dad,* 33.

25. Duncan, *Hi Dad,* 26–29. There is no connection between the medieval Holy Order of Knights Templar and the Order of DeMolay. Land was a member of the Masonic Knights Templar in Kansas City and head of the Kansas City Scottish Rite DeMolai Council, Knights Kadosh, and adopted the name for the youth group.

26. Duncan, *Hi Dad,* 67.

27. Duncan, *Hi Dad,* 144. For a list of inductees into the DeMolay Hall of Fame, visit www.demolay.org.

28. Duncan, *Hi Dad,* 135.

29. Margaret Kendrick, *Our Place in Time: 75 years of the History of the International Order of Rainbow for Girls* (Macalaster, OK: IORG, 1998) 15–16.

30. Kendrick, *Our Place in Time,* 13–14. There were Rainbow chapters in Mexico, Australia, the Philippines, and Morocco. For a list of famous Rainbow girls, visit www.iorg.org.

31. *Official History of the International Order of Job's Daughters,* 5–7, 38, 88, 168.

32. Christopher J. Kauffman, *Faith and Fraternalism: The History of the Knights of Columbus, 1882–1982* (New York: Harper & Row, 1982) 256, and David Gray, *Inside Prince Hall* (Lancaster, VA: Anchor Communications, 2004) 149.

33. From *Your Son Is My Brother* motion picture, produced and directed by Sid and Al Rogell, Masonic Service Association, 1944.

34. William R. Denslow, *10,000 Famous Freemasons* (Fulton: Missouri Lodge of Research, 1957–58) vol. 1, (Arnold) 31, (Bradley) 122–23; vol. 2, (King) 24–25, (Marshall) 138, (MacArthur) 111–12. Generals Marshall and MacArthur were not initiated in Masonic lodges, but were made "Masons at Sight" by a Grand Master. Marshall received the honor in 1941 after attending a Masonic banquet in Washington, DC. He mentioned that his father was an active Mason in Uniontown, PA, but he never had the time to join. The Grand Master attending the banquet responded by conferring the honor upon him. MacArthur was made a

Mason at Sight by the Grand Master of the Philippines in 1936. He later affiliated with Manila Lodge No. 1, became a Scottish Rite Mason in the Philippines and was made a life member of Nile Shrine in Seattle, WA.

35. Solomon Belchman, "Masons Organizing Clubs in South Pacific," *New York Masonic Outlook*, Aug.-Sept. 1944, 11. A list of known clubs also appears in *New York Masonic Outlook*, May 1945, 13. Included here are clubs in North Africa, New Guinea, Italy, Iceland, Aleutian Islands and on the USS Jean Lafitte. See also the 1945 index for *The New Age* magazine for a list of clubs in China, Paris, Iran and the Philippines.

36. Allen E. Roberts, *Freemasonry's Servant: The Masonic Service Association of the United States, The First Fifty Years* (Washington, DC: MSA, 1969) 62-70.

37. Denslow, *10,000 Famous Freemasons*, vol. 1, (Dewey) 312; vol. 4, (Thurmond) 240, (Truman) 255-56; (Wallace) 291. In 1940, Dewey stated, "I believe that if there were 50 million Masons in the United States instead of three million, there would be no fear of any invasion of foreign ideas contrary to the spirit of religious and personal freedom of America." As quoted in Denslow, vol. 1, 312.

38. Allen E. Roberts, *Brother Truman* (Highland Springs, VA: Anchor Communications, 1985) 92, 169, 226, and David McCullough, *Truman* (New York: Simon & Schuster, 1992) 191. Truman was also a member of the Elks, Eagles and American Legion. Truman wrote the introduction to Denslow's *10,000 Famous Freemasons*. His sister, Mary Jane, was Grand Worthy Matron for the Order of the Eastern Star in Missouri.

39. Thomas Smith Webb, *The Freemason's Monitor; or, Illustrations of Masonry* (Boston, Joshua Cushing, 1808) 75.

40. For an overview of this period, see David Halberstam, *The Fifties* (New York: Villard Books, 1993).

41. See Vance Packard, *The Status Seekers* (New York: David McKay Co., 1959).

42. S. Brent Morris, "Boom to Bust in the Twentieth Century: Freemasonry and American Fraternities," *A Radical in the East* (Ames: Iowa Research Lodge No. 2, 1994) 30-34. Membership in Job's Daughters rose from 47,793 in 1945 to 142,949 in 1960. See *Official History of the IOJD*, 109, 165. DeMolay membership increased from 115,416 in 1954 to 162,386 in 1964. See *1978 Proceedings of the International Supreme Council of the Order of DeMolay*, 36.

43. For an understanding of this phenomenon in Freemasonry and other American voluntary associations, see Alvin Schmidt, *Fraternal Organizations* (Westport, CT: Greenwood Press, 1980) 17-18, and Packard, *The Status Seekers*, 179-193.

44. Yogi Berra and Joe Garagiola, *The Yogi Book: "I Really Didn't Say Everything I Said"* (New York: Workman Publishing Co., 1998) 16.

45. Morris, *Radical in the East*, 30-34.

46. For an understanding of the development of the Scottish Rite's dramatic appeal, see C. Lance Brockman, "Creating Scenic Illusion for the Theater and the Fraternity," in *Theater of the Fraternity* (Minneapolis: Frederick R. Weisman Art Museum, University of Minnesota, 1996).

47. In 2001, the 32° Scottish Rite membership in the Northern Masonic Jurisdiction was 279,922, of which 3,629 have received the 33°. In the Southern Jurisdiction, there were 359,639 32° members, of which 5,152 men have been honored with the 33°. *Proceedings of the Supreme Council, 33°, NMJ, USA* (Lexington, MA: 2001); *Transactions of the Supreme Council, 33°, SJ, USA* (Washington, DC: 2001).

48. George A. Newbury and Louis L. Williams, *A History of the Supreme Council, 33°, of the Ancient Accepted Scottish Rite of Freemasonry for the Northern Masonic Jurisdiction of the USA* (Lexington, MA: Supreme Council, 33°, NMJ, 1987) 212-14, and William L. Fox, *Lodge of the Double-Headed Eagle: Two Centuries of Scottish Rite Freemasonry in America's Southern Jurisdiction* (Fayetteville: University of Arkansas Press, 1997) 202-4, 267-68.

49. For an overview of regimentation of the 1950s, see Halberstam, *The Fifties*. See also C. Wright Mills, *White Collar: The American Middle Class* (New York: Oxford University Press, 1951); Walter Isaacson, *The Wise Men: Six Friends and the World They Made* (New York: Faber & Faber, 1986), and David Halberstam, *The Best and the Brightest* (New York: Random House, 1972).

Notes to Chapter 11

1. Robert D. Putnam, "Bowling Alone: America's Declining Social Capital," *Journal of Democracy*, Jan. 1995.

2. For an overview of this period, see Bruce J. Schulman, *The Seventies: The Great Shift in American Culture, Society, and Politics* (New York: DeCapo Press, 2002), and Robert D. Putnam, *Bowling Alone: The Collapse and Revival of American Community* (New York: Simon & Schuster, 2000).

3. Putnam, *Bowling Alone*, 438. For example, between 1960 and 2000, the number of lodges decreased in Massachusetts from 347 to 290, in Illinois from 910 to 600, and in California from 696 to 400. *List of Regu-*

lar Lodges Masonic (Bloomington, IL: Pantagraph Printing, 1960) 21, 97, 129. *List of Regular Lodges Masonic* (2000) 24, 37, 58.

4. *Proceedings, 14th Annual Convention* (St. Louis, MO: Rotary International, 1923) 231. President Harding was also a Freemason. William R. Denslow, *10,000 Famous Freemasons* (Fulton: Missouri Lodge of Research, 1957) vol. 2, 180–81.

5. Jeffrey A. Charles, *Service Clubs in American Society: Rotary, Kiwanis and Lions* (Urbana: University of Illinois Press, 1993) 24–32.

6. Putnam, *Bowling Alone,* 50–52.

7. As quoted in Charles, *Service Clubs in American Society,* 25.

8. Mary I. Wood, *The History of the General Federation of Women's Clubs* (New York: Norwood Press, 1912) 329. See also Karen J. Blair, *The Clubwoman as Feminist: True Womanhood Redefined, 1868–1914* (New York: Holmes & Meier, 1980). Following the GFWC was the Junior League. Founded in 1903 by Mary Harriman, the 19-year-old daughter of railroad tycoon E.H. Harriman, the Junior League's first mission was to improve the health and education of urban poor. During the First World War, it partnered with the American Red Cross to help servicemen.

9. Charles, *Service Clubs in American Society,* 29–32. "In 1925 the nation's Lions clubs reported 904 different activities directed to children's welfare, 1,141 projects of civic improvement, and 498 actions on behalf of the blind, poor and the handicapped." Rotary and Kiwanis reported similar statistics. Charles, 70.

10. Charles, *Service Clubs in American Society,* 76. See also W.A.S. Douglas, *World's Biggest Doers* (Chicago: Wilcox and Follett, 1959).

11. For a history of the Kiwanis, see L.A. Hapgood, *The Men Who Wear the K* (Indianapolis: Kiwanis International, 1981).

12. For the range of Rotary's activities, see *Rotary Basic Library,* 7 vols. (Evanston, IL: Rotary International, 1987).

13. For an overview of the growth of government, see Frederick L. Allen, *Since Yesterday, The 1930s in America* (New York: Harper & Brothers, 1940); John Morton Blum, *V Was for Victory: Politics and American Culture during World War II* (New York: Harvest Books, 1977), and John A. Andrew, *Lyndon Johnson and the Great Society* (New York: Ivan R. Dee, 1998).

14. Putnam, *Bowling Alone,* 118.

15. *Preston's Illustrations of Masonry,* CD-ROM, Andrew Prescott, ed. (Sheffield, UK: Academy Electronics Publication, 2001) 1775 ed., 72.

16. Lynn Dumenil, *Freemasonry and American Culture,* 1880–1930 (Princeton, NJ: Princeton University Press, 1984) 132–33, 174. Masons in the 1920s argued that the institution must break through the barriers between Masonry and the outside world in order to promote cultural harmony in America as a whole.

17. Fred Van Deventer, *Parade to Glory: The Story of the Shriners and Their Hospitals for Crippled Children* (New York: William Morrow & Co. 1959) 174, 281.

18. Van Deventer, *Parade to Glory,* 178–90.

19. Van Deventer, *Parade to Glory,* 189.

20. Van Deventer, *Parade to Glory,* 196.

21. Allen E. Roberts, *Freemasonry's Servant: The Masonic Service Association of the United States: The First Fifty Years* (Washington, DC: MSA, 1969) 35.

22. *Coil's Masonic Encyclopedia* (Richmond, VA: Macoy, rev. ed., 1996) 409.

23. Amos T. Hall in *Proceedings of Prince Hall Grand Lodge of California* (1952) 25.

24. George A. Newbury and Louis L. Williams, *A History of the Supreme Council, 33°, of the Ancient Accepted Scottish Rite of Freemasonry for the Northern Masonic Jurisdiction of the USA* (Lexington, MA: Supreme Council, 33°, NMJ, 1987) 215–17, and William L. Fox, *Lodge of the Double-Headed Eagle: Two Centuries of Scottish Rite Freemasonry in America's Southern Jurisdiction* (Fayetteville: University of Arkansas Press, 1997) 280.

25. For a listing of Masonic charitable activities, see S. Brent Morris. *Masonic Philanthropies* (Lexington, MA, and Washington, DC: Supreme Councils, 33°, NMJ and SJ, 2nd ed., 1997).

26. Morris, *Masonic Philanthropies,* 68–69, 98.

27. William A. Muraskin, *Middle-Class Blacks in a White Society: Prince Hall Freemasonry in America* (Berkeley: University of California Press, 1975) 221–23.

28. Muraskin, *Middle-Class Blacks in a White Society,* 192–93.

29. Muraskin, *Middle-Class Blacks in a White Society,* 230.

30. *Proceedings of Prince Hall Grand Lodge of California* (1958), 27; Joseph Mason Andrew Cox, *Great Black Men of Masonry* (New York: Alpha Books, 1982) 236–37. Other civil rights leaders who were Freemasons included Medger Evers (141–42), Benjamin Hooks (194–95), Ralph Abernathy (24) and Adam Clayton Powell (270–71).

31. Loretta Williams, *Black Freemasonry and Middle-Class Realities* (Columbia: University of Missouri Press, 1980) 21.

32. Thomas Smith Webb, *The Freemason's Monitor; or, Illustrations of Masonry* (Boston: Joshua Cushing, Printer, 1808) 81.

33. Denslow, *10,000 Famous Freemasons*, Skelton, vol. 4, 144; Peale, vol. 3, 321 (Rev. Peale served as the Imperial Grand Chaplain of the Shrine); Warren, vol. 4, 297–98 (Justice Warren served as Grand Master of California in 1935–36); Goldwater, vol. 4, 394. Alan E. Iding, *Forward Freemasonry: A History of Freemasonry in Wisconsin* (Dousman: Grand Lodge of Wisconsin, 1996) vol. 1, 198. Van Deventer, *Parade to Glory*, 261.

34. For an overview of this period, see Todd Gitlin, *The 1960s: Years of Hope, Days of Rage* (New York: Bantam, 1987), and Schulman, *The Seventies*.

35. S. Brent Morris, "Boom to Bust in the Twentieth Century: Freemasonry and American Fraternities," *A Radical in the East* (Ames: Iowa Research Lodge No. 2, 1994) 30–34.

36. In eight years (1969–77), DeMolay membership dropped by 23 percent from 155,587 to 118,674. See *Proceedings of the International Supreme Council of the Order of DeMolay, 1978* (Kansas City, MO) 36.

37. See Fox, *Lodge of the Double-Headed Eagle*, Chapter 15. See also Pamela M. Jollicoeur and Louis L. Knowles, "Fraternal Associations and Civic Religions," *Review of Religious Research*, Fall 1978. For Masonic support of monuments, see Morris, *Masonic Philanthropies*, 34–37, 39, 85.

38. In 1970, 84 lodges met in Philadelphia, 57 met in Detroit, and 35 in St. Louis. By 2000, however, the number of lodges fell to 41 in Philadelphia, 16 in Detroit, and 10 in St. Louis. *List of Regular Lodges Masonic* (1970) 210, 151–52, 63, and *List of Regular Lodges Masonic* (2000) 95, 61, 70. In 1955, there were more than 300,000 Prince Hall Masons in the United States. Muraskin, *Middle-Class Blacks in a White Society*, 29. In 1977, there were 276,835 members in 4,815 lodges. *Official Proceedings of the International Conference of Prince Hall Grand Masters* (1977) 28. In 1997, there were 202,657 members in 4,259 lodges in the United States. David Gray, *Inside Prince Hall* (Lancaster, VA: Anchor Communications, 2004) 157–58.

39. Kwame Anthony Appiah and Henry Louis Gates Jr., eds., *Africana: The Encyclopedia of Africa and African-American Experience* (New York: Basic Civitas Books, 1999). The authors make no mention of Freemasonry or Prince Hall. The only article on fraternities discusses college black fraternities and sororities.

40. *Constitutions of the Grand Lodge of Masons in Massachusetts* (Boston, 1989) 2.

41. *Membership Statistics Report* (Silver Spring, MD: Masonic Service Association, 1981). In 1965, there were 3,987,690 Masons in the United States, and in 1980, there were 3,241,528, a drop of 736,162. Some Freemasons were concerned about the problem even before 1965, as evidenced by the 1960 MSA publication, *An Introduction to the Problems of Declining Membership and Poor Attendance.*

42. Dudley G. Davis, "Grand Masters Hear Results of National Survey," *The Northern Light,* May 1989, 4–7.

43. Richard H. Curtis, "Ohio's One-Day Class," *The Northern Light,* Aug. 2002, 6–7; Jim S. Deyo and Dennis V. Chornenky, "One-Day Class: Logical Evolution or Masonry Lite?" *The Northern Light,* May 2004, 4–6.

44. *Proceedings of Imperial Shrine Council of North America* (Tampa, FL, 2000).

45. See Morris, *Masonic Philanthropies,* 94–103.

46. Ralph Head, "A New Kind of Freemasonry," *California Freemason,* March 1989, 2.

47. Morris, *Masonic Philanthropies,* 18. Compounding the loss of membership was the realization that in 1994 the average age of a Shriner was 62 years old. See Fox, *Lodge of the Double-Headed Eagle,* 373.

48. Peter Brimelow, "Judicial Imperialism," *Forbes,* June 1, 1987, 109, and David B. Sentelle, "On Senate Confirmation of Men and Masons," *Short Talk Bulletin,* April 1988.

49. Fox, *Lodge of the Double-Headed Eagle.* 400; Richard H. Curtis, "Can a Southern Baptist Be a Mason?" *The Northern Light,* Aug. 1993, 4–7, and Gary Leazer, *Fundamentalism & Freemasonry: The Southern Baptist Investigation of the Fraternal Order* (New York: Evans, 1995). See also James L. Holly, *The Southern Baptist Convention and Freemasonry* (Taylors, SC: Mission and Ministry to Men, Inc., vol. 2, 1993, includes complete text of vol. 1).

50. John J. Robinson was unfamiliar with Freemasonry until he started to research the medieval Knights Templar for his book *Born in Blood* (New York: Evans, 1989). His fascination with the fraternity and his eventual desire to join is recorded in his book *A Pilgrim's Path* (New York: Evans, 1993).

51. An Internet search (*www.google.com*) on May 29, 2004, for the word "conspiracy" associated with "Freemasonry" returned 39,200 hits. To understand the basic tactics of anti-Masons, see Arturo de Hoyos and S. Brent Morris, *Is It True What They Say about Freemasonry?* (New York: Evans, rev. ed., 2004).

52. See Michael Baigent and Richard Leigh, *Holy Blood, Holy Grail* (New York: Delacorte Press, 1982); Robinson, *Born in Blood,* and David Ovason, *The Secret Architecture of Our Nation's Capital* (New York: Harper Collins, 2000).

53. Ronald Hutton, *The Triumph of the Moon: A History of Modern Pagan Witchcraft* (Oxford: Oxford Univer-

sity Press, 1999) 61–65. See Charlotte Allen, "The Scholars and the Goddess," *Atlantic Monthly,* Jan. 2001.

54. As early as the 1860s, white Masons attempted to recognize the legitimacy of Prince Hall Freemasonry. The Grand Lodge of Washington in 1898 and the Grand Lodge of Massachusetts in 1948 were on the verge of recognizing their Prince Hall Grand Lodge counterparts but were persuaded by other grand lodges to cancel their intent. See Gray, *Inside Prince Hall,* 168–73, and Thomas S. Roy, *Stalwart Builders: A History of the Grand Lodge of Masons in Massachusetts, 1733–1970* (Boston: Grand Lodge of Massachusetts, 1971) 351–52, 355. For the case against recognition, see Henry Wilson Coil Sr. and John M. Sherman, ed., *A Documentary Account of Prince Hall and Other Black Fraternal Orders* (Fulton: Missouri Lodge of Research, 1982).

55. *Proceedings of the Grand Lodge of Connecticut* (1989) 30.

56. Gray, *Inside Prince Hall,* 174–76.

57. Dan Frost, "Farewell to the Lodge," *Heredom: Transactions of the Scottish Rite Research Society,* Washington, DC, 2000–2001) 31–38; John L. Belton, "Masonic Myths Debunked," *Heredom,* (2001) 9–31; Ted H. Hendon, "Of Freemasons, Odd Fellows and Passenger Pigeons," *The Philalethes,* Oct. 1999, 115–16, and Thomas W. Jackson, "Charity as a Core of Our Craft," *The Philalethes,* April 2004, 36–37, 43.

58. *Preston's Illustrations of Masonry,* CD-ROM, Andrew Prescott, ed. (Sheffield, UK: Academy Electronics Publications, 2001) 1772 ed., 209.

Suggested Reading for American Freemasonry and Fraternalism

There are tens of thousands of books on, or related to, Freemasonry ranging from local lodge and grand lodge histories to philosophy, music and the art of the craft. Listed here are the primary books used in researching this book. They were selected through two criteria. First, those most important to the history of American Freemasonry and fraternalism, and, second, those that are most widely available. The works cited here are little more than portals into larger areas of study. Most of these books are available commercially or in large college or university libraries. State Masonic grand lodges are also valuable research resources. Many support libraries and are glad to receive visitors. Lastly, although I chose to avoid using Internet websites, most of the printed citations, their authors and publishers can be found through Internet keyword searches.

Basic References

The basic building blocks of the history of American Freemasonry are the annual state grand lodge proceedings. Combined with the proceedings of the York and Scottish Rites, the Shrine, the Order of the Eastern Star and numerous other affiliated clubs and bodies, they capture American Freemasons in all their eloquence, petty-mindedness, charity, sentimentality and bureaucracy. Most state grand lodges hold full sets of proceedings from every state and every Masonic body ranging from at least 1870 to 2000.

Anson, Jack L., and Robert Marchesani Jr., eds. *Baird's Manual of American College Fraternities*, 20th ed. Indianapolis, IN: Baird's Manual Foundation, Inc., 1991.

Cerza, Alphonse. *A Masonic Reader's Guide*, vol. 34 of *Transactions of the Missouri Lodge of Research*. Trenton: Transactions of the Missouri Lodge of Research, 1978–79.

Coil, Henry. *Coil's Masonic Encyclopedia*, revised edition, edited by Allen E. Roberts. Richmond, VA: Macoy Publishing and Masonic Supply Company, 1996.

Denslow, William R. *10,000 Famous Freemasons*, 4 vols. Trenton: Missouri Lodge of Research, 1957–1960.

Encyclopedia of Associations: An Associations Unlimited Reference, vol. 1, *National Organizations of the U.S.*, 35th edition, parts 1–3. Detroit, MI: Gale Group, 1999.

Heaton, Ronald E. *Masonic Membership of the Founding Fathers*. Silver Spring, MD: Masonic Service Association, 1965.

Henderson, Kent, and Tony Pope. *Freemasonry Universal: A New Guide to the Masonic World*, 2 vols. Victoria, Australia: Global Masonic Publications, 1998–2000.

[Kaulback, Michael S.]. *Masonic Libraries: A Listing of Masonic Libraries in the United States, Canada and England*. Silver Spring, MD: Masonic Service Association, 1998.

Linder, Erich J. *The Royal Art Illustrated: The Iconography of Freemasonry*. Translated from the German by Arthur Lindsay. Gaz, Austria: Akademisch Druck- u. Verlagsanstalt, 1976.

List of Lodges Masonic. Bloomington, IL: Pantagraph Printing & Stationery Co., 1910–.

Mackey, Albert G. *Encyclopedia of Freemasonry and its Kindred Sciences*. Philadelphia: McClure Publishing Co., 1917.

———. *The History of Freemasonry*, 7 vols. New York: Masonic History Company, 1898.

Macoy, Robert. *A Dictionary of Freemasonry* (1873; reprint, New York: Bell Publishing Co., 1989).

Morris, S. Brent. *Masonic Philanthropies: a Tradition of Caring*, 2nd edition. Lexington, MA: Supreme Council, 33°, Northern Masonic Jurisdiction; Washington, DC: Supreme Council, 33°, Southern Jurisdiction, 1997.

National Fraternal Congress of America. *2000 Statistics of Fraternal Benefit Societies.* Naperville, IL: National Fraternal Congress of America, 2001.

Pruess, Arthur, comp. *A Dictionary of Secret and Other Societies* (1924; reprint Detroit, MI: Gale Research Co., 1966).

Schmidt, Alvin J. *The Greenwood Encyclopedia of American Institutions: Fraternal Organizations,* advisory editor Nicholas Babchuk. Westport, CT: Greenwood Press, 1980.

Stevens, Albert C., ed. *The Cyclopaedia of Fraternities: A Compilation of Existing Authentic Information . . . of More than Six Hundred Secret Societies in the United States,* 2nd edition. New York: E.B. Treat & Co., 1907.

Walgren, Kent, *Freemasonry, Anti-Masonry and Illuminism in the United States; 1734–1850: A Bibliography,* 2 vols. Worcester, MA: American Antiquarian Society, 2003.

Watkins, Larissa P. *American Masonic Periodicals, 1811–2001: A Bibliography of the Library of the Supreme Council, 33°, Southern Jurisdiction,* edited by S. Brent Morris. New Castle, DE: Oak Knoll Press; Washington, DC: Library of the Supreme Council, 33°, Southern Jurisdiction, 2003.

General Works

Most books written about Freemasonry are written by Freemasons and often suffer three general limitations. First, the author is usually writing for other Freemasons and the text is filled with Masonic jargon and technical terms familiar only to the initiated. Second, Masonic authors rarely understand accepted fact-finding research techniques or have an appreciation for broader historical themes. Lastly, many Masonic writers prefer to work within the traditions of mythological Masonic history rather than contradict or revise them. Because of these inconsistencies, many Masonic books may be historically inaccurate. Nevertheless, the books are still worth reading, for an author may have uncovered some valuable information. The books listed here are only to aid the reader in how to select the good, reject the bad and avoid the fantastic.

Anderson, James. *The Constitutions of the Free-Masons: In the Year of Masonry 5723 and the New Book of Constitutions of the Ancient and Honourable Fraternity of Free and Accepted Masons, in the Vulgar Year of Masonry 5738* (1738, facsimile edition, Abingdon, UK: Burgess & Son, Ltd., 1976).

Baynard, Samuel Harrison Jr. *History of the Supreme Council, 33°, Ancient Accepted Scottish Rite of Freemasonry, Northern Masonic Jurisdiction of the United States of America and its Antecedents,* 2 vols. Boston: Supreme Council, 33°, Northern Masonic Jurisdiction, 1938.

Beito, David T. *From Mutual Aid to the Welfare State: Fraternal Societies and Social Services, 1890–1967,* Chapel Hill: University of North Carolina Press, 2000.

Blair, Karen J. *The Clubwoman as Feminist: True Womanhood Defined, 1868–1914.* New York: Holmes and Meier Publishers, 1980.

Brockman, C. Lance. *Theatre of the Fraternity: Staging the Ritual Space of the Scottish Rite of Freemasonry, 1896–1929.* Minneapolis: Frederick R. Weisman Art Museum; University of Minnesota, 1996.

Brooks, Charles H. *The Official History and Manual of the Grand United Order of Odd Fellows in America.* (1902, reprint, Freeport, NY: Books for Libraries Press, 1971).

Brown, William Adrian. *History of the George Washington Masonic National Memorial, 1920–1974, Half Century of Construction.* Alexandria, VA: William Adrian Brown, 1980.

Brownell, John H., ed. *Gems from the Quarry and Sparks from the Gavel: Carefully Selected and Collated Orations, Essays, Histories, Addresses,* 3 vols. Detroit, MI: John H. Brownell, 1893.

Bullock, Steven C. *Revolutionary Brotherhood: Freemasonry and the Transformation of the American Social Order, 1730–1840.* Chapel Hill: University of North Carolina Press, 1996.

Carnes, Mark C. *Secret Ritual and Manhood in Victorian America.* New Haven, CT: Yale University Press, 1989.

Carr, Harry. *The Freemason at Work.* London: Lewis Masonic, 1976.

Cerza, Alphonse. *The Courts and Freemasonry: Case Histories That Have or Could Affect Freemasonry.* Highland Springs, VA: Anchor Communications, 1986.

Chalmers, David Mark. *Hooded Americanism: The First Century of the Ku Klux Klan.* Durham, NC: Duke University Press, 1987.

Charles, Jeffrey A. *Service Clubs in American Society: Rotary, Kiwanis, and Lions.* Urbana: University of Illinois Press, 1993.

Claudy, Carl H. *Introduction to Freemasonry,* 3 vols. Washington, DC: Temple Publishers, 1931.

———. *"Where Your Treasure is . . . ," 12 Masonic Plays.* Washington, DC: Temple Publishers, 1946.

Clawson, Mary Ann. *Constructing Brotherhood: Class,*

Gender, and Fraternalism. Princeton, NJ: Princeton University Press, 1989.

Coil, Henry W., Sr. *A Documentary Account of Prince Hall and Other Black Fraternal Orders,* edited by John M. Sherman. Trenton: Missouri Lodge of Research, 1982.

——. *Freemasonry Through Six Centuries,* 2 vols. Fulton, MO: Ovid Bell Press, 1966–67.

Cook, Lewis C. Wes, ed. *Colonial Freemasonry,* vol. 30, *Transactions of the Missouri Lodge of Research.* Trenton: Missouri Lodge of Research, 1974.

Croly, Jane Cunningham. *The History of the Woman's Club Movement in America.* New York: H.G. Allen & Co., 1898.

Curl, James S. *The Art and Architecture of Freemasonry: An Introductory Study.* London: B.T. Batsford, 1991.

Davies, Wallace Evan. *Patriotism on Parade: The Story of Veterans and Hereditary Organizations in America, 1783–1900.* Cambridge, MA: Harvard University Press, 1955.

DeHoyos, Arturo, and S. Brent Morris. *Is it True What They Say About Masons? The Methods of Anti-Masons,* revised. New York: M. Evans and Co., 2004.

Dermott, Laurence. *Ahiman Rezon.* (1756, facsimile reprint, Bloomington, IL: Masonic Book Club, 1972).

DiBernardo, Giuliano. *Freemasonry and Its Image of Man: A Philosophical Investigation.* Translated from the Italian by Guy Astor and Giuliano DiBernardo. Tunbridge Wells, Kent, UK: Freestone, 1989.

Dumenil, Lynn. *Freemasonry and American Culture, 1880–1930.* Princeton, NJ: Princeton University Press, 1984.

Duncan, Herbert Ewing. *Hi Dad! A Biography of Frank S. Land.* Fulton, MO: International Supreme Council, Order of DeMolay; Missouri Lodge of Research; Ovid Bell Press [printer], 1970.

Dyer, Colin. *William Preston and His Work.* Shepperton, UK: Lewis Masonic, 1987.

Engle, Willis D. *The History of the Order of the Eastern Star,* 2nd edition. Indianapolis, IN: Willis D. Engle, 1901.

Ferguson, Charles W. *Fifty Million Brothers: A Panorama of American Lodges and Clubs.* New York: Farrar & Rinehart, Inc., 1937.

Fox, William L. *Lodge of the Double-Headed Eagle: Two Centuries of Scottish Freemasonry in America's Southern Jurisdiction.* Fayetteville: University of Arkansas Press, 1997.

Fox, William L., ed. *Valley of the Craftsmen: A Pictorial History of Scottish Rite Freemasonry in America's Southern Jurisdiction, 1801–2001.* Washington, DC: Supreme Council, 33°, Southern Jurisdiction, 2001.

Franco, Barbara. *Masonic Symbols in American Decora-*

tive Arts. Lexington, MA: Scottish Rite Masonic Museum of Our National Heritage, 1976.

——. *Bespangled, Painted and Embroidered: Decorated Masonic Aprons in America, 1790–1850.* Lexington, MA: Scottish Rite Masonic Museum of Our National Heritage, 1980.

——. *Fraternally Yours: A Decade of Collecting.* Lexington, MA: Scottish Rite Masonic Museum of Our National Heritage, 1986.

Gray, David. *Inside Prince Hall.* Lancaster, VA: Anchor Communications, LLC, 2004.

Haggard, Forrest D. *The Clergy and the Craft.* Fulton, MO: Ovid Bell Press, 1970.

Haffner, Christopher. *Workman Unashamed: The Testimony of a Christian Freemason.* Shepperton, UK. Lewis Masonic, 1989.

Hamill, John. *The Craft: A History of English Freemasonry.* Wellingborough, UK: Crucible imprint of the Aquarian Press, 1986.

Hamill, John, and Robert Gilbert, eds. *Freemasonry: A Celebration of the Craft.* St. Alban's, Hertfordshire, UK: Mackenzie Publishers, 1992.

Hamilton, John D. *Material Culture of the American Freemasons.* Lexington, MA: Museum of Our National Heritage, 1994.

Harris, Paul P. *My Road to Rotary: The Story of a Boy, a Vermont Community, and Rotary.* Chicago, IL: A. Kroch and Son, 1948.

——. *This Rotarian Age.* Chicago: Rotary International, 1935.

Horne, Alex. *King Solomon's Temple in the Masonic Tradition.* London: Aquarian Press, 1971.

Huss, Wayne. *The Master Builders: A History of the Grand Lodge of Free and Accepted Masons of Pennsylvania,* 3 vols. Philadelphia, PA: Grand Lodge of Pennsylvania, 1986.

Hutchens, Rex R. *A Bridge to Light.* Washington, DC: Supreme Council 33°, Southern Masonic Jurisdiction, U.S.A., 1988.

——. *Pillars of Wisdom: The Writings of Albert Pike.* Washington, DC: The Supreme Council, 33°, Southern Jurisdiction, 1995.

Jackson, A.C.F. *English Masonic Exposures, 1760–1769.* London: Lewis Masonic, Ltd., 1986.

Jacob, Margaret C. *Living the Enlightenment: Freemasonry and Politics in Eighteenth-Century Europe.* New York: Oxford University Press, 1991.

Johnson, Melvin M. *The Beginnings of Freemasonry in America: Containing a Reference to all that is Known of Freemasonry in the Western Hemisphere Prior to 1750.* New York: George H. Doran Company, 1924.

Katz, Jacob. *Jews and Freemasonry in Europe, 1723–1939.*

Translated from the Hebrew by Leonard Oschry. Cambridge, MA: Harvard University Press, 1970.

Kauffman, Christopher. *Faith and Fraternalism: The History of the Knights of Columbus 1882–1982.* New York: Harper & Row, 1982.

———. *Columbianism and the Knights of Columbus.* New York: Simon and Schuster (Academic Reference Division), 1992.

Kaufman, Jason, *For the Common Good?: American Civic Life and the Golden Age of Fraternity.* New York: Oxford University Press, 2002.

Kendrick, Margaret. *Our Place in Time: 75 years of the History; International Order of the Rainbow for Girls.* McAlester, OK: International Order of the Rainbow for Girls, 1998.

Leyland, Herbert T. *Thomas Smith Webb: Freemason, Musician, Entrepreneur.* Dayton, OH: Otterbein Press, 1965.

Lipson, Dorothy Ann. *Freemasonry in Federalist Connecticut, 1789–1839.* Princeton, NJ: Princeton University Press, 1977.

Lobingier, Charles Sumner. *The Supreme Council 33°, Southern Jurisdiction, U.S.A.* Louisville, KY: Standard Print, 1931.

MacNulty, W. Kirk. *The Way of the Craftsman: A Search for the Spiritual Essence of Craft Freemasonry.* London: Central Regalia, 2002.

———. *Freemasonry: A Journey through Ritual and Symbol.* New York: Thames and Hudson, 1991.

Masonic Renewal Task Force Reports. *Phase I Research: Attitudes of Non-Masons toward joining organizations such as Freemasonry; Phase II Research: Attitudes of Masons toward Freemasonry.* Silver Spring, MD: Masonic Service Association, 1990.

McLeod, Wallace, ed. *The Old Gothic Constitutions; Facsimile Reprints of Four Early Printed Texts of the Masonic Old Charges.* Bloomington, IL: Masonic Book Club, 1985.

Melish, William B. *History of the Imperial Council Ancient Arabic Order Nobles of the Mystic Shrine for North America, 1872–1921.* Cincinnati, OH: Abingdon Press, 1921.

Moore, William D. *Structures of Masculinity: Masonic Temples, Material Culture, and Ritual Gender Archetypes in New York, 1870–1930.* (Ph.D. dissertation, Boston University, 1999) Ann Arbor, MI: UMI Dissertation Services, [printers], 1999.

Moore, William D., and John D. Hamilton. "Washington as the Master of His Lodge: History and Symbolism of a Masonic Icon," *George Washington American Symbol,* edited by Barbara J. Mitnick. New York: Hudson Hill Press, in association with the Museums at Stoney Brook and the Museum of Our National Heritage, 1999.

Morris, Robert. *The Poetry of Freemasonry.* Chicago: Knight and Leonard, [printers], 1884.

Morris, S. Brent. *A Radical in the East.* Ames: Iowa Research Lodge No. 2, Siegler Printing and Publishing, 1994.

Muraskin, William. *Middle-Class Blacks in a White Society: Prince Hall Freemasonry in America.* Berkeley: University of California Press, 1975.

The National Masonic Conventions; The Birth and Places of Deliberation, 1843–1846. [Baltimore, MD]: Grand Lodge, AF&AM, of Maryland, 1943.

Newbury, George A., and Louis L. Williams. *History of the Supreme Council, 33°, of the Ancient Accepted Scottish Rite of Freemasonry for the Northern Masonic Jurisdiction of the United States of America.* Lexington, MA: Supreme Council, 33°, Northern Masonic Jurisdiction, 1987.

Newton, Joseph Fort. *The Builders: A Story and Study of Freemasonry.* New York: Macoy Publishing and Masonic Supply Company, Inc., 1930.

Official History of the International Order of Job's Daughters. Omaha, NE: Supreme Guardian Council of 1961, 1966.

Pettibone, James, ed. *The Lodge Goat, Goat Rides, Butts, and Goat Hair; Gathered from the Lodge Room of Every Fraternal Order, More Than a Thousand Anecdotes, Incidents and Illustrations from the Humorous Side of Lodge Life.* Cincinnati, OH: C.B. Pettibone, 1907.

Piatigorsky, Alexander. *Freemasonry: The Study of a Phenomenon.* London: Harvill Press, 1999.

Pike, Albert. *Morals and Dogma of the Ancient and Accepted Scottish Rite of Freemasonry First Three Degrees.* Charleston, SC: Supreme Council, 33°, Southern Jurisdiction, 1871.

Pound, Roscoe. *Masonic Addresses and Writings of Roscoe Pound.* New York: Macoy Publishing and Masonic Supply Company, 1953.

———. *Lectures of Masonic Jurisprudence.* Anamosa, IA: National Masonic Research Society, 1920.

Prescott, Andrew, ed. *Preston's Illustrations of Masonry,* (CD-ROM), Sheffield, UK: Academy Electronics Publications Ltd., 2001.

Preston, William. *Illustrations of Masonry* (1775, facsimile reprint, Bloomington, IL: Masonic Book Club, 1973).

Pritchard, Samuel. *Masonry Dissected* (1730, reprint with commentary by Harry Carr, Bloomington, IL: Masonic Book Club, 1977).

Putnam, Robert D. *Bowling Alone: The Collapse and Re-*

vival of American Community. New York: Simon & Schuster, 2000.

Ratner, Lorman, comp. *Antimasonry: The Crusade and The Party.* Englewood Cliffs, NJ: Prentice-Hall, 1969.

Ridley, Jasper Godwin. *The Freemasons: A History of the World's Most Powerful Secret Society.* New York: Arcade Publishing, 2001.

Roberts, Allen E. *Brother Truman: The Masonic Life and Philosophy of Harry S. Truman.* Highland Springs, VA: Anchor Communications, 1985.

——. *The Craft and Its Symbols: Opening the Door to Masonic Symbolism.* Richmond, VA: Macoy Publishing and Masonic Supply Company, Inc., 1974.

——. *Freemasonry in American History.* Richmond, VA: Macoy Publishing and Masonic Supply Company, Inc., 1985.

——. *Freemasonry's Servant: The Masonic Service Association of the United States, The First Fifty Years.* Washington, DC: Masonic Service Association, 1969.

——. *G. Washington: Master Mason.* Richmond, VA: Macoy Publishing and Masonic Supply Company, Inc., 1976.

——. *House Undivided: The Story of Freemasonry and the Civil War.* Richmond, VA: Macoy Publishing and Masonic Supply Company, Inc., 1961.

Robinson, John J. *A Pilgrim's Path: One Man's Road to the Masonic Temple.* New York: M. Evans, 1993.

Ross, Theodore A. *Odd Fellowship: Its History and Manual.* New York: M.W. Hazen Co., 1900.

Sachse, Julius Friedrich. *Benjamin Franklin as a Freemason.* Philadelphia, PA: New Era Printing Co., 1906.

——. *Washington's Masonic Correspondence . . .* Philadelphia: New Era Printing, 1915.

Sadler, Henry. *Masonic Facts and Fiction: Comprising a new Theory of the Origin of the 'Antient' Grand Lodge* (1887, reprint Wellingborough, UK: Aquarian Press, 1985).

Skocpol, Theda, and Morris P. Fiorina, eds. *Civic Engagement in American Democracy.* Washington, DC: Brookings Institute Press, 1999.

Skully, Francis J. *History of the Grand Encampment of Knights Templar of the United States of America; the 850th anniversary of Templary; the Story of Knighthood from the days of the Ancient Templars to the 44th Conclave of the Modern Templars in 1949.* Greenfield, IN: William Mitchell Printing Co., 1952.

Steblecki, Edith J. *Paul Revere and Freemasonry.* Boston: Paul Revere Memorial Association, 1985.

Stevenson, David. *The First Freemasons: Scotland's Early Lodges and Their Members,* 2nd edition. Edinburgh: Grand Lodge of Scotland, 2001.

Street, Oliver Day. *Symbolism of the Three Degrees.* Kingsport, TN: Southern Publishers, Inc., 1922.

Van Deventer, Fred. *Parade to Glory: The Story of the Shriners and Their Hospitals for Crippled Children.* New York: William Morrow and Co., 1959.

Vaughn, William Preston. *The Antimasonic Party in the United States, 1826–1843.* Lexington: University Press of Kentucky, 1983.

Wade, Wyn Craig. *The Fiery Cross: The Ku Klux Klan in America.* New York: Simon & Schuster, 1987.

Walkes, Joseph A. Jr. *Black Square and Compass: 200 Years of Prince Hall Freemasonry.* [N.p.]: Joseph A. Walkes Jr., 1979.

——. *History of the Shrine: Ancient Egyptian Arabic Order Nobles of the Mystic Shrine, Inc., Prince Hall Affiliated, A Pillar of Black Society, 1893–1993.* Detroit, MI: Ancient Egyptian Arabic Order Nobles of the Mystic Shrine of North and South America and Its Jurisdictions, Inc., (P.H.A.), 1993.

Webb, Thomas Smith. *The Freemason's Monitor or Illustrations of Masonry* (1797, reprint, Bloomington, IL: Masonic Book Club, 1996).

Weisberger, R. William, Wallace McLeod, and S. Brent Morris, eds. *Freemasonry on Both Sides of the Atlantic: Essays Concerning the Craft in the British Isles, Europe, the United States, and Mexico.* Boulder, CO: East European Monographs, 2002; distributed by Columbia University Press.

Wesley, Charles H. *The History of the Prince Hall Grand Lodge of the State of Ohio, 1849–1960: An Epoch in American Fraternalism.* Wilberforce, OH: Central State College Press, 1961.

Williams, Loretta J. *Black Freemasonry and Middle-Class Realities.* Columbia, MO: University of Missouri Press, 1980.

Yates, Keith L. *The Fogarty Years: A History of the A.O.U.W., America's First Fraternal Life Insurance Society.* Seattle, WA: Evergreen Printing Co., 1972.

——. *An Enduring Heritage: The First One Hundred Years of the North American Benefit Association.* Port Huron, MI: North American Benefit Association, 1992.

Masonic Articles in Periodicals

Perhaps more extensive than Masonic histories are Masonic periodicals and articles. Many local lodges as well as York Rite, Scottish Rite and Shrine bodies publish newsletters and bulletins. By reviewing Larissa P. Watkins, *American Masonic Periodicals, 1811–2001: A Bibliography of the Library of the Supreme Council, 33°, South-*

ern Jurisdiction, the reader will receive an excellent understanding of the availability and range of Masonic related serials.

Compounding Masonic periodicals are the proceedings of lodges of research and other Masonic historical societies. The oldest and most prestigious is Quatuor Cononati Lodge No. 2076 in London, chartered in 1886. Since its founding, the lodge has published its proceedings as *Ars Quatuor Coronatorum* (AQC) and has set the standards for all other Masonic research. In the United States, many grand lodges support research lodges. There are also two national Masonic research societies: the Philalethes and the Phylaxis. Lastly, the Scottish Rite Research Society began publishing its transactions, *Heredom,* in 1992 and is considered one of the leading American Masonic research organizations. The following citations may be of interest for further study.

Bullock, Steven C. "I Sing the Mason's Glory: Freemasonry and Musical Life in Early New England," *New England Music The Public Sphere, 1600–1900,* vol. 21, *The Dublin Seminar for New England Folklife Annual Proceedings 1996:* 80.

Camp, Bayliss J., and Orit Kent. "What a Mighty Power We Can Be: Individual and Collective Identity in African-American and White Fraternal Rituals." *Social Science History* (fall 2004).

Carnes, Mark. "Iron John in the Gilded Age." *American Heritage* 37 (September 1993): 37.

Cooper, Robert L. D. "The Knights Templar in Scotland: The Creation of a Myth." *Ars Quatuor Coronatorum: Transactions of the Quatuor Coronati Lodge No. 2076,* 115 (September 2002): 94.

Davis, David Brion. "Some Themes of Counter-Subversion: An Analysis of Anti-Masonic, Anti-Catholic, and Anti-Mormon Literature." *Mississippi Valley Historical Review* (now known as *Journal of American History*) 47 (1960–61): 205.

Gilbert, R.A. "'The Monstrous Regiment': Women and Freemasonry in the Nineteenth Century." *Ars Quatuor Coronatorum: Transactions of the Quatuor Coronati Lodge No. 2076,* 115 (September 2002): 153.

Gowans, Alan. "Freemasonry and the Neoclassical Style in America." *Antiques Magazine* (February 1960): 172.

Hackett, David G. "The Prince Hall Mason and the African American Church." *Church History* 69, no. 4 (December 2000): 770.

Harwood, W.S. "Secret Societies in America." *North American Review* 164 (May 1897): 63.

Hill, Walter B. "The Great American Safety-Valve." *Century Magazine* 44 (July 1892): 383.

Kaufman, Jason. "Rise and Fall of a Nation of Joiners: The Knights of Labor Revisited." *Journal of Interdisciplinary History* 31, no. 4 (spring 2002): 553.

Kaulback, Michael S. "The First Knights Templar in the United States." *Ars Quatuor Coronatorum: Transactions of the Quatuor Coronati Lodge No. 2076* 107 (1994): 224.

Liazos, Ariane, and Marshall Ganz. "Duty to the Race: African American Fraternal Orders and the Legal Defense of the Right to Organize." *Social Science History* (fall 2004).

Meyer, B.H. "Fraternal Beneficiary Societies in America." *American Journal of Sociology* 6 (March 1901): 646.

Moore, William D. "Funding the Temples of Masculinity: Women's Roles in Masonic Fair in New York State, 1870–1930." *Heredom: Transactions of the Scottish Rite Research Society* 5 (1996): 35.

———. "American Masonic Ritual Paintings." *Folk Art Magazine* (winter 1999/2000): 58.

Putnam, Robert D. "Bowling Alone: America's Declining Social Capital." *Journal of Democracy* 6, no. 1 (January 1995): 65.

Putney, Clifford. "Service Over Secrecy: How Lodge-Style Fraternalism Yielded Popularity to Men's Service Clubs." *Journal of Popular Culture* 47, no. 1 (summer 1993): 179.

Schlesinger, Arthur M. "Biography of a Nation of Joiners." *American Historical Review* 50 (October 1944): 1.

Shaftesley, John. "Jews in English Freemasonry in the 18th and 19th Centuries," *Ars Quatuor Coronatorum: Transactions of the Quatuor Coronati Lodge No. 2076,* 92 (1979): 46.

Simmel, Greg. "The Sociology of Secrecy and of Secret Societies." *American Journal of Sociology* 11 (1906): 441.

Skocpol, Theda, and Jennifer Oser. "Organization Despite Adversity: The Origins and Development of African American Fraternal Associations." *Social Science History* (fall 2004).

Upton, William H. "Prince Hall's Letter Book." *Ars Quatuor Coronatorum: Transactions of the Quatuor Coronati Lodge No. 2076* 13 (1900): 61.

Wilson, John. "Voluntary Associations and Civil Religion: The Case of Freemasonry." *Review of Religious Research* 22, no. 2 (December 1980): 125.

Index

Photography Credits

David Bohl: 6, 9, 25, 26, 27, 32, 35, 37, 40, 41, 43, 45, 46, 50, 51, 55, 56 (bottom), 59, 60, 65, 69, 70, 72, 74, 75, 76, 77, 78, 79, 80, 83, 86 (bottom), 88, 91, 92, 94, 95, 96, 97, 98, 99, 102, 105, 106, 107, 108, 109, 110, 112, 113, 114, 115, 116, 117 (top), 118, 119, 121, 124, 125, 126, 127, 130, 131, 135, 136, 137, 139, 140, 141, 143, 147, 149, 150, 151, 152, 153, 155, 160, 161, 162, 172, 173, 177, 181, 184, 186, 187, 188, 189, 192, 193, 194, 195, 196, 199, 203, 204, 207, 209, 211, 212, 213, 217, 218

Lee B. Ewing: 2, 39, 54, 178

Joe Ofria Photography: 133, 183

John M. Miller: 23, 52, 57, 81, 86 (top), 90, 101, 123, 165, 170

Arthur W. Pierson: 44, 48, 128

Bill Wasserman: 117 (bottom), 144, 154, 180